CRIMES
OF THE
EDUCATORS

CRIMES
OF THE
EDUCATORS

HOW UTOPIANS ARE USING GOVERNMENT SCHOOLS
TO DESTROY AMERICA'S CHILDREN

SAMUEL BLUMENFELD & ALEX NEWMAN

 WND BOOKS

CRIMES OF THE EDUCATORS

Published by WND Books®, Washington, D.C. WND Books is a registered trademark of WorldNetDaily.com, Inc. ("WND")

Book designed by Mark Karis

Scripture quotations are from THE ENGLISH STANDARD VERSION. © 2001 by Crossway Bibles, a division of Good News Publishers.

Excerpts from *Reading in the Brain: The Science and Evolution of a Human Invention* by Stanislas Dehaene, copyright 2009 by Stanislas Dehaene. Used by permission of Viking Penguin, a division of Penguin Group (USA) LLC.

WND Books are available at special discounts for bulk purchases. WND Books, Inc., also publishes books in electronic formats. For more information call (541) 474-1776 or visit www.wndbooks.com.

Hardcover ISBN: 978-1-938067-12-9
eBook ISBN: 978-1-938067-13-6

Library of Congress Cataloging-in-Publication Data
Blumenfeld, Samuel L.
  Crimes of the educators : how liberal utopians have turned public
education into a criminal enterprise / by Samuel L. Blumenfeld, Alex
Newman.
      pages cm
  Includes index.
  ISBN 978-1-938067-12-9 (hardcover)
1. Education--Aims and objectives--United States. 2. Education--Moral
and ethical aspects--United States. 3. Public schools--United States.
I. Newman, Alex, 1985- II. Title.
  LA217.2.B58 2014
  371.010973--dc23
                                    2014020569
Printed in the United States of America

14 15 16 17 18 19 MPV 9 8 7 6 5 4 3 2 1

DEDICATED TO

Charlotte Iserbyt
John Taylor Gatto
Geraldine Rodgers
Edward Miller
Charles Richardson
Patrick Groff

and those unforgettable public school teachers (of a forgotten era) who
taught me to read with phonics and write in cursive

Can the liberties of a nation be thought secure when we have removed their only firm basis, a conviction in the minds of the people that these liberties are the gift of God; that they are not to be violated but with His wrath?
—THOMAS JEFFERSON

If the representatives of the people betray their constituents, there is then no recourse left but in the exertion of that original right of self-defense which is paramount to all positive forms of government.
—ALEXANDER HAMILTON, *Federalist No. 28, 1787*

CONTENTS

INTRODUCTION   *XI*

1   TREASON: THE DELIBERATE DUMBING DOWN OF A NATION   1

2   HOW JOHN DEWEY CREATED A HOUSE OF LIES   11

3   PORTRAIT OF A FAILED SYSTEM   25

4   HOW DUMBED DOWN ARE WE?   35

5   CHILD ABUSE: TURNING NORMAL CHILDREN INTO DYSLEXICS   39

6   SIGHT VOCABULARY: THE POISON OF PRIMARY EDUCATION   50

7   HOW DO CHILDREN LEARN A SIGHT VOCABULARY? ANY WAY THEY CAN!   57

8   RIGHT BRAIN VS. LEFT BRAIN: HOW TO AVOID DYSLEXIA   65

9   EDWARD MILLER PROVED THE SIGHT METHOD CAUSES DYSLEXIA   73

10   THE VICTIMS OF EDUCATIONAL MALPRACTICE   87

11	THE READING CONSPIRACY MARCHES ON	92
12	THE POLITICS OF THE WHOLE LANGUAGE METHOD	101
13	CALIFORNIA'S LITERACY DISASTER: WHEN UTOPIANS RULE, THE CHILDREN SUFFER	110
14	COOPERATIVE LEARNING: COMMUNIST IDEOLOGY IN THE CLASSROOM	118
15	THE GREAT AMERICAN MATH DISASTER	122
16	DRUG PUSHING: THE "CURE" FOR ADD AND ADHD	127
17	CONTRIBUTING TO THE DELINQUENCY OF MINORS	135
18	DESTROYING A CHILD'S RELIGIOUS BELIEFS: A SPIRITUAL CRIME	147
19	THE UNSETTLING PHENOMENON OF TEEN SUICIDE	161
20	THE MAKING OF THE BLACK UNDERCLASS	168
21	EUGENICS AND THE CREATION OF THE BLACK UNDERCLASS	180
22	THE ROLE OF BEHAVIORAL PSYCHOLOGY IN THE DEWEY PLAN	190
23	WHY JOHNNY CAN'T TELL RIGHT FROM WRONG	198
24	BIG BROTHER'S DATA-COLLECTION SYSTEM AND THE ROAD TO TOTALITARIANISM	209
25	WHEN UTOPIANS ARE IN POWER, EXPECT TYRANNY	220
26	MULTICULTURALISM: THE NEW CULTURAL GENOCIDE	225
27	COMMON CORE: CONSUMER EXTORTION ON STEROIDS	233
28	COMMON CORE STANDARDS: AN EDUCATIONAL FRAUD	245
29	REBELLION AGAINST "OBAMACORE" MAKES STRANGE BEDFELLOWS	259
30	THE FUTURE OF EDUCATION: FREEDOM OR GLOBAL ENSLAVEMENT?	271
31	THE FUTURE OF EDUCATION: HOPE REMAINS	289
	APPENDIX A: A TEACHER'S TESTIMONIAL ON THE TEACHING OF READING	295
	APPENDIX B: JOHN DEWEY'S PLAN TO DUMB DOWN AMERICA	305
	NOTES	322
	INDEX	340

INTRODUCTION

It is easier to believe a credible lie than an incredible truth.

Progressive utopians are criminals! They are genocidal psycho-paths who have killed more human beings in the last one hundred years than any other ideologues in history. They don't limit their murder just to individuals, but to entire nations, as in National Socialist Germany's war of extermination against the Jews, the Soviet Union's war against anticommunists, Cambodia's slaughter of the educated middle class, and communist China's cultural war. And all of this was done in the name of creating a new, utopian society. In the United States the socialist utopians adopted a new and unique method of conquering a nation:

by dumbing down its people, by destroying the brainpower of millions of its citizens.

The plan to dumb down America was launched in 1898 by socialist John Dewey, outlined in an essay titled "The Primary-Education Fetich."[1] In it he showed his fellow progressives how to transform America into a collectivist utopia by taking over the public schools and destroying the literacy of millions of Americans. The plan has been so successfully implemented that it is now a fact that half of America's adult population are functionally illiterate.[2] They can't read their nation's Constitution or its Declaration of Independence. They can't even read their high school diplomas.

The method of achieving this was by simply changing the way children are taught to read in their schools. The utopians got rid of the traditional intensive phonics method of instruction and imposed a look-say, sight, or whole-word method that forces children to read English as if it were Chinese. The method is widely in use in today's public schools, which is why there are so many failing public schools that cannot teach children the basics. This can only be considered a blatant and evil form of child abuse.

And this abuse escapes detection because of the cleverness and deception of its perpetrators. In his 1898 essay, Dewey warned his colleagues about being too hasty in carrying out the plan. He wrote, "Change must come gradually. To force it unduly would compromise its final success by favoring a violent reaction."[3]

In other words, deception would have to be used in order for this long-range, complex plan to be successfully implemented. Educators learned quickly how to deceive trusting parents and taxpayers and how to manipulate politicians. They also knew that the children would be powerless to resist their abuse. And teachers have been taught to blame academic failure on the children, not themselves. Indeed, many of them revel in the idea that they are transforming America to suit their own social fantasies.

Of course, most teachers are unaware that they are complicit in this evil conspiracy. They simply do what they were taught to do by their professors of education. Few become aware that their professors deceived them and prepared them to create failure. Most of these teachers are as much victims of the system as the students they are teaching.

The purpose of this book is to expose the kind of crimes that are being committed every day against American children and the nation in the name of education. Most parents trust the public schools because they are supposed to represent the cherished values of our democratic republic. But the unhappy truth is that today's public schools have rejected the values of the Founding Fathers and adopted values from nineteenth-century European social utopians that completely contradict our own concepts of individual freedom. And they have invented new values under the umbrella of "social justice" in order to advance society toward their idea of moral perfection.

What are the crimes being perpetrated by the educators against America and its children? The first, most serious crime is *treason*. In April 1983, the National Commission on Excellence in Education said in its final report, *A Nation at Risk*: "If an unfriendly foreign power had attempted to impose on America the mediocre educational performance that exists today, we might well have viewed it as an act of war. As it stands, we have allowed this to happen to ourselves."[4]

In other words, our educators are engaged in a deliberate dumbing down of America. They are sabotaging the intellectual growth of our children and depriving Americans of the most productive use of their own lives. This is a criminal act of war against the American people and should be called what it is: treason.

The deliberate dumbing down of an entire nation is genocidal in its impact on that nation's culture and intellectual future. No group of educators should have been permitted to impose on American schools a program that is the antithesis of true education. But when deception is practiced on a scale that is beyond public understanding, it becomes a crime as specific as perjury under oath.

A second serious crime is *child abuse* by deliberately inflicting physical harm on a child's brain by using teaching methods designed to produce dyslexia and learning disabilities. Brain scans now prove beyond a doubt that the sight, or whole-word, method of teaching reading creates dyslexia and functional illiteracy by forcing children to use their right brains to perform the functions designed for their left brains. Deliberately impairing a child's brain ought to be a punishable offense.

A third serious crime is *contributing to the delinquency of a minor* by teaching pornographic sex education and "alternative" lifestyles that lead to premarital sex, venereal disease, depression, emotional crises, and unwanted pregnancies. More children are now born out of wedlock than ever before, creating one of America's most serious social problems. More American children are living in poverty because their parents have adopted an irresponsible lifestyle based on secular-humanist morality.

A fourth serious crime is *destroying a child's belief in biblical religion,* a moral and spiritual crime that leads children into atheism, nihilism, secular humanism, and satanism, all of which can result in self-destructive, murderous behavior. School shootings, massacres, arson, teen suicide, student depression, and self-destructive behavior are the results of a school curriculum that denies the existence of God, His loving protection, and life with a purpose.

A fifth serious crime is *pushing psychiatric drugs* on millions of children by requiring them to take such powerful, mind-altering stimulants as Ritalin or Adderall to alleviate such school-induced disorders as attention deficit disorder (ADD) and attention deficit/ hyperactivity disorder (ADHD). These drugs are as potent as cocaine and have even caused sudden death among teen athletes.

A sixth serious crime is *extortion*, committed when educators defraud taxpayers of billions of dollars in the name of school improvement and reform that never take place. Instead, these educators use the money to buy more miseducation. The present reform movement promotes the implementation of Common Core State

Standards, which will not improve education but cost the taxpayers billions of dollars. You cannot have high standards without high literacy, and high literacy is not a goal of the new curriculum.

How do you deal with such criminality? First you have to make the public aware that it exists. Then you must make your political leaders aware of what is going on in the schools. Most political leaders wear blinders when dealing with education. For example, when it comes to reauthorizing the Elementary and Secondary Education Act of 1965, our Washington legislators tinker with its many titles in the hope that somehow education can be improved. But what they fail to understand is that what goes on in the schools is based on an agenda that progressive utopians put in place decades ago and have no intention of deviating from. Only a massive outcry by an awakened public will force our state and national legislators to recognize the crimes taking place in the name of education and put a stop to them.

There is no doubt that what goes on today in the public schools of America are criminal activities of such a serious nature that millions of American children will suffer the consequences for their entire lives. We all recognize obvious child abuse when we see it. But the kind of abuse that goes on in our schools escapes detection because its perpetrators are so cunning and deceptive when serving up their disinformation. Indeed, it is much easier to believe a credible lie than an incredible truth.

Our progressive educational leaders have learned how to deceive parents and the taxpaying public and get away with it. They know that the children are powerless to resist their abuse. And they know how to blame academic failure on the children and not themselves. Indeed, they revel in the idea that they are, as Obama put it, "fundamentally transforming America" to be more in line with their totalitarian views. Only an enlightened public will be able to put a stop to this degradation of American education.

Parents, taxpayers, our progressive educational leaders are lying to you—and getting away with it. What's worse, your kids can't do a thing about it because *they* are the ones being blamed for poor performance in school. Of course, the educators have a solution—but will it really "fundamentally transform America"? Or has it *already* destroyed the American educational system? We say the latter is true, and only an enlightened public will be able to put a stop to this degradation of American education.

1

TREASON: THE DELIBERATE DUMBING DOWN OF A NATION

It is criminal to steal a purse, daring to steal a fortune, a mark of greatness
to steal [the mind of a nation]. The blame diminishes as the guilt increases.
—FRIEDRICH SCHILLER

John Dewey (1859–1952) is generally lauded as the father
of progressive education. But unfortunately he is father of
much more. In the late 1800s, he and his socialist colleagues
decided to embark on a long-range conspiracy to radically
change America by imposing their own utopian vision of a
collectivist society. In "The Primary-Education Fetich," which
we discussed in the introduction, Dewey stated that the only way
to undermine the capitalist system was to get rid of the emphasis
primary schools placed on the development of high literacy and
independent intelligence. Why? Because both of these sustained

individualism. What was needed, they believed, was a new curriculum that emphasized socialization and taught children to read by a whole-word method that would lower the nation's literacy level and make its children more amenable to collectivist values. That the conspirators' utopian fantasy would destroy our constitutional republic did not faze them at all. They considered themselves peerless intellects and socialism a morally superior way of life.

The most important question we must ask ourselves today is, did Dewey and his colleagues have a right to implement a scheme to destroy our form of government, which protects our people's God-given rights to life, liberty, and the pursuit of happiness? Was their utopian fantasy more worthy of devotion than the values of a free society? Dewey preceded such tyrants as Vladimir Lenin, Fidel Castro, Mao Tse-tung, Pol Pot, and other communist leaders, who used brutal force to impose their utopian nightmares on their entire nations, killing millions in the process. But he knew that socialism could not be imposed on America by force. And so he told his followers that "change must come gradually." That was the only strategy that would lead them to success.

Success was an egalitarian, collectivist society as described in Edward Bellamy's 1888 novel, *Looking Backward*, a fantasy of a communist America in the year 2000 in which all private property would be nationalized. In Bellamy's story it is assumed that Americans would adopt a communist way of life through consensus and by force of reason. So why did Dewey believe there would be a violent reaction to such a utopian plan if the public became aware of it? Of course, in all countries where communism has been imposed, there have been violent reactions. But these regimes have learned how to deal with anti-utopianism: kill off the most effective resisters, or put them in reeducation work camps, and organize mobs to intimidate the general public.

But in America, the greatest, richest, and freest nation on earth, the imposition had to be subtle, slow, patient, and "democratic." The primary vehicle for this gradual change would be the public schools, where the dumbing-down process could be carried out without parents knowing what was being done to their children.

All of this required a massive cooperative effort by progressive educators at all levels of the education system to carry out the plan. Of course, there would be debate among them on how best to implement this radical program. For this purpose, in 1902 they established their own private forum, the National Society for the Study of Education, in which they could discuss the various changes in curriculum needed to advance the plan. The society's yearbooks provide members of the conspiracy—and *conspiracy* is the right word here, because it is secret, immoral, and involves more than one person—with what is being discussed by progressive experts in each area of the school curriculum. Since Dewey and his colleagues were convinced that nobody would believe in the existence of such a conspiracy, they felt free to discuss their plans without fear of discovery by parents.

But as Abraham Lincoln reportedly said, "You can fool all of the people some of the time. You can even fool some of the people all of the time. But you can't fool all of the people all of the time."

In reality, Dewey's plan was to impose on America a form of cultural genocide never before imposed on any nation. The way to do it was to disparage high literacy and teach children to read by a method that would prevent them from achieving the kind of high personal literacy needed to develop their independent intelligence.

Dewey was joined in this endeavor by a new breed of "progressive" educator who came on the scene around the turn of the twentieth century. They were members of the Protestant academic elite, concentrated mainly at Teachers College, Columbia University, who no longer believed in the religion of their fathers even though many of them came from good Christian families. Some of their fathers were ministers and missionaries. These atheist renegades were also behaviorists who rejected individual freedom. Control of human behavior was one of their chief goals.

Dewey's mother was a devout Calvinist who plied her son with strong Calvinist doctrines, which he then spent all of his professional life trying to erase from his brain. He became one of those Protestant academics who rejected the religion of the Bible and put their new faith in science, evolution, and psychology. Indeed, Dewey's academic colleagues, G. Stanley Hall, James McKeen Cattell, Charles Judd, and James Earl Russell, traveled to Germany to study the new behaviorist psychology under Professor Wilhelm Wundt at the University of Leipzig. It was these men who later imposed the new psychology on American education and transformed it permanently from its academic function to one dedicated to behavioral and social change.

John Dewey was introduced to the new psychology by his teacher at Johns Hopkins University, G. Stanley Hall. In 1887, at the tender age of twenty-eight, Dewey felt that he knew enough about psychology to write a textbook on the subject, titled fittingly *Psychology*. In 1894, he was appointed head of the departments of philosophy, psychology, and education at the University of Chicago, which had been established two years earlier by a gift from John D. Rockefeller. In 1896, Dewey created his famous experimental Laboratory School, where he could test the effects of the new progressive curriculum on real children.

It was Dewey's exhaustive analysis of individualism that led him to believe that the socialized individual could be produced only by first getting rid of the traditional emphasis on language and literacy in the primary grades and turning children toward socialized activities and behavior. The long-term utopian plan required destroying America's political, social, and moral culture of religious freedom, individual rights, unobtrusive government, and high literacy for all.

Destroying the brainpower of a nation is an act of war against that nation. At no time in history has such a treacherous crime been committed against a free and trusting people. Fortunately, those born before the Dewey reading programs were put in the schools were taught to read in the traditional manner and were able to use our free-enterprise system to create our present high standard of living. But how much richer would America be if everyone who came after had that good education?

In 1983, the National Commission on Educational Excellence stated in its report, *A Nation at Risk*, "Our society and its educational institutions seem to have lost sight of the basic purposes of schooling, and of the expectations and disciplined effort needed to attain them."[1] In other words, although we have in every city, town, and hamlet in America tax-supported public schools and compulsory attendance laws, our educators—indeed, our entire society—seem to have forgotten why we have them. Not only do we have schools; we have teachers colleges, educational psychologists, and educational labs combined with tons of educational research. In short, our educational establishment is the best financed in the world. Yet, virtually no one in that establishment seems to know why schools exist. What they do know is that the system, as dysfunctional as it is, can provide many lucrative jobs for degreed practitioners of something called *education*.

Dewey's philosophy had evolved from Hegelian idealism to socialist materialism, and the purpose of his experimental school was to show how education could be changed to produce little socialists and collectivists instead of little capitalists and individualists. It was expected that these little socialists, when they became voting adults, would dutifully nullify our constitutional government and change the American economic system into a socialist one.

To Dewey, the greatest obstacle to socialism was the private mind that seeks knowledge in order to exercise its own private judgment and intellectual authority. High literacy gave the individual the means to seek knowledge independently. It gave members of society the means to stand on their own two feet and think for themselves. This was detrimental to the "social spirit" needed to bring about a collectivist society. Dewey wrote in *Democracy and Education* in 1916:

[W]hen knowledge is regarded as originating and developing within an individual, the ties which bind the mental life of one to that of his fellows are ignored and denied.

When the social quality of individualized mental operations is denied, it becomes a problem to find connections which will unite an individual with his fellows. Moral individualism is set up by the conscious separation of different centers of life. It has its roots in the notion that the consciousness of each person is wholly private, a self-enclosed continent, intrinsically independent of the ideas, wishes, purposes of everybody else.[2]

And he wrote in *School and Society* in 1899:

[T]he tragic weakness of the present school is that it endeavors to prepare future members of the social order in a medium in which the conditions of the social spirit are eminently wanting. . . .

The mere absorbing of facts and truths is so exclusively individual an affair that it tends very naturally to pass into selfishness. There is no obvious social motive for the acquirement of merely learning, there is no clear social gain in success thereat.[3]

It seems incredible that a man of Dewey's intelligence could believe that the sort of traditional education that produced our Founding Fathers and the wonderful inventors of the nineteenth century lacked "social spirit" when it was these very individuals who created the freest, happiest, and most prosperous nation in all of human history, which was no small accomplishment of the capitalist individualistic system. In reality, it was the progressives' rejection of God that made them yearn for a utopia of their own making. And if high literacy was standing in the way, it had to go. Dewey wrote in 1896, after the Laboratory School had been in operation for nine months:

It is one of the great mistakes of education to make reading and writing constitute the bulk of the school work the first two years. The true way is to teach them incidentally as the outgrowth of the social activities at this time. Thus language is not primarily the expression of thought, but the means of social communication. . . . If language is abstracted from social activity and made an end in itself, it will not give its whole value as a means of development. . . . It is not claimed that by the method suggested, the child will learn to read as much, nor perhaps as readily in a given period by the usual method. That he will make more rapid progress later when the true language interest develops . . . can be claimed with confidence.[4]

Note that Dewey admitted that the reading program he was proposing would not be as effective as the traditional method. But blinded by his vision of a utopian socialism, he was capable of deliberately miseducating the child to suit his progressive social agenda. It is doubtful that he was incapable of seeing what was truly happening in the mind of a child between ages four and seven and why the teaching of reading and writing was quite appropriate at those ages. All children, except the very seriously impaired, develop their innate language faculty very rapidly from ages two to six. In fact, by the time they are six, they have developed vocabularies in the thousands of words, and can speak with clarity and grammatical correctness without having had a single day of formal education.

In other words, children are dynamos of language learning and can easily be taught to read between ages four and seven, provided they are taught in the proper phonetic way. Also, Dewey's notion that the primary function of language is social communication is patently false. If we accept the Bible as our source of information, it becomes obvious that the primary purpose of language—which was God's gift to Adam—was to permit Adam to converse with God and know his Creator. The second purpose of language was to permit Adam to know objective reality and develop his practical use of language by naming the animals. God made Adam a scientist and lexicographer even before He created Eve.

The third purpose of language was to permit Adam to know Eve, the social function of language. The fourth purpose of language was to permit Adam to know himself through introspection and inner dialogue. For Dewey and his colleagues, only the social function of language was important, and therefore children would be instructed in reading and language in a manner that emphasized their social functions. Today, the whole language philosophy of reading carries out the Dewey objective most efficiently.

In May 1898, Dewey's far-reaching plan to dumb down America, "The Primary-Education Fetich," argued that the traditional curriculum of the primary school had to be radically changed and showed progressives how to implement the plan in this long-range crusade to remake American education as an instrument to bring about socialism. He wrote:

> There is . . . a false educational god whose idolators are legion, and whose cult influences the entire educational system. This is language study—the study not of foreign language, but of English; not in higher, but in primary education. It is almost an unquestioned assumption, of educational theory and practice both, that the first three years of a child's school-life shall be mainly taken up with learning to read and write his own language. If we add to this the learning of a certain amount of numerical combinations, we have the pivot about which primary education swings. . . . It does not follow, however, that because this course was once wise it is so any longer. . . .
>
> The plea for the predominance of learning to read in early school-life because of the great importance attaching to literature seems to me a perversion. . . . It is simply superstition: it is the remnant of an outgrown period of history.[5]

Dewey had no problem recruiting other utopians to the cause. They formed a kind of socialist brotherhood in which they all contributed their resources and ideas to this utopian crusade. Many of them had read Karl Marx's *Communist Manifesto,* published in 1848, and his *Das Kapital,* first published in German in 1867. Indeed, the publication of *Looking Backward* in 1888 spurred the creation of Nationalist Clubs throughout America. These socialist political groups specifically advocated the nationalization of private property.

Utopian fantasy had captivated the minds of many well-educated Americans, and it would shape the future of American education.

Their model of utopia was Bellamy's radical egalitarianism. And that is what Lenin gave to the Russians and Castro gave to the Cubans: equal poverty for all. Unexpectedly, the post-Mao communist leaders in China rejected the egalitarianism of their Great Leader and adopted a more free market–oriented economy in order to become a rich and powerful nation. In other words, the Chinese had learned that the only road to economic wealth and power is capitalism, not communism. Unfortunately, that message has not been received by present-day American utopians who constantly harp about economic inequality and how the rich are not paying their fair share in taxes. Yet, according to the Joint Committee on Taxation, as reported by the Tax Foundation on April 17, 2014, those earning over $200,000 a year pay 70 percent of federal income taxes.[6]

Indeed, capitalism has made America's poor the richest they have ever been. They have cars, TV sets, refrigerators and freezers, subsidized housing, air conditioners, health care, food stamps, credit cards, free progressive education (even though it keeps them poor), and other benefits.

The idea that a group of socialist educators would take it upon themselves to embark on a conspiracy to dumb down an entire nation speaks volumes about the evils of socialism. Of course, they embarked on this endeavor before the Bolshevik Revolution, before the evil of communism would show its true totalitarian colors. But even after the revolution, Dewey visited the Soviet Union and came back extolling its virtues.

In 1935 Dewey reaffirmed his commitment to socialism. In *Liberalism and Social Action* he wrote:

> The last stand of oligarchical and anti-social seclusion is perpetuation of this purely individualistic notion of intelligence. . . .
>
> The only form of enduring social organization that is now possible is one in which the new forces of productivity

are cooperatively controlled and used in the interest of the effective liberty and cultural development of the individuals that constitute society. Such a social order cannot be established by an unplanned and external convergence of the actions of separate individuals, each of whom is bent on personal private advantage. . . . Organized social planning . . . is now the sole method of social action by which liberalism can realize its professed aims.[7]

But it wasn't until the 1980s that parents began to become aware of the plan to socialize America. It was my (Samuel's) 1984 book, *NEA: Trojan Horse in American Education*, exposing the socialist aims of the National Education Association, that convinced many parents to take their children out of public schools and to begin educating them at home. Today, we have a vibrant home-school movement where reading is taught with intensive phonics and belief in God is upheld.

2
HOW JOHN DEWEY CREATED A HOUSE OF LIES

School is a liar's world.
—JOHN TAYLOR GATTO, *THE UNDERGROUND HISTORY OF AMERICAN EDUCATION* (2000)

One of the great problems Dewey and his colleagues had was convincing conservative teachers to adopt the new progressive curriculum that they endorsed. Deceiving the public about the aims of utopian socialism was easy enough. But teachers were needed to implement the Dewey plan. Thus, they had to be convinced that what the progressives were advocating was not only approved but highly recommended by a respected authority—educational psychologists.

Dewey wrote that what was needed first was a "full and frank statement of conviction . . . from physiologists and psychologists" that could be used to convince teachers and principals of the need to downgrade literacy in the primary grades.[1] This need was soon supplied in 1908 by psychologist Edmund Burke Huey, who had studied under G. Stanley Hall at Clark University and did his doctoral dissertation on the psychology and physiology of reading. His book, *The Psychology and Pedagogy of Reading*, published in 1908, became the bible of look-say, whole-word instruction. Huey wrote:

> A survey of the views of some of our foremost and soundest educators reveals the fact that the men of our time who are most competent to judge are profoundly dissatisfied with reading as it is now carried on in the elementary school. . . .
>
> The immense amount of time given to the purely formal use of printed and written English has been a prime source of irritation. It seems a great waste to devote, as at present, the main part of a number of school years to the mere mechanics of reading and spelling. . . .
>
> Besides, as child nature is being systematically studied, the feeling grows that these years of childhood, like the Golden Age of our race, belong naturally to quite other subjects and performances than reading, and to quite other subjects than books; and that reading is a "Fetich of Primary Education" which only holds its place by the power of tradition and the stifling of questions asked concerning it.[2]

What is this "Golden Age of the race" in which there was no need for books or reading? Before there was literacy there was no civilization. Was that the Golden Age? This is the sort of intellectual quackery that was going to be used to destroy "stifling" tradition in the primary school. Huey continued:

> In an article on "The Primary Education Fetich" in *Forum*, Vol. XXV, [Dewey] gives his reasons for such a conclusion. While the fetich of Greek is passing, there remains, he says, the fetich of English, that the first three years of school are to be given largely to reading and a little number work. . . . Reading has

maintained this traditional place in the face of changed social, industrial, and intellectual conditions which make the problem wholly different. . . .

Against using the period from six to eight years for learning to read and write, Professor Dewey accepts the opinion of physiologists that the sense-organs and nervous system are not adapted then to such confining work, that such work violates the principle of exercising the fundamental before the accessory, that the cramped positions leave their mark, that writing to ruled line forms is wrong, etc. Besides, he finds that a certain mental enfeeblement comes from too early an appeal to interest in the abstractions of reading.[3]

Huey then suggested that children be taught to read through the same sort of stages that the human race went through before the alphabet was invented. He wrote sanctimoniously:

The history of the languages in which picture-writing was long the main means of written communication has here a wealth of suggestion for the framers of the new primary course. . . .

It is not indeed necessary that the child should be able to pronounce correctly or pronounce at all, at first, the new words that appear in his reading, any more than that he should spell or write all the new words that he hears spoken. If he grasps, approximately, the total meaning of the sentence in which the new word stands, he has read the sentence.[4]

In 1908 these co-called educators justified teaching children to read without accuracy. It is obvious that Dewey knew exactly the kind of reading instruction that would destroy high literacy and reduce young readers to word guessers. Huey went on:

Usually this total meaning will suggest what to call the new word, and the word's current articulation will usually have been learned in conversation, if the proper amount of oral practice shall have preceded reading. And even if the child substitutes words of his own for some that are on the page, provided that these express the meaning, it is an encouraging sign that the reading has been real, and recognition of details will come as it is needed. The shock that such a statement will give to many a practical teacher of reading is but an accurate measure of the hold that a false ideal has taken of us, viz., that to read is to say just what is upon the page, instead of to *think*, each in his own way, the meaning that the page suggests. . . .

Until the insidious thought of reading as word-pronouncing is well worked out of our heads, it is well to place the emphasis strongly where it belongs, on reading as *thought-getting* independently of expression.[5]

Huey's words are an exact definition of the pedagogical philosophy behind *whole language*, the most recent reading program of the progressives. So, there you have the look-say, whole language philosophy of reading summed up very neatly in 1908 by Professor Huey, whose book is still considered the authority on reading instruction and is read in colleges of education. It is not known whether Dewey or Huey had ever taught a child to read. They certainly made no references to such experiences in their writings. But their views have dominated reading pedagogy in the teachers colleges of America since then.

In 1991, the authors of *Whole Language: What's the Difference* gave us their own definition of *reading*. They wrote, "Whole language represents a major shift in thinking about the reading process. Rather than viewing reading as 'getting the words,' whole language educators view reading as essentially a process of creating meanings. . . . It is a transaction, not an extraction of the meaning *from* print, in the sense that the *reader-created* meanings are a fusion of what the reader brings and what the text offers."[6]

In other words, today's whole language teachers are completely faithful to the view of reading as given by Dewey in 1898 and Huey in 1908. What all of this shows is the continuity of the Dewey plan and how it is still being faithfully carried out by the education elite to this very day.

Naturally, it took some time before the new philosophy of reading could be translated into textbooks for the schools. The development of these textbooks took place mainly at the University of Chicago and at Teachers College, Columbia University, in New York. In Chicago it was William Scott Gray, protégé of Wundtian educational psychologist Charles H. Judd, dean of the school of education, who produced the *Dick and Jane* readers. At Teachers College, it was Arthur I. Gates, protégé of Edward L. Thorndike, father of behaviorist educational psychology, who produced the Macmillan reading program.

By the time the books were published, there were enough progressive superintendents of schools in place to make sure that the new books were adopted. However, this was during the Depression, and many school districts could not afford these new, expensive, colorful basal reading programs. But when the economy improved after World War II, virtually every school district in America was teaching children to read by these crippling look-say programs.

In June 1928 Dewey visited the Soviet Union with a group of educators. The Soviet commissar of education had invited a group of American educators to visit Soviet schools in Leningrad and Moscow. Upon his return to the United States, Dewey wrote a series of six articles for the *New Republic* summarizing his impressions of Soviet education. What most attracted Dewey's attention in the Russian schools was that they were made to serve the needs and interests of a communist society. George Dykhuizen, in his biography of Dewey, wrote, "The curriculum, he found, stressed the central role of work in human life, relating it on the one hand to materials and natural resources and on the other to social and political history and institutions. Classroom methods and procedures were designed to develop habits and dispositions that would lead people to 'act cooperatively and collectively as readily as now in capitalistic countries they act "individualistically."'"[7]

Dewey believed that American public schools could be transformed to resemble the Soviet ones. Dykhuizen wrote, "Summing up his impressions, Dewey suggested that the most instructive way to view events in Russia was as a great national experiment whose outcome was still in doubt. Like all experiments, the Soviet one involved continuous adjustments, risks, inconveniences, and uncertainties; because of this Dewey was frank to admit that 'for selfish reasons I prefer seeing it tried in Russia than in my own country.'"[8]

Apparently, Dewey was not quite ready for the dictatorship of the proletariat, with its slave-labor camps, intense class warfare, secret police, controlled media, and collectivist farming.

John Dewey died on June 1, 1952, three years before Rudolf Flesch made the public aware of the devastating impact his ideas on reading were having on America's schoolchildren. To the very end, Dewey clung to his idea of imposing on America the utopian evil of egalitarianism as fantasized in *Looking Backward*.

The extent of the book's influence can be measured by the fact that in 1935, when Columbia University asked John Dewey, historian Charles Beard, and *Atlantic Monthly* editor Edward Weeks to independently prepare lists of the twenty-five most influential books since 1885, *Looking Backward* ranked as second on each list after Marx's *Das Kapital*. In other words, *Looking Backward* was considered the most influential American book in that fifty-year period.

Dewey characterized the book as "one of the greatest modern syntheses of humane values." Even after the rise of Hitler's National Socialism in Germany and Marxist-Leninist communism in Russia, Dewey still clung to Bellamy's vision of a socialist America. In his 1934 essay, "The Great American Prophet," Dewey wrote:

> I wish that those who conceive that the abolition of private capital and of energy expended for profit signify complete regimenting of life and the abolition of all personal choice and all emulation, would read with an open mind Bellamy's picture of a socialized economy. It is not merely that he exposes with extraordinary vigor and clarity the restriction upon liberty that the present system imposes but that he pictures how socialized industry and finance

would release and further all of those personal and private types of occupation and use of leisure that men and women actually most prize today. . . .

It is an American communism that he depicts, and his appeal comes largely from the fact that he sees in it the necessary means of realizing the democratic ideal. . . .

The worth of Bellamy's book in effecting a translation of the ideas of democracy into economic terms is incalculable. What *Uncle Tom's Cabin* was to the anti-slavery movement Bellamy's book may well be to the shaping of popular opinion for a new social order.[9]

Dewey, who spent his professional life trying to transform Bellamy's fantasy into American reality, is responsible for the dysfunctional public education we have today—a minimal interest in the development of intellectual, scientific, and literacy skills, and a maximal effort to produce socialized, politically correct individuals who can barely read.

Today, the University of Chicago stands as an island of academic tranquility in Chicago's South Side, surrounded by a sea of social and urban devastation caused by the philosophical emanations from Dewey's laboratory and other departments. Charles Judd, the university's Wundtian professor of educational psychology, labored mightily to organize the radical reform of the public school curriculum to conform to Dewey's socialist plan.

The simple truth is that most parents know why they send their children to school: to learn to read, write, and do arithmetic, at the very least. Everybody, except the educators, seems to know what happens next. You teach history, geography, grammar, French or Spanish, and lots more to fill twelve years of schooling.

The *Nation at Risk* report stated in 1983:

Some 23 million American adults are functionally illiterate by the simplest tests of everyday reading, writing, and comprehension.

About 13 percent of all 17-year-olds in the United States can be considered functionally illiterate. Functional illiteracy among minority youth may run as high as 40 percent. . . .

Over half the population of gifted students do not match their tested ability with comparable achievement in school.

The College Board's Scholastic Aptitude Tests (SAT) demonstrate a virtually unbroken decline from 1963 to 1980. Average verbal scores fell over 50 points and average mathematics scores dropped nearly 40 points.[10]

And the nation kept getting dumber. In 1988 Arthur Sulzberger, publisher of the *New York Times*, told his fellow newspaper publishers, "Today up to 60 million Americans—one third of the adult population—cannot read their local newspaper. As we edge closer to the 21st century, life is becoming more complex and will become more difficult for adults who cannot read."[11]

In September 1993, the National Center for Education Statistics (NCES) released the results of its study of "Adult Literacy in America." It found that some ninety million American adults were barely literate. They had only the most rudimentary reading and writing skills after spending years in our public schools. Education Secretary Richard W. Riley remarked: "This should be a wake-up call for all Americans to consider going back to school and getting a tune-up." If the schools were unable to teach these ninety million students to read to begin with, why should they go back for a so-called "tune-up"? How lame can a secretary of education be? According to a *Washington Post* article of September 9, 1993, "The conclusions underscore alarms raised in recent years by business leaders and education specialists alike about the literacy and quality of the American workforce and about millions of high-school students earning diplomas though barely able to read and write."[12]

In 2003 the National Center for Education Statistics (NCES) reported that only 13 percent of American adults are highly literate, 33 percent have intermediate literacy skills, 33 percent were reading at the basic level, and 22 percent were reading below basic level. In other words, 55 percent of American adults were virtually illiterate.[13]

In 2007 the National Endowment for the Arts released its own survey of literacy in America. According to its report, *Reading at Risk*, the number of seventeen-year-olds who never read for pleasure increased from 9 percent in 1984 to 19 percent in 2004. Almost half of Americans between the ages of eighteen and twenty-four never read books for pleasure.[14]

Endowment chairman Dana Gioia told a reporter, "This is a massive social problem. We are losing the majority of the new generation. They will not achieve anything close to their potential because of poor reading."

According to the *Washington Post*, "SAT reading scores for graduating high school seniors [in 2011] reached the lowest point in nearly four decades, reflecting a steady decline in performance in that subject on the college admissions test, the College Board reported."[15]

And according to SAT scores, even the smart are getting dumber. In 1972 2,817 students achieved the highest verbal score of 750 to 800. In 1994 it was down to 1,438. America has been literally losing its brains. As for those at the bottom of the scale, in 1972, the number of students who achieved the lowest verbal score of 200–290 was 71,084. In 1994 that number was up to 136,841. And so, the smart are getting dumber and the dumb are getting dumber. The number of test takers in 1972 was 1,022,820. In 1994 it was 1,050,386.[16]

In 1994, the College Board decided to "recenter" the scoring scale. What had happened since the original 200–800 scale was made in 1941 is that in 1994 the students' average scores were well below the 500 average of previous generations, which simply reflected the steady dumbing down taking place in American education. In 1994 the verbal "average" was 423, some 77 points below the 500 average, and the math "average" of 479 was 21 points below the 500 average.[17]

This meant that even the 469 average verbal score made by

independent school test takers was well below the 1941 average of 500! And yet, those same test takers scored 54 points above the 1994 average of 423. In other words, in 1994 the average student was a lot dumber than the average student of 1941, and the smarter students in 1994 were dumber than the average students of 1941. The College Board explained:

> Beginning with the high school class of 1996, the College Board will recenter the scales, based on a more contemporary reference group. This means that the average score will once again be at or about the center of the scale—500—for a new reference group from the 1990s…
>
> Setting the average verbal and math scores at 500 means that most students' scores will be higher. So if a student scored a verbal score of about 430 and a math score of about 470 before recentering, the score would be about 500 for both verbal and math when the test is recentered.[18]

Now you see it; now you don't. It's reminiscent of a shell game, using numbers to deceive the public. Everyone's score will suddenly go up. But the average will still remain an average so colleges will be able to tell who is or is not above or below average for purposes of acceptance. But what they won't know is how much dumber these students are than their counterparts in 1941.

Fast-forward to 2011. According to the College Board, the SAT reading scores for the high school class of 2011 were 497—the lowest on record. The math score of 514 was the lowest since 2006. In context of the 800-point text, the three-point decline from the previous year's verbal score of 500 to 2011's 497, is nothing to worry about.

The average verbal score in 2011 was 497. If we wish to see what that score would be in pre-centering terms, we would simply subtract 87 points from 497 which would give us a pre-centered score of 410, 90 points below the 500 average in 1941. In other words, students in 2011 were scoring 90 points lower on average than students of the Greatest Generation in 1941.

And according to the College Board, only 43 percent of SAT takers in the class of 2013 graduated from high school academically prepared for the rigors of college course work. This number has remained virtually unchanged during the last five years.[19]

Even Boston, touted as the Athens of America, is grappling with a school system in disarray. According to the *Boston Globe*, "Reading has been particularly problematic in Boston's classrooms. Only slightly more than 30 percent of third- and fourth-graders were proficient in reading on the MCAS, according to last spring's results, the most recent data available." So even the children of Boston are being dumbed down by their schools.[20]

That all of this dumbing down is deliberate and not some sort of huge national accident has been proven by the work of courageous, indomitable whistle-blower Charlotte Iserbyt, who served on the school board of her hometown, Camden, Maine, where her sons were attending school. As a conservative she discovered that she was being lied to by the liberal superintendent. She then went on to serve as a senior policy advisor in the Office of Educational Research and Improvement (OERI), US Department of Education, during President Ronald Reagan's first term. Concerning her appointment Iserbyt wrote:

> My reputation of being an "education activist" firmly established, Reagan conservatives in D.C. invited me to become part of the demolition team established to carry out President Reagan's promise to "abolish the U.S. Dept. of Education." . . .
>
> Off I went to Washington to serve as Sr. Policy Advisor in the most important office dealing with education in the world! I had zero credentials for such a job which would ordinarily be held by the former President of Stanford, Harvard, Columbia, whatever . . .
>
> Had I not been plopped into that job I would NEVER have had access to all the incredible documents (ones dating back many years and ones outlining the present restructuring of

education), all the federally-funded grants going around the world to change all nations' classical education systems to Skinnerian outcomes-based global education. I finally got myself fired for leaking an important technology grant, and that was the end of my career in the U.S. Dept. of Education. However, before I leaked the technology grant to *Human Events* I removed all the other incriminating education documents from my office to my apartment and many of them became the basis for the *Deliberate Dumbing Down of America: A Chronological Paper Trail.*[21]

Iserbyt's mammoth tome, based on research and documents she retrieved from the Department of Education, proves that the dumbing-down process has been engineered by American progressives determined to mold American children into members of the future utopian world socialist government.

Still, most Americans are under the impression that communism was invented by Karl Marx and Lenin and first practiced in the Soviet Union. The truth, however, is quite different.

Communism as an economic and political philosophy was created by Robert Owen (1771–1858), a British manufacturer who believed that all of man's ills were caused by religion. He became a social messiah when he "discovered" what he considered to be the basic truth about human character: that a man's character is made for him by society through upbringing, education, and environment, and not by himself, as the religionists taught. Children in a cannibalistic society grow up to be adult cannibals. Children in a selfish, competitive society grow up to be selfish and competitive. No one is innately depraved or evil, as Calvinists believe. An infant is a glob of plastic that can be molded to have whatever character society wishes him or her to have.

Owen started publishing his ideas in 1813, and in 1816, to prove that he was right, he established his famous Institution for the Formation of Character at New Lanark in Scotland. Through a secular, scientific curriculum coupled with the notion that each pupil must strive to make his fellow pupils happy, Owen hoped to turn out little rational, cooperative human beings, devoid of selfishness, religious superstition, and all of the other traits found in capitalist man.

In 1825, Robert Owen came to America to establish his communist colony at New Harmony, Indiana. The experiment received a great deal of newspaper publicity and attracted a large number of utopian followers. It was called "an experiment in social reform through cooperation and rational education." But in less than two years it failed. The problem, Owen decided, was that people raised and educated under the old system were incapable of adapting themselves to the communist way of life, no matter how much they professed to believe in it.

Therefore, the Owenites decided that a government system of rational, secular education would have to precede the creation of a socialist society. They subsequently launched a strong campaign to promote a national system of secular education. Owen's son, Robert Dale Owen, and feminist Frances Wright set up headquarters in New York City, helped organize the Workingmen's Party as a front for Owenite ideas, published a radical weekly paper called the *Free Inquirer*, and lectured widely on socialism and national education.

Their anti-biblical views turned so many people away from Owenism, however, that they were forced to adopt covert techniques to further their ends. One of the men attracted to their cause was writer and editor Orestes Brownson, whose remarkable religious odyssey took him from Calvinism to Universalism to Socialism to Unitarianism and finally to Catholicism. Years later, describing his short experience with the Owenites, Brownson wrote:

> But the more immediate work was to get our system of schools adopted. To this end it was proposed to organize the whole Union secretly, very much on the plan of the Carbonari of Europe, of whom at that time I knew nothing. The members of this secret society were to avail themselves of all the means in their power, each in his own locality, to form public opinion in favor of education by the state at the public expense, and to get such men

elected to the legislatures as would be likely to favor our purposes. How far the secret organization extended, I do not know; but I do know that a considerable portion of the State of New York was organized, for I was myself one of the agents for organizing it.[22]

Thus, we know that as early as 1829, the communists and socialists had adopted subversive techniques to further their ends in the United States, techniques that John Dewey and his progressive colleagues would continue to use right up to the present.

Public education was the result of an unholy alliance between Owenites, who wanted public schools to promote socialism; Unitarians, who wanted public schools to get rid of Calvinist influence; and Protestants, who wanted public schools to counter increasing Catholic immigration. The system we now have is anti-Christian, pro-socialist, and owned lock, stock, and barrel by the progressives and behavioral psychologists. It is a training system designed to treat children as little animals in conformity with the educators' prevailing belief in evolution.

This is clearly not an education system for a free society, and thus it must be changed or gotten rid of. How? American parents have shown that they still have the freedom to educate their children outside this corrupt government system. The faster they exercise that freedom, the better off we all shall be.

3
PORTRAIT OF A FAILED SYSTEM

Clearly, something very strange is happening in our schools.
—THEODORE DALRYMPLE, *LIFE AT THE BOTTOM* (2001)

According to Mary Sanchez of the *Kansas City Star* (quoted in *This Week* magazine, March 1, 2013), we are "a wealthy nation of dummies and dropouts," lagging far behind other countries' educational performance.[1] But in his State of the Union address of 2013, President Obama announced that he had an ambitious plan to close that gap. He proposed a program that would give all US three- and four-year-olds access to "high quality" preschool education. The new program would be run at the state level, with federal oversight. In other words, the dumbing down would begin earlier.

Obama's program is just another plan calculated to continue the deception being played on the American people by our political leaders. If our educational professionals cannot teach the five- and six-year-olds the basics in their present "high quality" programs, what makes anyone think they will be able to produce better results with a so-called high-quality curriculum on a preschool level?

Here is what our well-financed public education system has given us, according to data published by Jeb Bush's Foundation for Excellence in Education:

- *Eighty-one percent* of American eighteen-year-olds are *unprepared* for college coursework.[2]

- More than *25 percent* of students *fail to graduate from high school* in four years; for African-American and Hispanic students, this number is approaching *40 percent.*[3]

- According to American College Testing (ACT), *three-quarters* of American students who *do* achieve a high school diploma are *not ready* for college coursework and often need remedial classes at both the university and community college levels. Only *26 percent* are ready for college in all subjects.[4]

- More than a third of all Americans, *43 percent, read at the lowest two literacy levels* according to the 2003 National Assessment of Adult Literacy (NAAL).[5]

- In 2009 nationwide, *67 percent of fourth grade students, 75 percent of eighth grade students, and 74 percent of twelfth grade* students were not reading at a proficient level according to the National Center for Educational Statistics.[6]

- *Seventy percent* of those in prison and *70 percent* of those on welfare read at the two lowest literacy levels according to the 1992 National Adult Literacy Survey.[7]

- On the 2011 National Assessment of Educational Progress—known as the Nation's Report Card, *only 35 percent of eighth graders* performed *at grade level* or above in math, while *just 34 percent* of both fourth and eighth graders scored at grade level or above in English. This means that *65 percent* of eighth graders performed below grade level in math and *66 percent* of fourth and eighth graders performed below grade level in English.[8]

- According to tests in 2012 given to fifteen-year-olds by the Organization for Economic Cooperation & Development (OECD), US students were at *seventeenth place in the world in reading, twenty-seventh in math and twentieth in science.*[9]

- *Thirty percent* of high school graduates *can't pass the US military entrance exam,* which is focused just on basic reading and math skills.[10]

- Parents in the United States spend *five to seven billion dollars a year on tutoring programs.* Tutoring programs offering additional out-of-school instruction to students are drawing a growing number of clients as parents continue to be concerned about the quality of their children's schools.[11]

- The United States has more than *600,000 manufacturing jobs vacant* because there aren't enough qualified people to fill them.[12]

- The Alliance for Excellent Education estimates that if the *1.3 million high school dropouts* from the class of 2010 had earned their diplomas instead of dropping out, the *US economy* would have seen an additional *$337 billion in wages* over these students' lifetimes. But why would students stay in a school that can't teach them to read?[13]

- A survey conducted in 2012 by McKinsey & Company found that *87 percent* of educational institutions thought they had prepared their students well for employment, but *only 49 percent of employers agreed* that their new employees had the training they needed.[14]

- A Deloitte survey found that *63 percent of life science and aerospace firms report shortages of qualified workers.* In the defense and aerospace industries, many executives fear this problem will accelerate in the coming decade as *60 percent* of the existing workforce reaches retirement age.[15]

- On August 8, 2013, *The New York Times* revealed the scores from the new Common Core State math and English tests for students third through eighth grades. The new tests, supported by the Obama Administration, for the first time measure whether students are prepared to succeed in college and careers in today's economy, as opposed to measuring whether they are on track to graduate high school. Under the new, more rigorous test, *only 29.6 percent of students met proficiency standards in math and 26.5 percent of students met the standards in English.* In other words, *70 percent* of the students in the system are unprepared to succeed in our high-tech economy.[16]

- Across New York City, *only 15.3 percent of black students met the proficiency standards in math. In English, the percentage of proficient black students was 16.3 percent.*[17]

- The National Assessment of Educational Progress (NAEP) measures student achievement for grade 8 mathematics. Eighteen percent of New York City's white students scored at the Advanced level in 2013, as did 26 percent of the Asian students. Only 1 percent of the city's black and Latino eighth graders scored at Advanced levels. If 99 percent of black eighth graders are not performing math at advanced levels, the odds are slim that they will pass the admissions test for Stuyvesant and other selective schools.[18]

- According to Gov. Jeb Bush, president of the Foundation for Excellence in Education, "Our students have fallen behind their international peers in math and science. The result is that *only one quarter* of the students who do earn a high-school diploma are prepared for college."[19]

All of the above is the lamentable story of the failure of our public schools to educate American children. Those failures are not the result of an accident. They are the result of programs created by the best-organized and best-paid educators on the planet. All of these programs that create failure were conceived to produce precisely the results we are getting. But why are American educators able to get away with these crimes? It's because Americans cannot believe that our professional and highly respected educators could be involved in a conspiracy to deliberately dumb down the nation. They recognize that we are indeed being dumbed down, but they don't blame the educators. They blame the children and the culture. In short, this conspiracy is protected by its incredulity.

Perhaps no one in America is more qualified to report on the true condition of our government schools than John Taylor Gatto, the now-famous educator who spent thirty years teaching in six different schools in New York City and then quit because he could no longer take part in a system that destroys lives by destroying minds. How these millions of illiterates impact our society is what concerns Gatto the most.

In 1990 the New York Senate named John Gatto "New York City Teacher of the Year." The speech he gave at that occasion, "The Psychopathic School," amounted to a devastating indictment of public education as a failed system. In 1991 Mr. Gatto was again named New York State Teacher of the Year, at which occasion he gave a speech, "The Seven-Lesson Schoolteacher," so insightful of the wrongheadedness of public education that it will probably become a classic in educational literature. These two remarkable speeches were published in a book entitled *Dumbing Us Down: The Hidden Curriculum of Compulsory Schooling*, which perfectly describes the curriculum crafted by John Dewey and his colleagues.

Gatto was born in Monongahela, Pennsylvania, an industrial river town forty miles southeast of Pittsburgh. He wrote, "It was a place where independence, toughness, and self-reliance were honored, a place where pride in ethnic and local culture was very intense.

It was an altogether wonderful place to grow up, even to grow up poor."[20] Gatto's grandfather was the town printer and, for a time, the publisher of the town newspaper, the *Daily Republican,* a source of independent thinking in a stronghold of the Democratic Party.

The move from Monongahela to Manhattan was quite a jolt for Gatto. The difference in society and values turned Gatto into an anthropologist, and in the next twenty-six years he used his classes "as a laboratory where I could learn a broader range of what human possibility is . . . and also as a place where I could study what releases and what inhibits human power."[21]

Like so many university students, Gatto was taught by his professors that intelligence and talent were distributed throughout the population in bell-curve predictability. But his experience as a teacher taught him differently. He wrote:

> The trouble was that the unlikeliest kids kept demonstrating to me at random moments so many hallmarks of human excellence—insight, wisdom, justice, resourcefulness, courage, originality—that I became confused. They didn't do this often enough to make my teaching easy, but they did it often enough that I began to wonder, reluctantly, whether it was possible that being in school itself was what was dumbing them down. Was it possible I had been hired not to enlarge children's power, but to diminish it? That seemed crazy on the face of it, but slowly I began to realize that the bells and confinement, the crazy sequences, the age-segregation, the lack of privacy, the constant surveillance, and all the rest of the national curriculum of schooling were designed exactly as if someone had set out to prevent children from learning how to think and act, to coax them into addiction and dependent behavior.[22]

In other words, Gatto had figured out through his own deductive reasoning that the education system was so organized and constructed to deliberately dumb down the kids. This startling insight led him to develop a teaching style completely opposite of what was taught in the university. He wrote, "I dropped the idea that I was an expert, whose job it was to fill the little heads with my expertise, and began to explore how I could remove those obstacles that prevented the inherent genius of children from gathering itself."[23]

Naturally, Gatto's methods put him more and more in conflict with the system. He explains: "The sociology of government monopoly schools has evolved in such a way that a premise like mine jeopardizes the total institution if it spreads. . . . But once loose the idea could imperil the central assumptions which allow the institutional school to sustain itself, much as the false assumption that it is difficult to learn to read, or that kids resist learning, and many more."[24]

In his speech "The Seven-Lesson Schoolteacher," Gatto described the seven lessons that are taught in all public schools by all teachers in America, whether they know it or not. He wrote: "*The first lesson I teach is confusion.* Everything I teach is out of context. I teach the un-relating of everything. I teach dis-connections." He went on to say, "Even in the best schools a close examination of curriculum and its sequences turns up a lack of coherence, a host of internal contradictions."[25]

Gatto is right. Confusion is taught by the arbitrary content of the curriculum, beginning with whole language and invented spelling and a confusing mishmash called "social studies."

> *The second lesson I teach is class position.* . . . The children are numbered so that if any get away they can be returned to the right class. . . . My job is to make them like being locked together with children who bear numbers like their own. . . . If I do my job well, the kids can't even *imagine* themselves somewhere else, because I've shown them how to envy and fear the better classes and how to have contempt for the dumb classes. . . . That's the real lesson of any rigged competition like school. You come to know your place.[26]

Class position is enhanced by separating the gifted and talented (the rulers of tomorrow) from the vocational proles and peons whose future place in society will be determined by the psycho-visionary utopians. Many leading experts have commented on this. According to Sal Khan, founder of the Khan Academy of online education, "Advanced children are all put together; they all know each other and learn from each other's habits. At the low end, it's an intellectual wasteland."[27]

Gatto wrote, "*The third lesson I teach is indifference.* . . . When the bell rings I insist they drop whatever it is we have been doing and proceed quickly to the next work station. They must turn on and off like a light switch. . . . Bells inoculate each undertaking with indifference."[28]

Indifference is instilled by teaching students that they are the products of evolution and have no special purpose in life. Logic and reason give way to emotion as the principle means of knowing.

> *The fourth lesson I teach is emotional dependency.* By stars and red checks, smiles and frowns, prizes, honors, and disgraces, I teach kids to surrender their will to the predestinated chain of command.
>
> *The fifth lesson I teach is intellectual dependency.* . . . This is the most important lesson of them all: we must wait for other people better trained than ourselves, to make the meanings of our lives. . . . If I'm told that evolution is a fact instead of a theory, I transmit that as ordered, punishing deviants who resist what I have been told to tell them to think. . . . Successful children do the thinking I assign them with a minimum of resistance and a decent show of enthusiasm. . . . *Bad* kids fight this, of course, even though they lack the concepts to know what they are fighting. . . .Fortunately there are tested procedures to break the will of those who resist.[29]

Gatto points out that rarely do parents come to the aid of their resisting children. They generally believe that their kid's school is not one of the bad ones, and they tell their children to obey their teachers. Intellectual dependency creates politically correct thinking.

The sixth lesson I teach is provisional self-esteem. . . . The lesson of
report cards and tests is that children should not trust themselves
or their parents but should instead rely on the evaluation of certified officials. People need to be told what they are worth. . . .

The seventh lesson I teach is that one can't hide. I teach students
they are always watched, that each is under constant surveillance
by myself and my colleagues.[30]

No wonder students celebrate when they are released from
their prisonlike school at graduation. But can they cope with the
real world after having spent twelve years in the stifling, inhuman
system that did not educate them but simply indoctrinated them in
the worldview of the liberal utopians? Can the system be reformed?
Gatto wrote:

The current debate about whether we should have a national curriculum is phony. We already have a national curriculum locked
up in the seven lessons I have just outlined. Such a curriculum
produces physical, moral, and intellectual paralysis, and no curriculum of content will be sufficient to reverse its hideous effects. . . .
Look again at the seven lessons of school teaching . . . All of these
lessons are prime training for permanent underclasses, people
deprived forever of finding the center of their own special genius.[31]

Gatto's testimony has had a great influence on homeschoolers
but has not been able to stop the progressive juggernaut, which
maintains its power through its political connections. The union-
ized educators are the most-skilled lobbyists in Washington and
in every state capital. Some of their power has been undermined
by the charter school movement. But charter schools are public
schools, and thus cannot wander too far off the plantation. They
are more of a threat to the union than to the progressive utopians
who still control national curriculum development. When progressive doctors of education write on school reform, you know that
what they are doing is simply trying to justify their own salaries by

advancing the utopian cause. They are the best-paid "professionals" in America. The damage they have done to American education is beyond calculation.

Why has Congress permitted all of this to happen? Barry Goldwater, in his classic defense of conservatism, wrote in *Conscience of a Conservative,* published in 1960—five years before President Lyndon Johnson opened the federal coffers to public education:

> [F]ederal intervention in education is unconstitutional. . . . Therefore, any federal aid program, however desirable it might appear, must be regarded as illegal until such time as the Constitution is amended. . . . In the main, the trouble with American education is that we have put into practice the educational philosophy expounded by John Dewey and his disciples. In varying degrees, we have adopted what has been called "progressive education." . . . Responding to the Deweyite attack on methods of teaching, we have encouraged the teaching profession to be more concerned with how a subject is taught than with what is taught. Most important of all: in our anxiety to "improve" the world and insure "progress" we have permitted our schools to become laboratories for social and economic change according to the predilections of the professional educators. We have forgotten that the proper function of the school is to transmit the cultural heritage of one generation to the next generation, and to so train the minds of the new generation as to make them capable of absorbing ancient learning and applying it to the problems of its own day.[32]

We wish that every member of Congress would read Barry Goldwater's great 1960 testimony and return to constitutional government.

4
HOW DUMBED DOWN ARE WE?

Only a desperado would blindly trust his children to a collection of
untested strangers and hope for the best.
—JOHN TAYLOR GATTO

E. D. Hirsch Jr. relates in *Cultural Literacy* that, in the mid-1980s,
American business leaders wanted to know why their younger
middle-level executives could no longer communicate their
ideas effectively in speech or writing.[1] They wanted to know
why, despite the great advances in the technology of communication, the effectiveness of business communication had
been slipping, to the detriment of our competitiveness in the world.

To find answers, several large grants were awarded to the American Academy of Arts and Sciences of Cambridge, Massachusetts.
Teams of scholars were assembled, and the academy spent the next

twenty years trying to come up with the answers. The result was a 597-page book, *Educating All Children: A Global Agenda,* published in 2006. It contained a sweeping, dry, unreadable view of every aspect of world education, with no hint of why middle-level executives could no longer express themselves effectively.[2]

The project included highly credentialed experts in education—just not those who actually knew something about the problem. All they had to do was read Flesch's book *Why Johnny Can't Read,* or my own study, *The New Illiterates,* published in 1973, and they would have known what had to be done. But that would have been too easy and too cheap. The academy editors wrote:

> This volume reviews research related to the achievement of universal primary and secondary education globally: the current state of education, the quality and quantity of available data on education, the history of education and obstacles to its expansion, the means of expanding access and improving education in developing countries, estimates of the costs, and the potential consequences of expansion. This research implies that achieving universal primary and secondary education is both urgent and feasible. Achieving it will require overcoming significant obstacles, developing innovations in educational practices, and spending more money on education.[3]

In other words, the research team delivered dense dissertations about worldwide educational problems and posed new questions that might suggest new projects investigating the unknowable. That's how the establishment manages to make everything more complex than it has to be: by burying their scholarly musings under a mountain of mind-numbing data. And that is why there is such widespread, self-inflicted ignorance among the top leaders of this country. Those of us who have the answers are simply ignored and relegated to a form of social and professional exile that never before existed in American history.

But E. D. Hirsch apparently knows the source of the problem. In *Cultural Literacy,* published in 1987, he wrote of his son John's experience as a teacher of Latin in high school and eighth grade:

> In one of his classes he mentioned to his students that Latin, the language they were studying, is a dead language that is no longer spoken. . . . One girl raised her hand to challenge my son's claim. "What do they speak in Latin America?" she demanded.
>
> At least she had heard of Latin America. Another day my son asked his Latin class if they knew the name of an epic poem by Homer. One pupil shot up his hand and eagerly said, "The Alamo!" Was it just a slip for *The Iliad*? No, he didn't know what the Alamo was, either.[4]

Hirsch then quoted Ben Stein, who has his own stories to tell about ignorant youth:

> I spend a lot of time with teen-agers. Besides employing three of them part-time, I frequently conduct focus groups at Los Angeles area high schools to learn about teen-agers' attitudes towards movies or television shows or nuclear arms or politicians. . . .
>
> I have not yet found one single student in Los Angeles, in either college or high school, who could tell me the years when World War II was fought. Nor have I found one who could tell me the years when World War I was fought. Nor have I found one who knew when the American Civil War was fought. . . .
>
> Only two could tell me where Chicago is, even in the vaguest terms. (My particular favorite geography lesson was the junior at the University of California at Los Angeles who thought that Toronto must be in Italy. My second-favorite geography lesson is the junior at USC, a pre-law student, who thought that Washington, D.C. was in Washington State.) . . .
>
> Only two could even approximately identify Thomas Jefferson. Only one could place the date of the Declaration of Independence. None could name even one of the first ten amendments to the Constitution or connect them with the Bill of Rights.[5]

Our Constitution, not counting amendments, consists of only 4,400 words. It is one of the shortest in the world, and should be read by every student in an American middle school, where knowledge of the Constitution should be made mandatory in civics classes. But according to a survey made in the summer of 2010, 72 percent of a thousand people polled had never read the document, yet they all attended school.[6]

In his book *Just How Stupid Are We?* author Rick Shenkman wrote, "Young people by many measures know less than young people forty years ago. . . . Just 20 percent of young Americans between the ages of 18 and 34 read a daily paper. . . . When one college teacher required a class to listen to NPR for an hour, one student summed up the general reaction to the experience by calling it 'torture.'"[7]

Even our presidential speeches have been dumbed down. Shenkman added, "Studies show that the speeches of presidents today are pitched at the level of seventh graders; in the old days—a scant half-century ago or so—they talked at the twelfth grade level."[8]

As for our college graduates, the *Washington Post* reported:

> Literacy experts and educators say they are stunned by the results of a recent adult literacy assessment, which shows that the reading proficiency of college graduates has declined in the past decade, with no obvious explanation.
>
> "It's appalling—it's really astounding," said Michael Gorman, president of the American Library Association and a librarian at California State University at Fresno. "Only 31 percent of college graduates can read a complex book and extrapolate from it. That's not saying much for the remainder."[9]

No wonder the presidents' speeches have had to be dumbed down. So much for the intelligence level on which American politics are now conducted.

It may be a bit amusing to point out the appalling ignorance of our youth and functionally illiterate college graduates. But it is more of a tragedy than a comedy, for these ignoramuses are the leaders of tomorrow, and America never became the freest and richest nation on earth out of ignorance.

5
CHILD ABUSE: TURNING NORMAL CHILDREN INTO DYSLEXICS

It's a foolproof system all right.
—RUDOLF FLESCH

One of the great unrecognized crimes being committed every day in our public schools is turning perfectly normal, intelligent children into dyslexics, or lifelong functional illiterates. How is this done? Very simply: by using a sight, or whole-word, method of teaching reading.

The sight method of teaching reading was actually invented in the early 1800s by the Reverend Thomas H. Gallaudet, founder of the Hartford Asylum for the Deaf and Dumb. Gallaudet thought that he could apply to normal children some of the techniques used in teaching deaf-mutes to read.[1]

Since his deaf-mute pupils could not use the spoken language, they could not learn a sound-symbol system of reading unless they were taught the articulation method. However, Gallaudet had been trained to use the sign method. He taught his pupils to read by a purely sight method consisting of pictures and whole words. For the deaf pupil written language represented ideas, not language sounds. Indeed, the good reverend thought that such a method might work even better with normal children.

In 1835 Gallaudet published his *Mother's Primer,* the first whole-word primer to be published in America. Its first line reads, "Frank had a dog; his name was Spot." The dog Spot would later turn up in the Dick and Jane look-say readers. In 1836 the Boston Primary School Committee decided to try Gallaudet's primer on an experimental basis, and in the following year officially adopted it for use in Boston's primary schools. Seven years later, the decline in students' reading ability was so horrendous that a group of Boston schoolmasters published a blistering critique of the new method. The Boston schools got rid of the Gallaudet method and returned to the traditional method as used by Noah Webster in his celebrated *Blue-Backed Speller.*

But the deaf-mute teaching method did not die. It was kept alive in the new state-owned teachers colleges—or normal schools, as they were then called—until they were refurbished by the new generation of progressive educators.

The socialist professors claimed that their new method of teaching reading was based on a scientific experiment conducted in 1885 by a twenty-five-year-old American psychologist, James McKeen Cattell, who was studying under Prof. Wilhelm Wundt at the University of Leipzig in Germany. Wundt, founder of experimental psychology, believed that human beings could be studied like animals and could be conditioned to behave as society wanted. Man, in other words, was nothing more than a stimulus-response organism. This concept formed the basis of behavioral psychology and its views on behavior modification.

Cattell, a colleague of Dewey's, was eager to see how these principles could be applied to early education, particularly in the teaching of reading. In his experiment, he "discovered" that adult readers read words as whole units, or total word pictures, like Chinese characters. If that's the way adults read, he thought, why not teach children to read total word pictures from the very beginning? It sounded like a wonderful idea, except that he failed to realize that an adult reader recognizes the letters in the word so quickly that it *seems* as if he is reading them as wholes. Indeed, a fluent reader has had to first learn the letters and their sounds before becoming a proficient reader.

The progressives were in favor of this new approach to primary reading because it fitted in nicely with their philosophy of education. They strongly agreed with Dewey, whose aim it was to change the focus of education from the development of individual intellectual skills to the development of cooperative social skills. Socialism's objective had been from the very beginning to remake man from the competitive individual of a capitalist society to a cooperative being in a collectivist state. Education was considered the best way to achieve this transformation. Indeed, President Obama's idea of transforming America is also in line with the progressive aim to create a socialist America.

Dewey's famous Laboratory School at the University of Chicago (1896–1904), in which his ideas were tested on children, led to the writing of his book *School and Society*, which became the bible of progressive education. His ideas were later implemented at the Lincoln School (1916–1946) at Teachers College, Columbia University, in New York, where Dewey was invited to teach and set the direction for teacher education.

There he joined his two colleagues, James McKeen Cattell and Edward L. Thorndike, who became the chief architects of the progressive curriculum. Having gotten his PhD in psychology under Wundt in Leipzig, Cattell became head of the Department of Psychology, Anthropology, and Philosophy at Columbia in 1891.

Thorndike, who had studied how animals learn at Harvard under William James, completed his PhD at Columbia University in 1898 under Cattell's supervision. In 1899 he became an instructor in psychology at Teachers College, where he remained for the rest of his career, developing his human-animal training program known as the S-R (stimulus-response) learning process.

The Lincoln School, which opened in 1916 with support from the Rockefeller General Education Board, became the experimental school for Teachers College. John D. Rockefeller Jr., who greatly admired John Dewey and his radical education ideas, donated $3 million to the school.

Among the school's chief architects were Charles W. Eliot, a former president of Harvard University and an influential member of the New England Association of Colleges and Secondary Schools; his protégé, Abraham Flexner, a member of the controversial Rockefeller philanthropy, the General Education Board; Otis W. Caldwell, a professor of science education at Teachers College and the school's first director; and the dean of Teachers College, James E. Russell.

Mr. Rockefeller also sent four of his five sons to the school to be educated under the new progressive philosophy. All four boys, subjected to the new method of teaching reading, became dyslexic.

Jules Abels, in his book *The Rockefeller Millions*, revealed what the new teaching method did for the boys' literacy:

> The influence of the Lincoln School, which as a progressive school, encouraged students to explore their own interests and taught them to live in society has been a dominant one in their lives. . . . Yet Laurence gives startling confirmation as to "Why Johnnie Can't Read." He says that the Lincoln School did not teach him to read and write as he wishes he now could. Nelson, today, admits that reading for him is a "slow and tortuous process" that he does not enjoy doing but compels himself to do it. This is significant evidence in the debate that has raged about modern educational techniques.[2]

David Rockefeller wrote of his experience at the Lincoln School in his *Memoirs*, published in 2002:

> It was Lincoln's experimental curriculum and method of instruction that distinguished it from all other New York schools of the time. Father was an ardent and generous supporter of John Dewey's educational methods and school reform efforts. . . . Teacher's College of Columbia University operated Lincoln, with considerable financial assistance in the early years from the General Education Board, as an experimental school designed to put Dewey's philosophy into practice.[3]

Dewey's educational methods were conceived and calculated to dumb down the nation, and he started out by dumbing down the four Rockefeller boys. Nelson, of course, was able to hire Henry Kissinger to do his reading for him.

David Rockefeller wrote further:

> Lincoln stressed freedom for children to learn and to play an active role in their own education. . . . But there were some drawbacks. In my case, I had trouble with reading and spelling, which my teachers, drawing upon "progressive" educational theory, did not consider significant. They believed I was simply a slow reader and that I would develop at my own pace. In reality I have dyslexia, which was never diagnosed, and I never received remedial attention. As a result my reading ability, as well as my proficiency in spelling, improved only marginally as I grew older. All my siblings, except Babs and John, had dyslexia to a degree.[4]

David went on to become a banker and philanthropist, while Winthrop became a philanthropist and the thirty-seventh governor of Arkansas. Their wealth made it possible for them to deal with their reading handicaps by having great secretaries.

The experience of the Rockefeller boys is indicative of how progressive education can cripple individuals, who must live with their disability from then on. Nelson Rockefeller was especially victimized by the education he got at the Lincoln School. When he was governor of New York, he wrote a rather startling confession that appeared in *The Reading Teacher* in March 1972:

> I appreciate the opportunity to make some observations on the importance of reading—for I am a prime example of one who has had to struggle with the handicap of being a poor reader while serving in public office.
>
> On many occasions, upon confronting an audience, I have elected to announce that I have thrown away my speech in favor of giving the audience the benefit of my spontaneous thoughts.
>
> And, usually, I have added: "Besides, I went to a progressive school and don't read very well anyhow." This, of course, is a trial to my very able speech writer as well as a libel upon all the devoted teachers and professors who saw me through the years of my formal education. It is also usually a rather popular device, since it implies a desire to communicate with the audience on a much more intimate basis—but the truth is that it serves primarily to cover the fact that I really wish I could do a better job of reading a speech or other public statement.[5]

Why didn't the progressive educators admit that their teaching methods were creating dyslexia and go back to the traditional phonics method? Because what they had done to the Rockefeller boys in a private school, they intended to do to the rest of American children in the public schools.

The tragedy is that there are millions of Americans like the Rockefeller boys who must endure the crippling consequences of educational malpractice.

The fact that the progressives refused to stop what they were doing indicates that their intent was criminal. Indeed, they were politely but emphatically warned in February 1929 by Dr. Samuel T. Orton, a neuropathologist, in an article in the *Journal of Educational Psychology* titled "The 'Sight Reading' Method of Teaching Reading as a Source of Reading Disability." Dr. Orton couldn't have been more critical of the new teaching method. He wrote:

I wish to emphasize at the beginning that the strictures which I have to offer here do not apply to the use of the sight method of teaching reading as a whole but only to its effects on a restricted group of children for whom, as I think we can show, this technique is not only not adapted but often proves an actual obstacle to reading progress, and moreover I believe that this group is one of considerable educational importance both because of its size and because here faulty teaching methods may not only prevent the acquisition of academic education by children of average capacity but may also give rise to far reaching damage to their emotional life.[6]

Orton had discovered all of this in the 1920s while investigating cases of reading disability in Iowa, where the new teaching method was being widely used. But since the professors of education had no intention of changing their dumbing-down agenda, they simply argued that Orton didn't know much about education. And so they continued their plans to develop and publish their new basal reading programs for the public schools. Later they made use of Orton's own medical diagnoses and terminology to identify what was wrong with the kids having trouble learning to read. But they never admitted that it was the teaching method that was causing these problems to begin with.

And so, as early as 1929, the educators had had explicit warning from a prominent physician that the new whole-word method could cause serious reading disability. And they certainly must have known about the Gallaudet experiment in Boston in the 1830s and '40s. Despite this, the new basal reading programs, with their delightful illustrations, turned out to be huge commercial successes for the publishers as, virtually overnight, whole school districts switched to Dick and Jane, Alice and Jerry, Janet and Mark, Jimmy and Sue, Tom and Betty, and other whole-word basal series that were making their professor-authors rich. By the way, no one seems to know why, in the midst of the Great Depression, American schools suddenly decided to spend millions of dollars on a new experimental teaching method that had yet to prove its efficacy.

By the 1940s, however, the new method's harmful effects were quite evident. Schools everywhere were setting up remedial reading departments and reading clinics to handle the thousands of children with reading problems. In fact, remedial teaching had blossomed into a whole new educational specialty with its own professional status.

Researchers, seeking the causes of this epidemic of reading disability, began to develop a whole new lexicon of exotic terms to deal with this previously unknown educational phenomenon: *congenital word blindness, word deafness, developmental alexia, congenital alexia, congenital aphasia, dyslexia, strephosymbolia, binocular imbalance, ocular blocks, dyslexaphoria, ocular-manual laterality, minimal brain damage*, and anything else a gullible public would accept.

What cures were recommended for these horrible conditions? *Life* magazine, in a major article on dyslexia in 1944, described the cure recommended by the Dyslexia Institute at Northwestern University for one little girl with an IQ of 118: thyroid treatments, removal of tonsils and adenoids, and exercises to strengthen her eye muscles. It would have been a lot easier and cheaper to simply teach the little girl the letters and sounds of the alphabet in an intensive phonics program![7]

With the boom in remedial teaching also came the creation of professional organizations to deal with reading disability. In 1946 the National Association for Remedial Teaching was formed and, two years later, the International Council for the Improvement of Reading Instruction. The professors must have laughed all the way to the bank, having enormous fun deceiving an entire nation.

At this point one might ask, "How could these progressive educators get away with this blatant educational malpractice in a free country where parents and elected representatives are supposed to have ultimate control over the public schools?" In 1955 Rudolf Flesch gave the answer in *Why Johnny Can't Read*:

It's a foolproof system all right. Every grade-school teacher in the country has to go to a teachers' college or school of education;

every teachers' college gives at least one course on how to teach reading; every course on how to teach reading is based on a textbook; every one of those textbooks is written by one of the high priests of the word method. In the old days it was impossible to keep a good teacher from following her own common sense and practical knowledge; today the phonetic system of teaching reading is kept out of our schools as effectively as if we had a dictatorship with an all-powerful Ministry of Education.[8]

Apparently, government-monopoly education, even without a dictatorship, is quite capable of stifling dissent. In the matter of reading instruction, what we have had to contend with is a private monopoly of professors of education within a state-controlled and -regulated system. These professors have had a strong economic and professional interest in pushing and keeping their textbooks and methodology in the schools, and the state system made it easy for them to create a monopoly and maintain it indefinitely. As for the suffering their teaching methods were inflicting on millions of children, it didn't seem to bother them at all.

Teacher certification laws require young teachers to be trained by these professors, who not only prepare the curriculum for teacher training but also hold sway over the professional journals the teachers read and the organizations they join. In addition, the professors of education are organized professionally along national lines and therefore can assert a nationwide influence over the teaching profession as a whole. They also had the help of the National Education Association, which published numerous articles in its journal in favor of the new teaching method.

Nevertheless, Flesch's book was an eye-opener. Now, for the first time, parents knew why so many of their children were having such a difficult time learning to read. Flesch wrote, "The teaching of reading—all over the United States, in all the schools, in all the textbooks—is totally wrong and flies in the face of all logic and common sense."[9]

What was the reaction of the professors of education in 1955 to *Why Johnny Can't Read?* Unlike the parents, who praised the book, the professors denounced Dr. Flesch in no uncertain terms, accusing him of misrepresentation, oversimplification, and superficiality. At the same time they decided to consolidate the two previously mentioned reading organizations into one major professional organization: the International Reading Association. In a few short years, it would become the impregnable citadel of the whole-word method, protecting the professors' vested interests not only from Dr. Flesch but from all other critics who would dare question the professors' wisdom.

So if you've wondered why reading instruction in America has not gotten better since the publication of *Why Johnny Can't Read,* there's the reason. The profession is simply too well insulated from public or parental pressures. Today the International Reading Association has about sixty thousand members, publishes three professional journals, and holds an annual convention that draws as many as thirteen thousand attendees. It held its fifty-eighth annual convention in 2013 in San Antonio. If you peruse the *Reading Teacher,* the IRA's journal for classroom teachers, you will see how complex the teaching of reading has become. Complexity has become the reading establishment's defense against a return to anything as simple and effective as intensive, systematic phonics.

Another reason why there has been no improvement in reading instruction is because the academic elite don't believe that everyone should be taught to read. That's the opinion of Harvard professor Anthony Oettinger, chairman of the Harvard Program on Information Resources Policy and a member of the prestigious Council on Foreign Relations. He told an audience of telecom executives in 1982:

> Our idea of literacy, I am afraid, is obsolete because it rests on a frozen and classical definition . . . The present "traditional" concept of literacy has to do with the ability to read and write. But the real question that confronts us today is: How do we help citizens function well in their society? How can they acquire

the skills necessary to solve their problems? Do we, for example, really want to teach people to do a lot of sums or write in "a fine round hand" when they have a five-dollar hand-held calculator or a word processor to work with? Or, do we really have to have everybody literate—writing and reading in the traditional sense—when we have the means in our technology to achieve a new flowering of oral communication? What is speech recognition and speech synthesis all about if it does not lead to ways of reducing the burden on the individual of the imposed notions of literacy that were a product of nineteenth century economics and technology?[10]

Professor Oettinger doesn't want to impose on American children notions of literacy that were a product of nineteenth-century economics and technology. What he chooses to forget is that literacy was high in early America because of the need to be able to read the Bible and know the Word of God. To our forefathers the purpose of education was to pass on to the next generation the knowledge, wisdom, and values of the previous generation. To them, man was made in God's image, and therefore children had to be educated with that concept in mind.

We don't know of any parent who sends a child to school not to learn to read, write, and do arithmetic. Yet, a member of the Harvard elite is telling us that these are things not all children have to learn, and that the dumbing-down curriculum is just fine. The establishment does not think your kids should even be able to read. What would make anyone think that its members care whether the methods being used can cause dyslexia in children?

6

SIGHT VOCABULARY: THE POISON OF PRIMARY EDUCATION

Children should be able to learn sight vocabulary in context rather than in isolation.
—*UNESCO'S GUIDE TO TEACHING READING AT THE PRIMARY SCHOOL LEVEL*

n writing my book *The New Illiterates*, in which I (Samuel) did a painstaking, line-by-line analysis of the Dick and Jane readers, I came to the conclusion that anyone taught to read exclusively by that sight-word method was at risk of becoming dyslexic. Requiring a child to memorize a sight vocabulary, in my estimation, was putting that child on the high road to dyslexia, especially because it forced the child to use the right brain to perform a left-brain function.

The fact that the human brain is divided into two hemispheres, with specialized functions in each hemisphere, has become the subject of intense study among brain scientists, particularly those concerned with the issue of dyslexia. Dr. Stanislas Dehaene is the director of the Cognitive Neuro-Imaging Unit at Saclay, France. His pioneering study of the reading brain provides us with a fresh look at the teaching of reading and dyslexia. Dehaene wrote in *Reading in the Brain*:

> Literacy drastically changes the brain—literally! The literate brain obviously engages many more left-hemispheric resources than the illiterate brain—even when we only *listen* to speech. Most strikingly, literacy did not only alter brain activity during language listening tasks, but also affected the anatomy of the brain. The rear part of the corpus collosum, which links the parietal regions of both hemispheres had thickened in the literate subjects. This macroscopic finding implies a massive increase in the exchange of information across the two hemispheres—perhaps explaining the remarkable increase in verbal memory span in literates.[1]

So we know that literacy has a positive effect on brain development. But what does dyslexia do to the nonreader's brain? Dehaene wrote:

> The comparison of the dyslexic with their respective control groups reveal a clear anomaly. A whole chunk of their left temporal lobe was insufficiently active. Furthermore, this reduced brain activity was observed at the same location and to the same degree for all three nationalities. . . . [T]he left temporal lobe seems to be systematically disorganized. . . . This decrease in temporal lobe activity was found in adults who had suffered from lifelong reading deficits. But reduced activity can also be seen in young dyslexic children aged from eight to 12 years old.[2]

Using the right brain to perform a left-brain function causes cognitive confusion, which is viewed in the left brain as being disorganized and "insufficiently active." And it is the learning of the sight vocabulary that causes this symbolic and cognitive confusion and left-brain disorganization. Learning an alphabetic system is the function of the left temporal lobe, and memorizing a sight vocabulary thwarts that function. That is why I (Samuel) call a sight vocabulary "the poison of primary education." It does to the brain what the drug thalidomide did to the fetus that emerged from the womb without arms.[3]

Several years ago, I (Samuel) had a demonstration of how easy it is to turn a normal child into a budding dyslexic. A father in his early forties brought his five-year-old kindergartner to me for an evaluation. The boy had had ear infections, which the parents thought might interfere with his learning to read. He had some difficulty distinguishing m's and n's, and his teacher said that the boy "wasn't catching on." Previously, the parents had signed a statement that they would make sure that the child did the homework assigned by the teacher.

The boy's pediatrician recommended that the child be core evaluated. At a core evaluation, teachers, counselors, and psychologists discuss the child's problem with the parents. They then recommend an individualized learning program. The father had heard about me and wanted my advice about the need or desirability of a core evaluation. Having served as a teacher in a private school for children with learning and behavioral problems, I had participated in several core evaluations and was familiar with the process. But I wanted to meet the child and judge for myself whether or not he needed any kind of core evaluation.

The five-year-old turned out to be very friendly and, from all appearances, completely normal. First, I wanted to see if he could learn to read by intensive phonics. He was able to recite the alphabet, but he had not yet learned the letter sounds, and his ability to identify all of the letters correctly required more work on his part. This was quite normal for a five-year-old.

But I wanted to demonstrate to his father that the boy was quite capable of learning to read by phonics. So I turned to lesson one in my *Alpha-Phonics* book and I explained to the youngster that the letter *a* stood for a short *a,* which I then articulated quite distinctly. I asked the boy to repeat the sound, which he did. Then I pointed to the letter *m* and told the boy that the letter *m* stood for the "mmm" sound. And the boy was able to repeat the "mmm" with no problem. I then demonstrated that when we put the short *a* together with the "mmm," we get the word *am.*

I next introduced the letter *n* and its sound, "nnn." The boy repeated the sound quite nicely. I then joined the short *a* with the "nnn" to create the word *an.* The boy repeated the word. I told him that *an* was a word and asked him if he had ever used it. He said no. So I told him to listen to me, and I said, "I have *an* apple." He got the message.

Meanwhile, through all of this the boy sat on his dad's lap and was smiling happily. I went through the rest of the consonants in the lesson—*s, t,* and *x*—showed how the words *as, at,* and *ax* were composed of two sounds, articulated the sounds, had him repeat them, and demonstrated their use in short sentences. I asked him if he knew what an ax was. He did.

The purpose of the lesson was to show this anxious father that his son was quite capable of learning to read by phonics, emphasizing that it required patience and repetition. Namely, the use of flash cards was needed to produce automaticity—the development of a phonetic reflex. I did not think that the boy's hearing problem was even an issue. I was sure that his pronunciations would improve as he learned to read phonetically and that his very minor problem with *m* and *n* would clear up as he became a reader.

The father then showed me the papers his son had brought home from school. The math papers were simple counting exercises. There was also an exercise in categorizing. One exercise, which was supposed to test the youngster's ability to follow instructions, was somewhat confusing and got the child a failing grade in the exercise. That upset the father.

But what really perked my interest was the Dolch list of basic sight words, which the child was required to memorize. The teacher had given the child this list of ninety words, which were to be memorized with a parent's help—five words per week, from January to June. The first week's words were: *a, the, yellow, black,* and *zero.* The second week's words: *and, away, big, blue,* and *can.* Third week: *come, down, find, for, funny.* Fourth week: *go, help, here, I, in.* And so on. Now, the child had hardly learned the alphabet and was not aware that letters stood for sounds. So why was he being given this arbitrary list of words to memorize by sight? Most of the words were perfectly regular in spelling and could have easily been learned in the context of a phonics reading program. Did the teacher realize that she was in the process of turning this child into a dyslexic? Once he left her kindergarten class, she would probably never see him again.

E. W. Dolch was a professor of education in the early 1920s who composed a list of the most frequently used words in English.[4] It was thought that if children learned several hundred of these words by sight—that is, by whole-word recognition—before they even knew the alphabet or the letter sounds, they would have a jumping head start in learning to read.

But what Dolch didn't realize is that once the child began to automatically look at English printed words as whole configurations, like Chinese characters, or little pictures, the child would develop a whole-word or holistic reflex or habit, which would then become a block against seeing our alphabetic words in their phonetic structure. And that blockage would cause the symptoms of what is known as dyslexia.

You might ask, what is a reflex? A reflex is a quick, automatic, habitual response to stimuli. There are two sorts of reflexes: unlearned (unconditioned) and learned (conditioned). An unlearned reflex is innately physical, such as the automatic reaction of our eyes when we go from daylight into a dark tunnel. The response is involuntary, and thus not something that has to be learned. A learned reflex is the kind we develop through habitual use, for example, in learning to drive. When we see a red light ahead, we automatically apply our foot to the brake pedal. We do this without thinking, whether in the middle of a conversation, or on a cell phone, or listening to the radio. That's a learned reflex.

A learned reflex is not easy to unlearn. For example, an American who rents a car in England, where people drive on the left side of the road, must suppress his right-drive reflex if he is to avoid a head-on collision. In that case, the American driver can no longer rely on his normal reflexes and must think about every move he makes while driving. Likewise, when an American pedestrian in London wants to cross a road with heavy traffic, she habitually looks to the left, but in London she must look to the right to avoid being hit by one of those huge double-decker buses.

That learning to read involved the development of conditioned reflexes was well known by the professors of reading, especially when teaching a child to read by the sight method. In 1940, Prof. Walter Dearborn of Harvard University wrote:

> The principle which we have used to explain the acquisition of a sight vocabulary is, of course, the one suggested by Pavlov's well-known experiments on the conditioned response. This is as it should be. The basic process involved in conditioning and in learning to read is the same. . . .
>
> In order to obtain the best results from the use of the conditioning technique, the substitute stimulus must either immediately precede, or occur simultaneously with, the adequate stimulus. As we have explained before, the substitute stimulus in the case of learning to read is the word seen and the adequate stimulus is the word heard.[5]

And so, it was well understood by the professors of reading that, in learning to read, it was necessary to develop automaticity—a reflex. But the correct reflex to develop in learning to read an alphabetic writing system is a phonetic reflex, which comes about by learning the letter sounds and being drilled sufficiently in the consonant-vowel combinations so the learner can see a word's phonetic structure and can automatically sound out a multisyllabic word by articulating each syllabic unit. In other words, the child automatically associates the letters with sounds. When that phonetic reflex is acquired, reading becomes easy, fluent, enjoyable, and accurate. Maybe our educators should try it sometime.

7

HOW DO CHILDREN LEARN A SIGHT VOCABULARY? ANY WAY THEY CAN!

The word *horse* does not look like a horse...or a pony.
—PAT GROFF

While we know how children learn to read phonetically, no one seems to know how children learn a sight vocabulary. Indeed, teaching children to read in the twentieth and twenty-first centuries by a method preceding the invention of the alphabet does not make sense. After all, alphabetic writing has tremendous advantages over the older forms of writing. For the first time man had an accurate, precise means of transcribing the spoken word directly into written form. It was the most revolutionary invention in all of history. It did away with hieroglyphic and ideographic writing and accelerated the speed of intellectual development and the expansion of vocabulary, thus expanding knowledge and brainpower. It also made learning to read simple and available to the population as a whole.

In light of these advantages, it seems strange that professors of education in the early twentieth century would decide to teach American children to read English as if it were an ideographic writing system. How could you possibly teach children to read that way? To a logical mind the whole idea seems not only absurd but insane. Yet, that is what the professors did, and what most primary school teachers continue to do today.

Essentially, the sight method works as follows: The child is given a sight vocabulary to memorize. He or she is taught to look at and say the words without knowing that the letters stand for sounds. As far as the learner is concerned, the letters are a bunch of arbitrary squiggles arranged in some arbitrary, haphazard order. The learner's task is to see a picture in the configuration of the whole word—to make the word *horse* look like a horse.

Of course, the word *horse* does not look like a horse. So how does a child remember that the word is *horse*? Any way he can. There isn't a professor of education anywhere in the world who can tell you how a child learns a sight vocabulary. The only research we found that addressed that question was done by Josephine H. Bowden at the elementary school of the University of Chicago around 1912. A description of the studies was given by Prof. Walter F. Dearborn in 1914 as follows:

> In the first study the pupils, who had had no instruction in reading, were taught by a word method without the use of phonics and the problem was to determine by what means the children actually recognized and differentiated words when left to their own devices. The following quotation indicates the methods employed by the experimenter: "First, incidents; for example, one day when the child was given the cards to read from, it was observed that she read with equal ease whether the card was right side up or upside down. This incident suggested a test which was

later given. Second, comments of the child; for example, when she was asked to find in the context the word 'shoes,' she said that 'dress' looked so much like 'shoes' that she was afraid she would make a mistake. Third, questioning; for example, she had trouble to distinguish between 'sing' and 'song.' When she had mastered the words she was asked how she knew which was which. Her reply was, 'by the looks.' When questioned further she put her finger on the 'i' and the 'o.' These three types of evidence correspond to introspection with the adult. The fourth type of evidence is a comparison of the words learned as to the parts of speech, geometric form, internal form, and length. Fifth, misreading; for example, 'dogs' was read 'twigs,' and 'feathers,' 'fur.' Sixth, mutilations; for example, 'dogs' was printed 'digs,' 'lilac' was written 'lalci.'"

Some of the conclusions may be cited, first as regards the kind of words most easily learned on the basis of word forms. Four out of six children learned more "linear" words, *i.e.,* words like "acorns," "saw," in which there are no high letters, than of any other group. In but one case were the "superlinear" words more easily recognized. . . .

Misreadings or the mistaking of one word for another occurred most frequently in these early stages, first when the words were of the same length (which again controverts Messmer's findings); secondly, when words had common letters, the "g" and "o" of "igloo" caused it to be read as "dogs"; thirdly, when the initial letters of words were the same; and fourthly, when the final letters were the same. Words were recognized upside down nearly as easily as right side up, but [only] two children noticing any difference. The word seems to be recognized as a whole, and as the author notes, recognized upside down just as the child would recognize a toy upside down.

The general conclusions of the study may be quoted:

"The comments and the questions, as well as the misreading, seem to show that children learn to read words by the trial and error method. It may be the length of the word, the initial letter, the final letter, a characteristic letter, the position of the word in the sentence, or even the blackness of the type that serves as the cue. . . . There is no evidence in any of the cases studied that the child works out a system by which he learns to recognize words.

That he does not work out phonics for himself comes out quite clearly in the transposition test. Furthermore, only once did a child divide a word even into its syllables. There is some evidence that the child is conscious of the letter, except in the case of 'E,' who so analyzed the word 'six.' Sometimes, when the child seemed to have made a letter analysis, he failed to recognize the word a second time, and in some cases did not learn it at all."[1]

And so, it was obvious to the professors as far back as 1914 that the sight method was a totally horrendous, inaccurate, inefficient, and illogical way of teaching a child to read. And despite Dr. Orton's warning in 1929 that the sight method would harm many children, they proceeded to put their new reading programs in all the schools of America.

The writers of the new look-say reading programs realized that they had to beef up their sight-vocabulary primers with a battery of "word recognition strategies." They provided configuration clues: putting sight words in frames; picture clues: loading the page with illustrations depicting the words; context clues: inane stories in which the word could be easily guessed on the basis of context; and phonetic clues: teaching initial and final consonant sounds to reduce the ridiculousness of some of the guesses.

It is important to note that teaching phonetic clues is not the same as teaching intensive, systematic phonics. The latter helps the child acquire an automatic association of letters and sounds and teaches blending. The former provides phonetic information that is stored in the brain and requires effort to retrieve. Learning an isolated consonant sound without knowing the other sounds in the word makes no sense at all.

That this sight method of teaching reading can cause the symptoms of dyslexia is not difficult to surmise. What are the symptoms? Dr. Harold N. Levinson, founder of the Medical Dyslexic Treatment Center in Lake Success, New York, and author of *Smart but Feeling Dumb,* which he dedicated to the "40 million dyslexic Americans," lists the symptoms as follows: (1) memory instability for letters, words, or numbers; (2) a tendency to skip over or scramble letters, words, and sentences; (3) a poor, slow, fatiguing reading ability prone to compensatory head tilting, near-far focusing, and finger pointing; (4) reversal of letters such as *b* and *d*, words such as *saw* and *was,* and numbers such as 6 and 9 or 16 and 61; (5) word blurring or movement or double images; and (6) headaches, vertigo, or nausea brought on by reading.[2]

These symptoms sound just like the very mistakes made by those children back in 1912 who were trying to learn a sight vocabulary. Some of those kids even read the words upside down!

It is obvious that if you are told to look at a word as a picture, you may look at it from right to left as easily as from left to right. You will reverse letters because they look alike, and you have not been drilled to know them by sound as well as by sight. In alphabetic writing, the sounds in the word follow the same sequence in which the letters are written, which makes reversing letters virtually impossible. A sight reader will be a poor speller because the sequence of letters seems completely arbitrary, with no rhyme or reason. But to a phonetic reader the sequence of letters is most important because it follows the same sequence in which the sounds are uttered.

Other symptoms include transposing letters in a word, for example, reading *abroad* as *aboard,* *left* as *felt,* and *how* as *who;* confusing words with others of similar configuration, such as *through,* *though,* and *thought,* or *quit,* *quite* and *quiet,* or *realty* and *reality;* and guessing at unknown words.

Dr. Kenneth L. Goodman, America's top professor of reading and chief advocate of the sight method, calls reading a "psycholinguistic guessing game."[3] And that's exactly what it is for most American children in today's primary schools. The result is an explosion in special education, which has become the growth industry for educators so worried about the dropout problem. The primary schools create the learning disabilities, and the federal government is funding a new industry to deal with them. In the 1976–77 school year, there were 796,000 learning-disabled students in special education. In 1983–84 there were 1,806,000.[4] Dyslexia is booming!

Obviously, the prevalent methods of teaching reading cause dyslexia. I (Samuel) have visited many American cities on my lecture tours and have seen for myself the sight-word basal reading programs being used in today's primary classrooms all across the country. Yes, they now teach more phonics, but not in the intensive, systematic way that would produce the needed phonetic reflex. They teach letter sounds as information that the student may or may not use while looking at the words as little pictures. The educators call that a "balanced approach." But the scale is tipped in favor of the sight method.

Donald Potter, an educator in Odessa, Texas, specializes in tutoring reading-disabled children with phonics. He wrote in an e-mail to me:

> One of the cardinal signs of whole-language instruction is the confusion of "a" and "the." I know they look totally different, but the kids continually confuse them. I take it that the "determiner slot" in the sentences can be filled with either "a" or "the" and still make good sense. The kids have been taught to read with syntactic clues (along with graphemic and semantic). This training CAUSES them to make these substitutions. The parents (and researchers) are fooled into thinking that the kids have dyslexia when they are really just performing as they have been instructed in their "How to Guess Reading Classes." The a/the confusion is only one of many examples of syntactic substitutions. The sentence will always make sense, even though they have read the wrong word.[5]

This means that the minds of millions of American children are being crippled, their futures handicapped, their self-esteem destroyed by educators who should know better. This criminal malpractice is going on in virtually every community in the nation. And yet, there is little one can do about it. The professors of education won't listen; after all, they write the textbooks. The book publishers publish what the educators want and what the textbook committees will adopt. The classroom teachers know no other way to teach; the professional organizations promote these faulty methods; and principals, administrators, and superintendents leave the teaching of reading to the "experts."

Also, holistic readers are encouraged by their teachers to substitute words, as explained by a whole language advocate quoted in the 1986 *Washington Post* article "Reading Method Lets Pupils Guess; Whole-Language Approach Riles Advocates of Phonics." The article states, "The most controversial aspect of whole language is the de-emphasis on accuracy. American Reading Council President Julia Palmer, an advocate of the approach, said it is acceptable if a young child reads the word house for home, or substitutes the word pony for horse. 'It's not very serious because she understands the meaning,' said Palmer. 'Accuracy is not the name of the game.'"[6]

When does accuracy become the name of the game in Ms. Palmer's view of education? Probably never, for if you teach children in primary school, through invented spelling and word substitutions, that accuracy is not at all important, they may never acquire a sense of accuracy, unless forced to do so by the demands of the workplace.

What we do know is that when you impose an inaccurate, subjective ideographic teaching technique on a phonetic-alphabetic writing system, which demands accurate decoding, you create symbolic confusion, cognitive conflict, frustration, and a learning breakdown. In addition, I strongly suspect that attention deficit disorder, otherwise known as ADD, is a form of behavioral disorganization created by a teaching disorganization. It is the symbolic confusion, cognitive conflict, learning blocks, and frustration caused by holistic teaching methods that literally force children to react physically to what they instinctively know is harming them. They started school feeling very intelligent. Now they feel stupid. They may not know exactly what the teacher is doing that is harming them. But they certainly know that they are being harmed. And that is why they react.

But there is some hope. The enormous growth of the home-school movement has spurred the development of many new phonics programs, which are being used at home. Also, there are more and more private and church schools that teach children to read with intensive phonics. And here and there one finds a teacher in a public school who teaches phonics. But phonics in a public school is usually taught as "bootleg phonics"—that is, surreptitiously, if at all.

However, for the nation as a whole, there is little hope that the vast majority of schools will change their teaching methods in the foreseeable future. The fact that more and more children are being labeled learning disabled, dyslexic, or ADD, and are being given drugs each day in order to attend school, is a sad indication that the schools are committed to programs that damage children.

One would expect American business leaders, who need literate workers, to be at the forefront of those who are urging education reform. But the problem is that business professionals go to educational professionals for information, advice, and ideas and are given the usual song and dance in which the professional educators have become expert practitioners.

Professionals in other fields cannot believe that educational professionals are deliberately miseducating American children and causing dyslexia. And so, considering how poorly informed our business leaders are and how difficult it is to reach them, let alone brief them on this rather complex subject, there is little likelihood that they will act effectively on behalf of the children entrapped in the government schools.

8

RIGHT BRAIN VS. LEFT BRAIN: HOW TO AVOID DYSLEXIA

When children learn to read . . . their brains will never be the same again.
—STANISLAS DEHAENE, *READING IN THE BRAIN* (2010)

The human brain is divided into two hemispheres, each with different functions. The left brain is the center of language development. The right brain deals with spatial functions: art, distance, depth, perspective, and so forth. The human being is quite distinct from every other species in that we have the faculty of speech, the ability to use a variety of voice sounds to represent meaning. Thus, we develop spoken language. Other species can make vocal sounds, too, but only the human being has the unique brain faculty that permits the development of spoken language—the ability to use a sound-symbol system to represent objects, feelings, emotions, and ideas.

It is language that has permitted humankind to create civilization, write history, and communicate with one another in the most intimate manner. In other words, language permits us to have knowledge of the great power that created us, knowledge of the objective world, knowledge of others, and knowledge of ourselves. We think in terms of language. We formulate scientific knowledge by the use of language. We argue with our tongues. We pray with language. We develop complex philosophical ideas with language. We speak to ourselves in language. And that is why the distance between the highest jungle primate and the human being is eons apart.

Modern scientists have become quite interested in the functions of the brain and its development from infancy to adulthood. Investigations of brain damage and how it can affect behavioral functions have become the focus of intense scientific interest. Soldiers whose left-brain hemispheres have been injured will have speech difficulties. Victims of stroke will also suffer loss of normal speech. Anyone who has been around an individual who has suffered a stroke will be keenly aware of the stroke's effect on speech. However, with the invention of brain-scanning machines, we can now actually see how the brain functions under different normal and abnormal conditions.

Of late there has been considerable interest in the subject of dyslexia and how this disease affects brain functions. It is thought by some investigators that we can see the origin of dyslexia in some actual brain damage or distortion. They assume that this brain anomaly is the cause of dyslexia instead of being the result of the child being forced by educators to use the right brain to perform a left-brain function. This is done by forcing children to learn a sight vocabulary, to look at our alphabetic words as little pictures, when in reality our alphabetic words are symbolic representations of language sounds.

Back in the early 1800s, the Reverend Thomas H. Gallaudet was able to have his deaf pupils use their right brains to learn a sight vocabulary because they could not hear language. That permitted the deaf to associate the printed words with pictures and thereby learn a sight vocabulary. Of course, deaf children are also born with a language faculty that can be expressed by means other than sound, although some deaf are taught to articulate speech.

But when that sight method is applied to children with normal hearing, it creates reading problems. Why? Because a sound-symbol system cannot be learned as a picture-meaning system. Yet today, in American schools and in schools in Canada, England, Australia, and New Zealand, children are being taught to read as if our printed words were pictures instead of representations of spoken language.

Recent brain research has shown how faulty teaching methods can physically alter the brain. Two recent books provide the results of extensive research on dyslexia: *The Brain that Changes Itself* by Norman Doidge (Penguin, 2007) and *Reading in the Brain* by French neuroscientist Stanislas Dehaene (Viking, 2009).

Dr. Doidge deals with the adaptability of the brain, or its plasticity. The leading researcher in the field of neuroplasticity is Michael Merzenich. He has proven that dyslexia, even in adults, can be cured. Since I (Samuel) have tutored numerous dyslexics and cured them of their condition, I've known that the brain is plastic enough to change a sight reader into a phonetic reader. It means creating a phonetic reflex to replace the holistic one. This is not always easy to do. It depends on the individual. But first I teach the student the entire alphabetic system with *Alpha-Phonics*, my phonetic reading program. Then I show the student how to apply his new phonetic knowledge to the printed page. That may require weeks or months of getting rid of sight-reading habits and learning how to look at words in their phonetic structure.

Some years ago I tutored an eight-year-old child who found it painful to make the transition from sight reading to phonetic reading. He could not look at the page directly. He had to sit sideways. And sometimes he burst into tears. But eventually we succeeded. From that experience I learned why so many dyslexics do not want to undergo an intensive course in phonics. It might be too painful.

In 1996 Merzenich and his colleagues formed a company, Scientific Learning, devoted to using neuroplastic research to help people "rewire their brains." They developed a computerized training program for language-impaired and learning-disabled children called *Fast ForWord*. Doidge wrote, "The program exercises every basic brain function involved in language from decoding sounds up to comprehension—a kind of cerebral cross-training."[1] He wrote further:

> A Stanford group did brain scans of twenty dyslexic children, before and after *Fast ForWord*. The opening scans showed that the children used different parts of their brains for reading than normal children do. After *Fast ForWord* new scans showed that their brains had begun to normalize. (For instance, they developed increased activity, on average, in the left temporal-parietal cortex, and their scans began to show patterns that were similar to those of children who have no reading problems.)[2]

What does all of this mean? First, it means that stimulating the brain makes it grow. It also means that neuroscience has finally caught up to those of us who have been curing dyslexia the old-fashioned way: teaching the English alphabetic system by intensive phonics. But the one thing the neuroscientists have not investigated is how the schools induce dyslexia by the use of faulty teaching methods in the classrooms. Dr. Dehaene is well aware of the political factors involved in teaching reading. He wrote:

> Left-wing progressives supported the whole-language approach under the pretext that it protects children from the tyranny of decoding and spelling instruction, and that children should be free to learn at their own pace. In a similar vein, some teachers still think that the constraints exercised by our genes and brain structure on learning are "right-wing." These attitudes do not have much to do with the hard facts about reading acquisition.[3]

Concerning the brain's plasticity, Doidge emphasizes the importance of exercising the brain.

The irony of this new discovery is that for hundreds of years educators did seem to sense that children's brains had to be built up through exercises of increasing difficulty that strengthened brain functions. Up to the nineteenth and early twentieth centuries a classical education often included rote memorization of long poems in foreign languages, which strengthened the auditory memory (hence thinking in language) and an almost fanatical attention to handwriting, which helped strengthen motor capacities and thus not only helped handwriting but added speed and fluency to reading and speaking. . . . But the loss of these skills has been costly; they may have been the only opportunity that many students had to systematically exercise the brain function that gives us fluency and grace with symbols.[4]

What an extraordinary endorsement of classical education by a leading modern neuroscientist!

Dr. Dehaene's view on the way reading should be taught conforms with our own. He wrote, "We now know that the whole-language approach is inefficient: all children regardless of socioeconomic backgrounds benefit from explicit and early teaching of the correspondence between letters and speech sounds. This is a well-established fact, corroborated by a great many classroom experiments. Furthermore, it is coherent with our present understanding of how the reader's brain works."[5]

Dehaene is critical of the research conducted in the late nineteenth and early twentieth centuries that was used to justify using the look-say method in our schools. He wrote, "Recent research on the brain's reading networks proves it was wrong."[6] But how long will it take for today's educators to acknowledge what the brain scientists are telling us now?

For decades now we've known that the left hemisphere deals with language and reading and the right hemisphere deals with spatial phenomena. Dehaene wrote, "Words and faces also have different preferred hemispheres. When we recognize a word the left hemisphere plays the dominant role. For faces, the right hemisphere is essential. Although both hemispheres are initially equally stimulated, words quickly get funneled to the left and faces to the right. . . . This lateralization is another invariant and essential feature of reading."[7]

Simply put, the best way to prevent dyslexia, or reading disability, in healthy children is a good phonics-first program in the schools, such as Sue Dickson's remarkably effective Sing, Spell, Read & Write program, which she wrote for her first-grade class, or my own *Alpha-Phonics* program, which can be used to teach a child to read at home. And we know that children are ready to be taught to read with phonics quite early because their brains already have the required architecture. Dr. Dehaene wrote, "Before children are exposed to their first reading lesson, their prior linguistic and visual development [plays] an essential role in preparing their brains for this new cultural exercise."[8]

And that is why children feel so intelligent when they enter school. They already have a keen knowledge of their language. We also have a much better understanding of how the brain deals with the reading process. According to Dr. Dehaene:

> Modern brain imaging methods now reveal, in just a matter of minutes, the brain areas that activate when we decipher written words. . . . We have discovered that the literate brain contains specialized cortical mechanisms that are exquisitely attuned to the recognition of written words. . . . The insight into how literacy changes the brain is profoundly transforming our vision of education and learning disabilities. . . . There is no longer any reason to doubt that the global contours of words play virtually no role in reading. We do not recognize a printed word through a holistic grasping of its contour, but because our brain breaks it down into letters and graphemes.[9]

He added, "Cognitive psychology directly refutes any notion of teaching via a 'global' or 'whole language' method."

In other words, Dr. Dehaene repudiates the experiments that James McKeen Cattell conducted in Professor Wundt's laboratory in Leipzig in 1885 that became the pseudoscientific basis for abandoning traditional phonics in favor of the whole-word method, which spawned the Dick and Jane readers and created the greatest literacy disaster this nation has ever known. This method was also adopted throughout the English-speaking world, thus lowering the literacy levels in virtually all of these nations. And it is still being used today in American public schools despite the fact that children are born with dominant left hemispheres preparing them to use language after birth. Dr. Dehaene explained, "Not only is the left planum temporale already bigger than the right prior to birth, but the brains of infants are already powerfully and asymmetrically activated when they listen to speech in the first few months of life."[10]

That is why, when children are confronted with a teaching method that prevents the left hemisphere of their brains from performing its normal functions, they become learning disabled and suffer considerable pain.

On dyslexia, Dehaene wrote, "In dyslexics the left temporal lobe seems to be systematically disorganized." Citing the findings of a study of Italian, French, and English dyslexics by Professor Eraldo Paulesu of the University of Milan, he said, "All brain imaging studies of dyslexia find a reduction of brain activity in this area [left hemisphere] when it is compared to that of normal readers. . . . A whole chunk of their left temporal lobe was insufficiently active. Furthermore, this reduced brain activity was observed at the same location and at the same degree for all three nationalities. . . . [T]he left temporal lobe seems to be systematically disorganized."[11]

In other words, the faulty methods used in teaching children to read can physically impair their brains. They can become, in Dehaene's words, "spectacularly dysfunctional." This finding alone should shock our educators into understanding how damaging their teaching of a sight vocabulary is to the children in their charge. Finally, Dehaene wrote, "All children have similar brains. Their cerebral circuits are well tuned to systematic grapheme-phoneme correspondences and have everything to gain from phonics—the only method that will give them freedom to read any text."[12]

Of course, Dr. Dehaene is telling us something we've known since 1929 when Dr. Orton warned the educators that the sight method of teaching reading could cause reading disability. And we were further alerted by Dr. Flesch, who in 1955 told us why Johnny couldn't read. And we were even informed by the Boston schoolmasters in 1844 why the whole-word method produced reading problems. But now we have brain scientists affirming what we have been saying all these years. It will be interesting to see what the progressives at Teachers College have to say about all of this.

9

EDWARD MILLER PROVED THE SIGHT METHOD CAUSES DYSLEXIA

I think killing phonics was one of the greatest causes of illiteracy
in the country.
—DR. SEUSS

ack in 1973, after completing my book *The New Illiterates,*
I (Samuel) became convinced that the sight method of teaching
reading could cause dyslexia—that is, the inability to see
the phonetic structure of our alphabetically written words.
Without having been taught the alphabetic principle and
drilled in the letter sounds, it was impossible for a child to see
something he or she did not know existed.

As I mentioned in chapter 5 the sight method had been invented
back in the 1830s by the Reverend Thomas H. Gallaudet, the
director of the American Asylum at Hartford for the Education of

the Deaf and Dumb. The good reverend was able to teach the deaf to read by a sight method, juxtaposing a picture of a cat with the word *cat*. In that way the deaf were able to acquire a limited sight vocabulary and read primary texts.

He then thought that this method might work with normal children, sparing them the drudgery of learning the alphabet and the letter sounds before acquiring a considerable reading vocabulary. He produced a small primer based on this method in 1836, *The Mother's Primer*, and it was adopted by the Boston primary schools in 1837. Horace Mann was the secretary of the board of education, and he favored the new method.

But by 1844, the defects of this new teaching method were so apparent that the Boston schoolmasters issued a blistering attack against it, and urged a return to the traditional alphabetic-phonics method of teaching reading. I reprinted that critique in my book to demonstrate how early the defects of the sight method were recognized by responsible educators who were not seduced by the siren songs of the reformers.[1]

But in my lectures, I encountered parents who told me that their child was already dyslexic before entering school. How could that be? Were they born that way? I could not honestly answer that question until the fall of 1988, when a man named Edward Miller called me from his home in North Carolina.[2] Ed had seen me on a television interview in 1984 and was so astounded by what I had said about dyslexia that he decided to get my book on the National Education Association, *NEA: Trojan Horse in American Education*.

Miller was particularly interested in this subject because he himself was dyslexic and had been since the first grade. He had been taught to read in a rural school in North Carolina by a young teacher fresh out of college who used the sight method. At first Miller thought it was stupidity that was causing his reading problem. But in the fourth grade he proved that he was not stupid by memorizing the multiplication table and winning a prize in class.

From then on Miller saw his reading problem merely as a

handicap for which he compensated with all sorts of tricks. For example, he found that he could pass many essay tests by writing short, simple sentences in which all the words were correctly spelled. He might get a C for his efforts, but Cs were better than Fs.

Miller even made it through North Carolina State College. In fact, despite his reading disability, he was able to become a math teacher and finally an assistant administrator in a high school in Hollywood, Florida.

It was by reading an excerpt from Rudolf Flesch's book, *Why Johnny Can't Read*, in a newspaper in 1956 that Miller learned there were two ways of teaching reading: the phonetic way and the look-say, or sight way. He realized that he had been taught by the sight method and had adjusted to his reading handicap in as successful a way as possible.

But it wasn't until 1986 that Miller decided to investigate the matter of dyslexia further. His young grandson, Kevin, then in the first grade, had developed a reading problem. In his grandson's pain and suffering, he saw a duplicate of himself. He knew that Kevin had learned to read by the sight method because the boy could read his little sight vocabulary books rapidly. But when it came to the little phonetic books that Miller had given him, Kevin had extreme difficulty. Miller could see that his grandson was trying to guess the words. The process of sounding out the words was too painful.

In observing this phenomenon, Miller recalled what he had read in my NEA book about the Russian psychologists Luria and Pavlov, and how they had devised a way of artificially inducing behavioral disorganization by introducing two conflicting stimuli to the organism. Miller believed that he was seeing the same process at work in Kevin. He was sure that Kevin had learned a way of reading at an early age that was interfering with his attempt to decode the little phonetic books.

Kevin had apparently learned a way of reading that conflicted with the phonetic method, and it was causing "dyslexia." But Miller wondered how the boy could have developed such a strong automatic sight way of looking at words without any formal reading instruction. The answer came when Miller examined the little preschool books that Kevin had been reading, including the popular Dr. Seuss books, the contents of which Kevin had memorized by sight. Indeed, if Kevin had become a sight reader by having memorized the words in these books, he would have had a problem by entering a first-grade class in which the teacher was using a phonetic reading program. That explained how a child could enter school already "dyslexic."

To my mind, that was a very significant discovery by Miller. It answered the question I had previously been unable to answer. It also brought my attention to the entire field of preschool readers that millions of children are memorizing, thus causing reading problems that would affect their ability to learn at school, problems that parents would assume were caused by something wrong with their children.

Indeed, most parents are unaware that the Dr. Seuss books were created to supplement the whole-word reading programs in the schools. Most people assume that Dr. Seuss made up his stories using his own words. The truth is that a textbook publisher supplied Dr. Seuss with a sight vocabulary of 223 words that he was to use in writing the book, a sight vocabulary in harmony with the sight-reading programs the schools were using. Thus, the children would enter first grade having already mastered a sight vocabulary of several hundred words, thereby making first-grade reading a breeze.

Because the Dr. Seuss books are so simple and delightful, many people assume that they were easy to write. But Dr. Seuss debunked that idea in an interview he gave *Arizona* magazine in June 1981. He said:

> They think I did it in twenty minutes. That damned *Cat in the Hat* took nine months until I was satisfied. I did it for a textbook house and they sent me a word list. That was due to the Dewey revolt in the Twenties, in which they threw out phonic reading and went to word recognition, as if you're reading a Chinese pictograph instead

of blending sounds of different letters. I think killing phonics was one of the greatest causes of illiteracy in the country. Anyway, they had it all worked out that a healthy child at the age of four can learn so many words in a week and that's all. So there were two hundred and twenty-three words to use in this book. I read the list three times and I almost went out of my head. I said, I'll read it once more and if I can find two words that rhyme that'll be the title of my book. (That's genius at work.) I found "cat" and "hat" and I said, "The Title will be *The Cat in the Hat.*"[3]

So Dr. Seuss was quite aware of what the educators were up to. He was correct in citing John Dewey, the progressive educator, as the culprit in this insidious changeover from phonics to the sight method, which Seuss believed was one of the greatest causes of illiteracy in America. But somehow that insight, made by America's most famous writer of children's books, has escaped our educators.

Meanwhile, bookstores are now awash with colorful preschool books that turn children into sight readers without parents knowing what is being done to them. Knowledgeable moms and dads will teach their children phonics while also reading these beautifully illustrated books. But most parents will be completely unaware of the harm they are causing by allowing their children to memorize these books. They may even be pleased when their kids are able to "read" them easily and happily. Nowadays, publishers are selling books for preschoolers with audio recordings so children can learn to read by the sight method without their parents' help. There ought to be a warning on these books informing parents that their children can become dyslexic if they memorize these books by sight.

Meanwhile, Miller went to great lengths to bring his ideas about "educational dyslexia" to the powers that be in government and the universities, but found little enthusiasm or interest in his research. Some of these experts on dyslexia, doing research on large government grants, were not interested in any theories that might undercut their own well-financed projects.

So Miller decided to do something that would force the experts to recognize that the sight method of teaching reading could cause dyslexia. He began experimenting on a test that would demonstrate beyond any doubt that there was such a phenomenon as "educational dyslexia." It took about ten months of work before he finally devised an ingenious test that anyone could duplicate, that would indicate clearly whether a child, or adult, was a sight reader or a phonetic reader and at what point the child's reading mode became permanent. The test would also provide the means of scientifically measuring the severity of an individual's dyslexia.

The test consists of two sets of words: the first set is composed of 260 sight words taken from two of Dr. Seuss's books, *The Cat in the Hat* and *Green Eggs and Ham*. The second set contains 260 equally simple words drawn from Rudolf Flesch's phonetic word lists in *Why Johnny Can't Read*. The sight words are arranged in alphabetical order across the page. They include such multisyllabic words as *about, another, mother, playthings, something, yellow*; words from Flesch's book, also arranged alphabetically across the page, are all at first-grade level, single syllable and phonetically regular. In other words, for a child who knows his or her phonics, neither set of words would pose any problem.

By now hundreds of children have been given the MWIA, or the Miller Word Identification Assessment, and what it shows is that children who are taught by the sight method read the sight words rather quickly with few errors, but when they are then required to read the one-syllable, phonetically regular words, they slow down considerably and make many more errors. For example, on tests conducted by Miller, an eleven-year-old child was able to read the sight words at fifty-one words per minute with no errors, but read the phonetic words at seventeen words per minute with ninety-one errors. That child was clearly dyslexic. A second child, age seven, read the sight words at a speed of forty-four words per minute with no errors, but read the phonetic words at twenty-four words per minute with forty-seven errors.[4]

Both youngsters had become dyslexic. The fact that they could

t words at over thirty words per minute meant that
.dentification mode was automatic and, therefore, per-
ñxed. Their cognitive block against phonics had been
d by the way they had learned to read. Unless the blockage
.oved through intensive remedial intervention, it would
a major lifelong handicap, preventing them from pursuing
s that required accurate reading skills.

.n January 1990 Miller obtained permission to administer his
. to sixty-eight students at the Ronda-Clingman Elementary
.hool, a rural school with an enrollment of about six hundred
ıear the town of Ronda in Wilkes County, North Carolina. Of the
sixty-eight students, twenty-five were fourth graders, twenty-six were
second graders, and seventeen students were from different grades
in Title I. The results were alarming.[5]

Of the twenty-six second graders, five were phonetic readers,
eleven were permanently holistic readers (with a sight-reading speed
of over 30 words per minute) and therefore educationally dyslexic,
and ten were in a state of reading limbo; that is, they hadn't yet
developed automaticity in either word-identification mode and
could either become fluent phonetic readers or educationally dyslexic readers. The outcome would depend on how they were taught
to read in the next few months.[6]

Of the twenty-five fourth graders, fourteen were phonetic
readers and eleven were holistic—that is, educationally dyslexic.
None were in an indeterminate state. In other words, they had all
developed the degree of automaticity in their word-identification
mode that made their reading mode permanent. If this fourth-grade
class was typical of fourth-grade classes throughout North Carolina,
this meant that 44 percent of all students in the public schools of
that state would emerge at the end of their school careers educationally dyslexic; that is, functionally illiterate.[7]

Of the seventeen students in Title I, six were phonetic readers,
six were holistic (educationally dyslexic), and five were in limbo.
Of the latter, four were in first grade, indicating that their reading

instruction was leading them into educational dyslexia.[8]

What was happening at the Ronda-Clingman school was going on in every elementary school in North Carolina. Were the authorities concerned? Miller had actually gone to the state education authorities in September 1989 and demonstrated to them his theory on the artificial induction of dyslexia. Two months later he received a letter from Betty Jean Foust, the state's consultant for reading communication skills. She wrote:

> This letter is in response to your request that I review your materials and comment upon your theory of dyslexia. Members of the Department of Public Instruction believe in a multiple approach to teaching reading. We believe that phonics may help the beginning reader if it is done early and kept simple. We do not feel phonics are useful with older students. In my teaching experience, I have encountered several students who could not hear sounds; therefore, we used other methods for learning to read. In my opinion, all students do not need a phonics assessment. We have never promoted reading words out of context as your assessment does. Time is precious in our schools, and we need activities which promote achievement. Secondly, I believe all students can be taught to read. Some can read better than others, but all students can learn something. We need to guard against the use of dyslexia as a term for "catch all reading problems."[9]

Thus spake the state reading authority!

In January 1991, Miller gained permission to test sixty-two students at Dade Christian School, a private school in Miami, Florida. The school, with an enrollment of about one thousand students, is racially mixed, with many children from Spanish-speaking families. Of the sixty-two students tested, twenty-six were in fourth grade, nineteen were in second grade, and seventeen were in a special group selected from second and third grades because of the difficulties they were having in reading. Of the nineteen second graders, fourteen were established phonetic readers, four were holistic, and one was indeterminate; that is, in the limbo state. All of the sixteen children in the special group were educationally dyslexic. Of the twenty-six fourth graders, twenty-four were phonetic readers, and only two were educationally dyslexic.[10]

In other words, while in the public schools of North Carolina forty-four out of one hundred students were becoming educationally dyslexic because of their reading-instruction methods, only eight out of one hundred were becoming educationally dyslexic at the private school in Florida. But even that rate was too high. In any case, Miller had not ascertained how those two dyslexic students in the fourth grade had become that way, nor was he given the academic histories of the seventeen children in the special group.

The implications to be drawn from Edward Miller's theory on the artificial induction of dyslexia are most significant. In the first place, they imply that dyslexia is being caused by the reading-instruction methods presently being used in most American public schools, and that educational dyslexia can be prevented by the teaching of intensive, systematic phonics so that the children will become phonetic readers. As Miller has pointed out, a phonetic reader cannot become dyslexic.

If what Miller discovered is correct, then the millions of dollars the federal government is spending on finding the genetic causes of dyslexia are a total waste. In addition, the billions of Title I dollars the US Department of Education has spent in support of reading programs that are causing educational dyslexia are worse than a waste. They are being used to commit a horrible crime against the children of this country.

For years now, we have been telling the public that the dyslexia that afflicts millions of perfectly healthy children is being caused by the reading-instruction methods used in our schools. Whole language, which is presently sweeping through the primary schools of America like a plague, is the latest manifestation of this insane addiction to defective teaching methods. It is sad to know that millions of innocent children will be permanently damaged by these methods, used by teachers who believe they are doing the right thing.

In April 1992, Miller obtained permission to retest the same students at Ronda-Clingman he had tested in 1990 using the same first-grade test. Fifty-one of the original sixty-eight students were available for retesting.

The results showed that none of the students who were holistic readers in 1990 had become phonetic readers in the interim. Most of them were able to read these first-grade words faster, and their accuracy had improved in the phonetic part of the test. But more than half of the dyslexic students miscalled some of the very sight words they had read correctly in 1990. One student, who as a fourth grader had made twelve errors in 1990, made twenty-nine errors in 1992 as a sixth grader on the identical test. In other words, this student read better in the fourth grade than in the sixth grade! In fact, seventeen of the twenty-seven sixth graders did better in 1990 as fourth graders than they did two years later on the same first-grade test!

And nowhere was the dumbing-down process more obvious than among the good phonetic readers of the second and third grades of 1990, who were now in the fourth and sixth grades. Of the thirteen students who had achieved the best scores in 1990, nine made more errors on the very same test in 1992. One student who had made only two errors as a fourth grader in 1990 made eighteen errors two years later as a sixth grader. Whereas he had missed zero sight words in 1990, he missed eight in 1992. And whereas he had missed only two of the phonetic words in 1990, he missed ten in 1992. Obviously, whatever was being taught at Ronda-Clingman was not advancing the students' academic skills. On the contrary, many of the students had regressed.

The data also showed that twenty-eight of the fifty-one students tested missed more of the sight words in 1992 than in 1990, indicating that there is a limit on how many sight words an individual can retain in memory. Apparently, the dyslexic will retain only those sight words that are frequently seen. Simply put, words learned by sight but seen rarely are often forgotten.

Another important phenomenon Miller observed through his testing is that even the worst of the educationally dyslexic readers have a good deal of phonetic knowledge that they can only tap through conscious effort.

Miller obtained this vital data by having the children go back and spell the words they missed. Almost always they were able to reread the words correctly after spelling them. Obviously, there was enough phonetic information in the spelling alone that enabled the student to experience the word as a phonetic entity. The problem for the sight reader was that the holistic reflex overrode and thereby suppressed whatever phonetic knowledge the reader may have acquired through oral spelling. In fact, it was the holistic reflex that was creating the block against the phonetic experience.

One of the features of the whole language reading program is a writing exercise called *invented spelling*, in which the student is encouraged to write a word without regard to its correct spelling. If he orally spells the word as he has written it, he will not see that the sequence of letters makes phonetic sense. The whole concept of invented spelling simply reinforces a view, encouraged by his teacher, that letters in words are just arbitrary, nonsensical graphic conglomerations that depict a word. To the severely dyslexic, letters have no meaning, and that is why they become lifelong nonreaders. To inflict this kind of diabolical pedagogy on a healthy child who wants to learn to read is a horrendous crime.

Through his tests, Miller also developed a means of measuring an individual's phonetic knowledge and a scale that measures the severity of the dyslexic's handicap. Just as a physician can measure a fever with a thermometer on a scale of 98.7 to 108, Miller could measure the severity of the dyslexic condition on a scale of 1 to 100, based on the number of words miscalled on the phonetic portion of the word identification assessment.

The scale is applied only to students who have developed a holistic reflex. A score of 1 would indicate a very mild reading hand-icap, while a score of 100 would indicate an extremely severe case of educational dyslexia. A score of 8 or 10 may indicate a slight reading problem for a second grader, but for a sixth grader it would represent a more serious handicap since the measuring instrument is a first-grade test. Of the fifty-one students tested at Ronda-Clingman in 1992, thirteen had no handicap, seventeen showed handicaps from 8 to 13, and twenty students had handicaps from 21 to 100.

Although Miller went to great lengths to bring his findings to the attention of the powers that be in government, the foundations, and the private sector, he found no interest. It is hoped that this book will bring Miller's extraordinary work to the public at large so it can be used productively by Americans who want to solve our reading problem.

Miller's test dramatically illustrated the startling difference between a holistic sight reader and a phonetic one. And all of those he tested were perfectly healthy children. Are there children born with neurological problems that make learning to read a problem? Yes, but even many of these children can be taught to read by intensive phonics if instructed with great patience and understanding.

The best way for parents to prevent educational dyslexia is to teach their children to read phonetically before giving them the Dr. Seuss books or any other preschool books to read. They should avoid having their children memorize words by their configurations alone, because once that mode of viewing words becomes an automatic reflex, it will create a blockage against seeing the phonetic structure of the words.

A preschool child who has memorized a sight vocabulary will do well in kindergarten and first grade, and even in second grade. But as the child moves into the third grade, where reading demands are much greater, involving many new words that the child's overburdened memory cannot handle, the child will experience a learning breakdown.

But the problem can also show up in the first grade where the teaching method is phonics-based. This is often the case in many private and religious schools where reading is taught phonetically. If a child enters the first grade in such a school after having already memorized several hundred sight words from preschool readers, that child will most likely have already developed a blockage against looking at words phonetically. That's why we see "dyslexia" among some first graders.

When they entered school at the age of five or six, these children felt very confident, very intelligent. After all, they had all taught themselves to speak their own language very nicely without the aid of certified teachers or school. And when they enter school, they expect to be able to learn to read with the same competence. And normally, this is what happens when they are taught to read phonetically and begin to master our alphabetic system.

If they are taught to read holistically, mastering our alphabetically written words becomes a superhuman task. And because the teaching method seems to defy all logic and common sense, their minds react against such teaching just as their stomachs would if some sort of poison were eaten. The stomach throws up, rejecting the poison, and I suspect that ADD is a form of mental rejection of pedagogical poisoning.

What other defense does the child have against pedagogical poisoning? What Ritalin does is lower the defense against such poisoning. The child becomes a docile, defenseless victim of whatever nonsense the teacher is inflicting on the child. And the child is usually dumped into special education for the rest of his or her academic life.

Fortunately, homeschooling parents are in the best position to guard their children against the kind of pedagogy that is turning millions of healthy children into LDs (learning disabled). They can begin teaching their children to read phonetically as early as the child wishes. Above all, they must avoid having their preschoolers memorize words holistically without any knowledge of the letter sounds. If you tell children that letters stand for sounds, they will begin to understand what our alphabetic system is all about.

Ed Miller died in July 2010. He enters the pantheon of those unsung heroes who have provided humanity with the means to improve their lives and in particular the lives of schoolchildren.

That is not what can be said of those who, as professional educators, continue to inflict pain and suffering on the most vulnerable of our citizens. This deliberate dumbing down of American children must stop!

10
THE VICTIMS OF EDUCATIONAL MALPRACTICE

I loathed school.
—DAVID MAMET, *THE SECRET KNOWLEDGE* (2011)

The great tragedy in America is that the vast majority of Americans who acquire school-induced dyslexia are unable to develop their full potential as productive human beings. They are denied the rich cultural heritage to be found in books. Many remain stuck in the underclass for the rest of their lives. Others struggle to get and keep good jobs.

But in America, where free enterprise offers the ambitious unlimited opportunities to build businesses and thrive, high achievers have found ingenious ways to get around their school-acquired reading handicap. And many of them keep their illiteracy a secret. This was the case with self-made millionaire Jay Thiessens, owner of a successful manufacturing company, B&J Machine and Tool. Lewis Schiff wrote in his book *Business Brilliant*, "For most of his life, though, Thiessens harbored what he called 'a little secret.' The secret was that Thiessens was illiterate. Thanks to a few lenient teachers and a lot of vocational classes, he was handed a high school diploma in 1962 despite the fact that he could not read. Over the ensuing years, he developed a kind of mental block about reading and, by the age of fifty-six, he still could not make his way through a children's book."[1]

How can an obviously intelligent, ambitious young man spend twelve years in school and not learn to read? Apparently, progressive educators have found a way to make that happen on a scale that boggles the mind. Thiessens never knew that he was a victim of school-induced dyslexia. Schiff wrote further, "Thiessens' story is an extreme example of a very commonly observed fact. A lot of entrepreneurs were poor students when they were young and had particular difficulties with reading and writing. A 2007 study concluded that about 35 percent of U.S. small-business owners suffer from some form of dyslexia, compared with about 10 percent of the general population and just 1 percent of corporate managers."[2]

The reason for that is quite interesting. Since it is difficult for an illiterate to climb the corporate ladder if he or she can't read or write, these ambitious individuals are forced to create their own companies, where they can hire others to do the tasks that require literacy. Schiff continued:

> The most successful dyslexic entrepreneur in the United States is probably self-made billionaire Charles R. Schwab, founder of the brokerage that bears his name. When Schwab was applying to colleges as a young man, he had miserable verbal SAT scores and was accepted at Stanford only because he was recruited for the golf team . . . but he almost flunked out because he failed the same introductory English course twice. "It was a very debilitating, depressing thing for me to do that," Schwab recalls, "because I was thought of as pretty bright and I didn't realize how incompetent I was at the skill of writing."[3]

Schwab was forced to endure the pain of a needless handicap foisted on him by his progressive educators, who were more interested in advancing their agenda than teaching kids to read in the proper phonetic manner. As a reporter, I (Samuel) encountered a similar individual many years ago when doing a story on Boston's famous Quincy Market. He was the owner of the market's most popular restaurant, and during the interview he told me that he couldn't read even though he was a university graduate. I offered to tutor him with my *Alpha-Phonics* program, and he accepted the offer. I would go to his office after hours and teach him the sounds of our alphabet letters. When I taught him the short *a*, he asked if anybody else knew this. His ignorance of our alphabetic system was total. He then told me something that I will never forget. He said that he would rather be beaten than have to read.

That is the kind of pain inflicted on millions of American children by the progressive sadists who control our public schools. And as we know, socialist utopians have been responsible for inflicting more pain on the human race than adherents to any other political philosophy. And they continue to do that today in America.

Other successful dyslexics include brilliant entrepreneur Richard Branson, creator of Virgin Airlines; actor Tom Cruise; Olympic athlete Bruce Jenner; actress-singer Cher; impersonator Rich Little; film producer Stephen Spielberg; comedian Jay Leno; actress Whoopi Goldberg; and Major League Baseball pitcher Nolan Ryan, who said, "When I had dyslexia, they didn't diagnose it as that. It was frustrating and embarrassing. I could tell you a lot of horror stories about what you feel like on the inside."[4]

Famous actress Loretta Young wrote, "I hated school. . . . One of the reasons was a learning disability, dyslexia, which no one could understand. I still can't spell."[5]

Henry Winkler, another victim of school-induced dyslexia, was able to achieve great success as an actor despite his dyslexia. He says of his schooling, "It was extraordinarily difficult. It was like climbing Mount Everest with no clothes on. I didn't get math. Reading is still difficult. Spelling was out of the question. I had teachers who literally had no time or patience."[6]

However, he didn't realize he was dyslexic until he was an adult. He says:

> I was 31. My stepson was in third grade and was diagnosed. It was then that I realized: "Oh, my goodness, that was me." Then I saw I had been saying to him all the things that were said to me—"You're so smart, so verbal, you're just lazy." I learned just to be quiet and support him. . . .
>
> Be the most supportive that we can possibly be [with kids with learning disabilities]. Children's feelings about themselves when they meet with frustration again and again can become so damaged and so brutalized.

In other words, Winkler has accepted the notion that there is nothing wrong with the teachers or the schools. The problem is that many children, like his stepson, are born with learning problems that the schools can't properly deal with. The idea that these problems are deliberately caused by the whole-word reading programs in the schools never even crossed his mind. Why? The idea is too incredible. As we have said, it is easier to believe a credible lie than an incredible truth.

Playwright David Mamet wrote of his school experience in a way that probably echoes the experiences of millions of children:

> I loathed school. I never opened a schoolbook. I failed every test given to me. (I was sent back from second to first grade, and was enrolled in remedial reading classes.) It never occurred to me to point out the books that occupied all my leisure time, and suggest that perhaps they left one little time for Dick and Jane ("Oh Dick, see Spot run. Run, Spot, run. Jane see Spot run," et cetera).
>
> The habit, inculcated at school and at home, of thinking myself a failure persisted through my school career.[7]

It makes perfect sense that a literary genius would find his public school curriculum loathsome. But its brutality forced him to think of himself as a failure during all of his time in school. That is what the dumbing-down process does to intelligent kids. What it does to the average child is unspeakable.

Despite all attempts to expose the criminal educators who have deliberately turned perfectly healthy, intelligent American children into dyslexics, their crimes are still being committed every day in American public schools. What is needed is for the parents of these dyslexics to organize into a group and sue the education system by means of a class action suit. So far, the courts have rejected lawsuits by individual dyslexics against the education system. But a class action suit might fare better in our courts of law.

11

THE READING CONSPIRACY MARCHES ON

Intelligence is not all that important in the exercise of power, and is often, in point of fact, useless.
—HENRY KISSINGER

As America's mushrooming literacy crisis was becoming more and more obvious in the 1960s, questions were being asked, and solutions were being sought. The political class, however, knows of only one way to "address" problems: Spend more taxpayer money. In 1965, lawmakers in Washington, DC, followed the same approach to solving the nation's reading dilemma, and Congress passed the Elementary and Secondary Education Act (ESEA) with its now-infamous Title I compensatory education program. Flush with federal taxpayer dollars, the new Title I bureaucracy promptly began showering billions of dollars on government schools across the country. It was supposed to save students who were failing in reading from a life of functional illiteracy. Instead, as is often the case with government programs, the new federal cash cow was milked by vested interests. The seventeen thousand school districts on the federal dole indulged in an orgy of spending and hiring, resulting in a bonanza for the educational establishment and its suppliers.

On the other hand, despite all the federal funding, the literacy disaster among American children continued to grow. Indeed, within a decade, information on the results of the scheme was beginning to trickle out in newspapers from coast to coast: The disastrous decline in reading had not improved. In fact, based on SAT scores, the situation was actually in an alarming nosedive. By September 1, 1991, for example, a writer from the *Boston Globe* reported a dip in scores, but even more "ominous" was a drop in the verbal scores of even the nation's best students. "In 1972, College Board data showed that 116,630 students nationwide scored 600 or above—of the maximum possible 800—on the verbal SAT, compared with 74,836 in 1991," the *Globe* reported. "Overall this year, average verbal scores nationally dropped to 422, down 2, and math score to 474, also down 2. The verbal scores were the lowest in 20 years."[1] The *Globe* itself described the phenomenon as "a prolonged and broad-scale decline unequalled in US history."[2] And indeed, it was shocking: The mean verbal score on the SAT went from 467 in 1966–67 to 424 in 1980—a drop of 43 points in less than a decade and a half!

Within a few years of passing the ESEA, the utter lack of results from Title I in terms of improving literacy in America was becoming clearer. By 1969 a blue-ribbon Committee on Reading was appointed by the National Academy of Education to examine America's reading problems and offer recommendations on how to deal with them. "It is not cynical to suggest that the chief beneficiaries of the Elementary and Secondary Education Act (ESEA) have been members of the school systems—both professional and paraprofessional—for whom new jobs were created," explained the committee's 1975 *Toward a Literate Society* report, which was virtually ignored. "Seven years and as many billions of dollars later, the children of the poor have not been 'compensated' as clearly as the employees of the school systems through this investment."[3]

To deal with the obvious problems, the committee offered a rather radical recommendation: create a voucher system to help students buy reading instruction, a sort of "reading-stamps" program. "We believe that an effective national reading effort should bypass the existing education macrostructure," the committee continued in its report. "At a minimum, it should provide alternatives to that structure. That is, the planning, implementing, and discretionary powers of budgeting should not rest with those most likely to have a vested interest in maintaining the status quo, especially given their unpromising 'track record.'"[4]

Those statements proved historic: Never before in American educational history had a committee of educators pointed out the existence of "vested interests" impeding improvements in education. In essence, the committee was admitting in its report that the most serious impediment standing in the way of literacy in America was the educational establishment itself. The implications of the bombshell were monumental. If Americans hoped to improve education and produce literate citizens, the education establishment would need to be bypassed. The irony was incredible too. The education system, supposedly created to ensure universal literacy, was now being identified as an *impediment* to improving literacy. If and how $100 billion worth of institutionalized educational malpractice could be circumvented, though, was another matter entirely.

In fact, just such an effort had already been undertaken by the federal government in the 1970s during the Nixon administration with the so-called Right to Read program. Instead of eradicating illiteracy, however, that scheme failed as well—primarily because it was unsuccessful in overcoming the education establishment's monopoly over reading instruction. The program was eventually shut down in 1980 with little fanfare.

The next year, the educational establishment was once again put on trial with the publication of *Why Johnny* Still *Can't Read* by Dr. Rudolf Flesch. It was, essentially, an update on the ongoing literacy crisis. "Twenty-five years ago I studied American methods of teaching reading and warned against educational catastrophe," Flesch wrote. "Now it has happened."[5] This time, though, the educators and the education establishment mostly ignored their longtime nemesis, confident and secure in the knowledge that they were essentially untouchable. Their progressive power was firmly entrenched—especially with the tenure system.

Instead of reaching for the pitchforks and torches, America at large mostly yawned off the stunning indictment, probably because the nation had already started to accept widespread illiteracy and declining literacy levels as normal. In 1955 expectations were still high, with excellence understood to be the goal. By the next generation, even minimal competency was enough for much of the public. Plus, by the early 1980s, there were all sorts of new excuses for the decline that could be relied upon, ranging from television and the nuclear arms race to the breakdown of the family. The reading fiasco had been growing for so long—and appeared to be so hard to combat—that to many Americans, it seemed easier to simply adapt to the illiteracy epidemic than aim for the universal literacy that now seemed so far out of reach.

At the same time, policymakers in key states were ensuring that the reading crisis would be perpetuated for many years to come. In 1980 Texas's state textbook selection committee adopted five whole-word basal reading programs to be used throughout the state's public schools for the next five years. Incredibly, the decision came after Flesch had published in the November 1979 *Family Circle* magazine his list of the "dismal dozen" whole-word programs. In the piece, he advised parents to beware if they didn't want their children to become reading disabled. All of the Texas adoptions were among Flesch's "dismal dozen." Two years later, the California Board of Education adopted nine basal reading programs. Only one was phonics oriented. Thus, the government-school system in America's two largest states embarked on an unprecedented program of educational malpractice, ensuring the production of millions of functionally illiterate citizens. Making matters even worse, Texas and California have especially large Hispanic populations who urgently needed to learn English in the most effective way possible—through intensive, systematic phonics. Instead, they were denied access to the method that demonstrably would have made them fluent readers in English.

In 1982, President Ronald Reagan's secretary of education, Terrel H. Bell, ordered another survey of America's failing education system. An eighteen-member National Commission on Excellence in Education was created. In April 1983 it issued its highly critical report, *A Nation at Risk: The Imperative for Education Reform.* Its most damning statement was widely quoted by the media. "The educational foundations of our society are presently being eroded by a rising tide of mediocrity that threatens our very future as a Nation and a people," the report found. "If an unfriendly foreign power had attempted to impose on America the mediocre educational performance that exists today, we might well have viewed it as an act of war."[6]

In response to the full-blown indictment of the education system, some state governments did make adjustments, resulting in minor improvements in graduation rates and SAT scores. However, the sort of massive, systemic change that was really needed never came, and schools continued to rely on their harmful reading programs. As a result, serious improvements in education remained elusive. The reason for the lack of real reforms, though, is simple: the educational criminals implementing Dewey's plan to dumb down American students and fundamentally transform America had absolutely no intention of abandoning it.

In response to growing public outrage over the failure of education, educators demanded the same bogus solution they always demand: more money. Unsurprisingly, politicians—experts at squandering taxpayers' hard-earned dollars—promptly capitulated. As Flesch had already proven, the progressive education establishment was virtually impossible to change. Indeed, it would never even admit that anything *ought* to be changed. More money clearly did not solve the problem, and it will not solve it going forward. That means parents cannot rely on government schools to teach their children how to read with the proper, phonetic method.

Just one lonely lawmaker on Capitol Hill took a serious interest in the controversy over reading methods and tried to act on it: the late Sen. Edward Zorinsky of Nebraska. In July 1983 he introduced Senate Joint Resolution 138 to create a National Commission on Teacher Education. "The colleges of education and departments of education are not subject to scrutiny as are our public schools," he explained. "Therefore, a national Commission would be the most effective way to look into this matter. I also believe that we should not put this investigation into the hands of the education community alone. Representatives of business and industry as well as parents should be included in any study because they are also directly affected and can provide a fresh perspective."[7]

On June 7, 1984, the Subcommittee on Education, Arts, and Humanities of the Senate Committee on Labor and Human Resources held hearings on the issues. I (Samuel) was among the witnesses who testified, along with others, such as celebrated black educator Marva Collins, on the same story of educational malpractice in the teaching of reading at public schools. The hearings were published, and a digitized version is available today online.[8] However, as expected, nothing came of the testimonies. The education establishment had too many friends in Congress who could stop any attempt by parents or critics to change anything. Thus, Zorinsky's bill to form the commission failed.

Much more recently, in November 2007 the National Endowment for the Arts unveiled its own report, *Reading at Risk*, documenting the alarming state of literacy in the United States. The investigation found that the situation continues to deteriorate. "*Reading at Risk* is not a report that the National Endowment for the Arts is happy to issue," it stated. "This comprehensive survey of

American literary reading presents a detailed but bleak assessment of the decline of reading's role in the nation's culture. For the first time in modern history, less than half of the adult population now reads literature, and these trends reflect a larger decline in other sorts of reading. Anyone who loves literature or values the cultural, intellectual, and political importance of active and engaged literacy in American society will respond to this report with grave concern."[9]

In other words, America is becoming an increasingly illiterate nation, which does not bode well for its future. However, as Flesch recommended way back in 1955, the solution is actually very simple: beginning in primary school, teach every child how to read with intensive systematic phonics without pictures. Restoring high levels of literacy in America is literally that simple. After young Americans know how to read properly, they will read whatever interests them, thus expanding their intellectual horizons. However, in 2015, there are still no signs that the nation's public schools will be returning to intensive phonics anytime soon.

Instead, the *New York Times* of June 27, 2014, reported that New York City schools were seriously considering adopting a "new" approach to reading—now called "literacy learning"—developed at Teachers College, Columbia University. It is also called "balanced literacy." The new program was developed by literacy author and teacher Lucy Calkins, dubbed the "Teachers College Reading and Writing Project," and was being pushed for adoption by the new schools chancellor, Carmen Farina, a close friend of Calkins.[10]

If you want to see the program in action, the TCRWP website, as of this writing, had fifty-seven videos demonstrating all aspects of the program.[11] I watched a twenty-one-minute video of a lesson given by an attractive young teacher to twenty first graders seated on the floor. The teacher sat on a stool beside a large easel and opened the lesson by reading a poem, "A Circle of Friends," on a large pad. The children read along with their teacher. The lesson was called a "Shared Reading Experience." She then placed a large, colorful book on the easel, titled *The Scrubbing Machine*.

She then went through the book, showing each of its full-page colored illustrations. She read the small print at the bottom of each page, and then said, "Let's do what readers always do, predict."[12]

That was news to me. I thought that reading was decoding what the author had to say, not predicting what the author was going to say. So the children tried to predict how the story would end. They did that by looking at the pictures and not the text. She also told them that they had to solve the problem. The problem? The scrubbing machine would not stop. She told them to look for clues. The main character of the story was Mrs. Wishy-Washy. In other words, the whole purpose of the lesson was to teach the children that reading consisted of predicting the story and solving its problem. The children, trying to give the correct answers, seemed bewildered by the whole dumb exercise. These six-year-olds were intelligent little human beings. They had taught themselves to speak their own language and had watched hundreds of hours of television. Now they were being confronted with something quite nonsensical.

Next, the children went to their tables, found their books, and tried to predict and solve their problems. They all had different illustrated books telling different stories. The teacher sat on the floor with several children, helping them do their predictions. She then told them to write their predictions with invisible pens. Finally, they were told to read with their reading partners. The room then got a little noisy and chaotic. At the end of the lesson, the teacher told the class that they had all learned a great deal: they had learned how to predict and solve the problem.

In other words, the kids had been taught *about* reading, based on dubious premises. They had not been taught *how to* read. And all of this was done with the right side of the brain. Indeed, that's what the new "literacy education" is all about: teaching kids about reading, not teaching them how to read by mastering our phonetic system.

It should be noted that Teachers College is the home of the progressive radicals, where Dewey, Cattell, and Thorndike plotted to destroy American literacy and dumb down the American people.

If the schools of New York City adopt the TCRWP, they will be committing a horrendous crime against their children.

If you want to imbibe the latest thinking of our educators on literacy learning, the National Council of Teachers of English has created a special Center for Literacy Education. It has a very informative website that tells you how complicated the whole subject of literacy is. Literacy is now so complex that it requires hundreds of doctors of education to figure it out. The center's latest report, *Remodeling Literacy Learning*, is a perfect example of what the education establishment has become: an asylum for the educationally insane. Once you accept their mind-set you enter a world of esoteric nonsense that only the inner circle of disciples can understand. To subject perfectly healthy, intelligent children to the teachings of these insanities is a crime.[13]

12
THE POLITICS OF THE WHOLE LANGUAGE METHOD

There is no idea so stupid that you can't get some professor to believe it.
—H. L. MENCKEN

t's refreshing and encouraging to know that neuroscientists like Dr. Dehaene have denounced whole language as a faulty way to teach reading. He advocates teaching phonics first, which ensures that the child will become a fluent, efficient reader. But most parents haven't the faintest idea what whole language is. If they did know, they would oppose it strenuously.

The best way to define whole language is to simply quote its proponents, who've written books on the subject. They are not at all reticent about describing their idea of reading progress. In a book entitled *Whole Language, What's the Difference?* written by three whole language professors in 1991, they said:

Whole language represents a major shift in thinking about the reading process. Rather than viewing reading as "getting the words," whole language educators view reading as essentially a process of creating meanings . . . Meaning is created through a *transaction* with whole, meaningful texts (i.e., texts of any length that were written with the intent to communicate meaning).

It is a transaction, not an extraction of the meaning *from* the print, in the sense that the *reader-created* meanings are a fusion of what the reader brings and what the text offers . . . Although students who learn to read in whole language classrooms are, like all proficient readers, eventually able to "read" (or identify) a large inventory of words, learning words is certainly not the goal of whole language.[1]

Another passage from the same book may be even more illuminating:

From a whole-language perspective, reading (and language use in general) is a process of generating hypotheses in a meaning-making transaction in a sociohistorical context. As a transactional process . . . reading is not a matter of "getting the meaning" from text, as if that meaning were *in* the text waiting to be decoded by the reader.

Rather, reading is a matter of readers using the cues print provides and the knowledge they bring with them (of language subsystems, of the world) to construct a unique interpretation.

Moreover, that interpretation is situated: readers' *creations* (not retrievals) of meaning with text vary, depending on their purposes of reading and the expectations of others in the reading event. This view of reading implies that there is no single "correct" meaning for a given text, only plausible meanings.[2]

Now, you might think that all of this pedagogical insanity is taking place in some kind of political vacuum. Nothing could be further from the truth. Whole language practice is very politically oriented:

Learning is a social process . . . Although whole language educators accept the importance of learning through individual interactions with the environment (Piaget 1967), they lean more heavily on Vygotsky's ideas about the social nature of learning (Vygotsky 1978).

Whole language takes seriously Vygotsky's notion of the Zone of Proximal Development (Engstrom 1986) which entails stressing the importance of collaborations (between students and teachers and between peers) through which students can transcend their own individual limitations.[3]

You might ask, "Who is Vygotsky?" Lev Vygotsky (1896–1934) was a Soviet psychologist who worked with Pavlov's colleagues at the State Institute of Experimental Psychology in Moscow in the 1920s and '30s. James Wertsch, Vygotsky's biographer, wrote, "[It] is important to note that Vygotsky was a staunch advocate of dialectical and historical materialism. He was one of the creators of Marxist psychology . . . People such as Vygotsky and his followers devoted every hour of their lives to making certain that the new socialist state, the first grand experiment based on Marxist-Leninist principles, would survive."[4]

Vygotsky's colleague, Alexander Luria, wrote, "Vygotsky was . . . the leading Marxist theoretician among us . . . In [his] hands, Marx's methods of analysis did serve a vital role in shaping our course."[5]

Apparently, these same methods of analysis are also serving to shape the course of the whole language agenda. The three professors cited earlier stated:

The whole language theoretical premise underlying which topics are pursued and how they are treated is: "All knowledge is socially constructed."

Therefore all knowing is political. In an effort to promote critical literacy and thus to help children learn to read the world, not only the word (Shor & [Marxist revolutionary] Freire 1987), teachers who work with theme cycles try—no matter whether the topic is overtly "political" or not—to show how the topic is related to other more general questions.

They try to demystify social institutions by helping children investigate connections between surface facts and underlying social structures, between lived experience and structural features of class, gender and race. They know that not making connections is as political as making connections.[6]

No further explanation needed. "But what about phonics?" you might ask. Here's a view of phonics given in another book on whole language, *Evaluation: Whole Language, Whole Child.*

The way you interpret what the child does will reflect what you understand reading to be. For instance, if she reads the word *feather* for *father*, a phonics-oriented teacher might be pleased because she's come close to sounding the word out.

However, if you believe reading is a meaning-seeking process, you may be concerned that she's overly dependent on phonics at the expense of meaning. You'd be happier with a miscue such as *daddy*, even though it doesn't look or sound anything like the word in the text. At least the meaning would be intact.[7]

The response of any sane educator to that kind of imbecilic pedagogy is that any child who looks at the word *father* and says "daddy" can't read. It's as simple as that. But tell that to a whole language teacher. It is therefore commendable that Dr. Dehaene and other neuroscientists have not been fooled by whole language and are warning parents and educators, as Dr. Orton did in 1929, that this ludicrous form of teaching should be thrown out of the schools.

Most parents haven't the faintest idea that there is a political agenda behind their child's classroom reading instruction. They are also unaware that there is a war going on between conservatives and liberals over how reading should be taught. For example, in an article by whole language advocates in *Education Week* we read:

The accumulating evidence clearly indicates that a New Right philosophy of education has emerged in this country. . . . By limiting reading instruction to systematic phonics instruction, sound-symbol decoding, and literal comprehension, and by aiming its criticism at reading books' story lines in an effort to influence content, the New Right's philosophy runs counter to the research findings and theoretical perspectives of most noted reading authorities.

If this limited view of reading (and, implicitly, of thinking) continues to gain influence . . . the New Right will have successfully impeded the progress of democratic governance founded on the ideal of an educated—and critically thinking—electorate.[8]

First, what is the so-called New Right's philosophy of education that threatens to impede "the progress of democratic governance"? It's the same philosophy espoused by our Founding Fathers, who gave us our limited form of government as outlined in the US Constitution. In those days, education was considered primarily a private, religious, and parental concern. In fact, homeschooling was the rule, and children were taught to read and write at home or at a dame school before they went on to any kind of formal education. And since there was a strong religious component in education, it was implicitly assumed that the purpose of education was to pass on to the future generation the knowledge, wisdom, and values of the previous generation.

That, of course, is no longer the case. When the progressives took over American education at the beginning of the 1900s, their goal was to use the schools as the means of changing America from a capitalist, individualistic, believing nation into a socialist, collectivist, atheist, or humanist nation.

And so, when educators write of "democratic governance," what form of government are they talking about? John Dewey often used the word *democracy* as a euphemism for socialism and, as we know, communist countries often referred to themselves as "democracies," like the late, unlamented German Democratic Republic. A November 1987 article in *The Reading Teacher* describes the socialist purpose behind whole language: "Whole Language views the learner as profoundly social. Thus practice congruent with Whole Language includes participating in a community of readers during small group literature study, peer writing workshops, group social studies projects with built in plans for collaborative learning."[9]

The purpose of whole language is to get rid of individualism. Reading is not, as whole language people claim, a social or collectivist activity. It's an individual activity in which the reader is engaged with the author on a one-on-one basis. Indeed, reading is the one activity in which an individual can retreat into his or her own world of thought and pleasure by absorbing the words and experiences of authors living and dead.

In reality a "community of readers" is really a community of believers all believing in the same thing. The same article speaks of a "political vision woven through whole language beliefs. . . . Its goal is empowerment of learners and teachers."

What does learning to read have to do with political power? Why should a child in primary school, struggling to master the three Rs, be concerned with "empowerment"? A January 1989 article in *Phi Delta Kappan* by whole language guru Frank Smith makes it quite clear that whole language is a political movement: "Literacy is power. Literacy can do more than transform thought; it can transform the world. Literacy can raise social consciousness and provide a means for the expression and fulfillment of this consciousness. . . . Paulo Freire's pedagogic technique raises social consciousness not as a way of using literacy but as a means of acquiring it."[10]

Smith's reference to Paulo Freire is quite revealing, for Freire was a leading Marxist theoretician who used adult literacy campaigns in the Third World to foment Marxist revolution. He had worked with socialist and revolutionary governments in Tanzania, Guinea-Bissau, and Angola.

Freire was considered a "master dialectician" by his progressive American admirers and colleagues, who revered him as a sort of Brazilian incarnation of John Dewey. In the introduction to *Literacy: Reading the Word and the World*, written with radical professor Donaldo Macedo of the University of Massachusetts, Freire wrote:

In order to overcome at least partly, this "crisis of democracy," a critical literacy campaign must be instituted. It must be a literacy campaign that transcends the current debate over the literacy crisis which tends to recycle old assumptions and values concerning the meaning and usefulness of literacy, that is a notion that literacy is simply a mechanical process which overemphasizes the technical acquisition of reading and writing skills . . . We call for a view of literacy as a form of cultural politics.[11]

That's about as good and clear a description of whole language theory and practice as one is likely to find anywhere. And in order for whole language to dominate the education process, teachers have to be empowered. Frank Smith wrote:

Of course, there is no way that students will be empowered until teachers themselves are empowered. And this will not happen until teachers are autonomous in their classrooms. . . . The basic question is, Who is to be in charge of classrooms—teachers or outsiders? . . . I see but one solution for all these problems. Teachers must become more professional; they must regain control of classrooms, assert themselves politically, and demand that all outside interference in educational practice be halted.[12]

Outsiders, of course, are parents who might object to their children being taught to read by a method that will turn them into functional illiterates. Implicit in the whole language philosophy is that phonics is outmoded and must be rejected. Kenneth Goodman, whole language guru-in-chief, wrote in *What's Whole in Whole Language*: "Phonics methods of teaching reading and writing reduce both to matching letters with sounds. It is a flat-earth view of the world, since it rejects modern science about reading and writing and how they develop."[13]

It is whole language that is comparable to a flat-earth view of the world, since that methodology preceded the development of the alphabet, an invention that made learning to read easy and accessible to everyone. The alphabet did for the ancient world what the computer has done for the modern world. But as we know, there has always been a political agenda behind the whole-word method of teaching reading. John Dewey wrote in *Democracy and Education* in 1916, "The notion that the 'essentials' of elementary education are the three Rs mechanically treated, is based upon ignorance of the essentials needed for realization of democratic ideals."[14]

Yet, it was the three Rs, "mechanically treated," that produced our highly literate Founding Fathers, who could write a Declaration of Independence and create the freest society in history where literacy became virtually universal. Sadly, that high literacy is a thing of the past and won't be revived as long as the public schools are in the hands of the socialists.

The fact that classroom indoctrination should include political content was made clear in an article in *Young Children*, titled "Children's Political Knowledge and Attitudes," coauthored by three professors. They wrote:

> There is a clear rationale for early childhood educators to explore and promote political socialization in young children, and to play an important role in it. Children have and express political knowledge and attitudes. . . . Early childhood educators have an important role in helping children understand their social and political environment. Teachers can choose to model positive citizenship, practice a consensus decision-making process, and foster feelings of altruism and benevolence, all the while providing language opportunities to help children learn politically oriented vocabulary.[15]

In other words, early childhood education should include political indoctrination by way of vocabulary development, which is very much in line with Freire's methodology. In the old days, children sang "My Country 'Tis of Thee," which promoted love of country and its founders. They also sang "America the Beautiful." But that's now old-fashioned, like religion. What's important now is *empowerment.* William T. Fagan wrote in an article titled "Empowered Students; Empowered Teachers": "Teachers have power over how reading and writing are taught, over how children experience reading and writing within the school text. . . . Teachers who impose a narrow view of reading or writing (word sounding, precision in spelling) may confuse children so that they begin to feel powerless in the school context."[16]

The idea that teaching phonics will make a child feel powerless is both ludicrous and imbecilic. When children gain mastery over our alphabetic system, they acquire tremendous intellectual power. But that's not what the utopians want. Indeed, Dewey's socialism was so extreme that he even denied an individual's ownership of his own mind. He wrote in 1916 in *Democracy and Education,* "When knowledge is regarded as originating and developing within an individual, the ties which bind the mental life of one to that of his fellows are ignored and denied. When the social quality of individualized mental operations is denied, it becomes a problem to find connections which will unite an individual with his fellows."[17]

That notion became the moral justification for cooperative learning, the prevalent form of education that promotes groupthink. That is why so many individualists hate public education, because it denies them the right to be themselves and own the products of their own brains.

Obviously, cooperative learning or groupthink does not produce a Steve Jobs or a Mark Zuckerberg. Even those who were made dyslexic by their schools manage to maintain ownership of their minds and become successful entrepreneurs. But millions of students are never permitted to gain the mastery they need in order to expand their minds. They are the victims of the self-styled utopians who think nothing of destroying a nation's intellectual power. To them cultural genocide is a sacred mission.

13

CALIFORNIA'S LITERACY DISASTER: WHEN UTOPIANS RULE, THE CHILDREN SUFFER

"It's easier to control a group than it is to control an individual."
—B. K. EAKMAN, *PUSH BACK*

Some years ago a lady in Southern California faxed me an article about California's literacy disaster describing what happened when whole language was introduced in California schools in 1987. The article, "The Blackboard Bungle" by Jill Stewart, appeared in the March 1996 issue of *LA Weekly*. Ms. Stewart wrote:

Since 1987, whole-language theory has swept California. . . . The theory's basic principles have been institutionalized in the form of a widely acclaimed reading "framework" adopted by the state

Board of Public Education that downplays the teaching of traditional reading skills. . . . "The core idea of whole language," says one of its most vocal proponents, Mel Grubb of the California Literature Project at Cal State Dominguez Hills, "is that children no longer are forced to learn skills that are disembodied from the experience of reading a story. The enjoyment and the wonder of the story are absorbed just as the skills are absorbed."[1]

Apparently, Mr. Grubb doesn't seem to know the difference between reading a story and learning how to read. Ms. Stewart continued:

> But whole language, which sounds so promising when described by its proponents, has proved to be a near disaster when applied to—and by—real people. In the eight years since whole language first appeared in the state's grade schools, California's fourth-grade reading scores have plummeted to near the bottom nationally, according to the National Assessment of Educational Progress (NAEP). Indeed, California's fourth-graders are now such poor readers that only the children in Louisiana and Guam—both hampered by pitifully backward education systems—get worse reading scores.[2]

And who is to blame for this "near disaster"—which is not near but actual? According to the article "the problems stem from a tragic misinterpretation of the state's 1989 reading framework." Was it a "tragic" misinterpretation or a deliberate misinterpretation? In 1987, California already had a horrendous reading problem. An article from the *San Francisco Examiner*, reprinted in the *Patriot Ledger*, reported: "Almost one in six adults in California is 'functionally illiterate,' and most of those who can't read are native English speakers who went to school in the United States, according to a new study by the state Department of Education. The report says 3.1 million Californians can't read well enough to understand advertising in newspapers, simple recipes or job applications."[3]

So California had a serious reading problem in 1987. That's

when the brilliant people who ran education in California decided to improve reading with whole language. Bill Honig, who was then superintendent of public instruction, oversaw the creation of the "reading framework." Years later, in face of a reading disaster brought on by his own administration, Honig distanced himself from whole language and advocated a phonics approach.

Back in September 1988, we wrote in the *Blumenfeld Education Letter*: "Functional illiteracy will be booming in California in the years ahead if the state adopts the look-say basal reading programs it has already approved. . . . Because of textbook selection decisions based on ignorance, millions of California children will be condemned to lives as functional illiterates. Such state sanctioned education malpractice will be doing more damage to more lives than one can possibly calculate."[4]

How is it that we were able to predict the disaster that lay ahead? And why is it that we who have this superior predictive ability are never called upon by the professional educators to help them make the right decisions? The reason is very simple: dumbed-down people rarely rely on people who know more than they do for fear that the smarter people will supplant them. Ms. Stewart wrote:

> Says Honig today: "Things got out of hand. School administrators and principals thought they were following the framework when they latched on to whole language, and our greatest mistake was failing to say, 'Look out for the crazy stuff, look out for the overreaction and the religiously anti-skills fanatics.' We totally misjudged which voices would take charge of the schools. We never dreamed it would be driven to this bizarre edge. When I tell people that we never even say the phrase 'whole language' anywhere in the 73-page document, they look at me like I'm mad."[5]

But if you are superintendent of public instruction for the state of California and you decide to create a "reading framework" for the entire state system, you'd better know something about how it is going to be implemented. The war between advocates of systematic phonics and the whole-word method had been going on at least since 1955 when *Why Johnny Can't Read* was published. Obviously, Honig was ignorant of this educational fact of life and was therefore clearly unqualified for the job of superintendent.

But how did whole language manage to take over California? According to the article, it began in 1986 when Honig invited a select group of educators "to brainstorm about ways to set California on a new course in reading." Honig said, "I told them to dream, and to forget about any old rules that weren't working." And dream they did. Cal State, Chico, professor Jesus Cortez relates: "Somebody stood up and said that we were there to create a new generation of superior thinkers and readers and writers who would run the businesses and set the policies of the 21st century. Creating that new generation was the dominant theme from day one."[6]

Not only were these people incompetent, but they were wacky visionaries as well! Stewart wrote: "The secondary-school representatives emerged as natural leaders because they, more than anyone, were driven by tremendous frustration over skyrocketing drop-out rates, the hatred many teenagers expressed for reading, and the shocking levels of remedial reading required by California's college freshmen. . . . They also knew that something had to be done about beginning grade school reading, but they weren't sure what."[7]

These were well-paid professional educators who had no idea how to teach a child to read. And obviously, none of these dummies had read Rudolf Flesch's book, or Professor Jeanne Chall's *The Great Debate: Learning to Read*, or my (Samuel's) *The New Illiterates*. Nor did anyone suggest looking into the many good private schools where children were being taught to read successfully with phonics programs. They were acting like a bunch of kids willing to try any wacky experiment that sounded good. Ms. Stewart wrote:

> "The group was charting new ground, and we wanted an inspirational document," recalls Jerry Treadway, a textbook author and a professor at San Diego State. "I remember specific meetings at

which Mel Grubb and other whole-language proponents convinced everyone that there was no distinction between learning how to read as a first-grader and the way a mature reader would handle the printed word. We decided that until we got kids to deal with language the way it is used by adults, as a whole thought, our reading programs wouldn't work. . . . We underwent a real interesting perceptual shift in the meetings, and what we finally stated, almost derisively, is that the traditional reading approach, the emphasis is on mere accuracy. We said, 'How absurd it is to care about individual words and accuracy.' Under whole language the rule was efficiency of the mind: Get the meaning using the least perception possible. Skip words. Absorb ideas instead. At the time, it sounded great."[8]

These are the numbskulls to whom California parents entrusted the minds of their children. These are so-called professionals incapable of thinking like sane adults responsible for the future of a nation. This is the mind-set of the liberal utopians who think nothing of ruining the lives of millions of young people just to see if their cockeyed ideas would work. And if they didn't? Well, it was a great try.

One tragic victim of California's faulty whole-word reading programs was Kari Jorgensen, former basketball star on the Fresno State women's basketball team, who committed suicide in January 1996 at age twenty-two after struggling all her life with dyslexia. For Kari, the written word had become an insurmountable barrier to growth. According to the *Fresno Bee*, "She dreaded the world of words. She feared it. She cursed it. But too many years went by masking her secret, too many days bottling her emotions. . . . Jorgensen's fear was the ridicule of others, so she turned to her ploys, anything to avoid the shame in her eyes."[9]

Kari's dyslexia could have been cured with lessons in systematic, intensive phonics. But no one in California's education system cared. They produce dyslexics by the million, so why should they care about one? Ms. Stewart continues:

Unfortunately, while the group pursued its ideas within this cloistered atmosphere of growing consensus, emerging research was showing that just the reverse was true about how children learn to read. . . .

In the end, the committee produced a thick document that was adopted by the state Board of Education and praised nationally on talk shows. Official textbooks were selected that were mostly literature; the book chosen by 80 percent of the school districts contained no lessons at all. Schools were expected to follow the new approach, and compliance officers began appearing in local classrooms.[10]

Compliance officers? Sounds like something out of a police state. But it didn't take long before the horrors of whole language became apparent. A grandmother by the name of Marion Joseph, a chief policy analyst under former state superintendent Wilson Riles, found out by happenstance that the primary schools were no longer using primers. She contacted several teachers to find out what was going on. She related, "I got almost without exception, 'Oh my God, Marion, we are having a terrible time. The new reading method is not working.' If they tried to teach phonics or word attack skills to the kids who weren't getting it from the storybook and the invented writings, compliance officers came in from their district office and ordered a stop to it. It was terrible stuff, virtually a new religion, a cult."[11]

Marion Joseph complained to Honig, and Honig began to talk to teachers and came to the conclusion that his reading framework had been "grossly misinterpreted." In 1993, Honig was forced to resign after his conviction on conflict-of-interest charges. Ms. Stewart wrote, "In the end, a rudderless group of state officials were left struggling to interpret a unique and untested reading philosophy that they themselves did not understand. At the schools, deep divisions broke out as district bureaucrats began dictating bizarre orders to teachers and principals."[12]

That was 1996. And how are California's schools doing today? According to Dan Walters at the *Sacramento Bee*, "State schools

Superintendent Tom Torlakson tried to put a positive spin on it, but the harsh reality is that academic test scores in California's public school system of 6 million students declined this year after years of apparent gains. Moreover, scores are likely to get worse when new Common Core standards are applied."[13]

> Like most other states, California is moving away from its own academic standards into the multistate Common Core of what students are expected to learn at each step through the system. And when they are tested on those standards, which will kick in later this year, chances are very high that proficiency levels will plummet.
>
> That's what happened in New York State, one of the first to make the transition. When New York tested on its own standards in 2012, for example, 65 percent of its elementary students were rated as proficient in mathematics and 55 percent in English. But this year, using the tougher Common Core standards, just 31 percent were proficient in those two areas.
>
> California students were already markedly lower in math and English than their New York counterparts, using state standards, so when California's Common Core testing kicks in, it wouldn't be surprising if proficiency drops to the 25 percent to 30 percent level.
>
> Moreover, black and Latino students have scores well below those of white and Asian American kids—what Torlakson and other educators call the "achievement gap"—so when Common Core standards become the norm, that gap may widen even more.[14]

So why are the Common Core State Standards being adopted if they are producing worse results? Apparently, the same imbeciles who implemented whole language are now in charge of implementing the Common Core State Standards, all of which will cost the nation billions of dollars. And there you have the key: more money for educational bureaucrats who cannot guarantee anything but lower test scores. Increased failure is just what American children need! Ms. Stewart reported back in 1996: "Jerry Treadway, of San

Diego State, recently became the most prominent whole-language proponent to publicly concede that whole-language theory was fundamentally flawed . . . . 'I don't mind saying it has been a disaster, as long as it's clear to everyone that it was done with the best of intentions by a lot of really committed people.'"[15]

Tell that to the millions of adult Californians who can't read. These "committed people" will now implement the Common Core State Standards just for the heck of it. What a crime!

As for actual 2013 test scores, according to the *LA Times*, the percentage of students in California at grade level in English slipped to 56.4 percent from 57.2 percent and in math to 51.2 percent from 51.5 percent.[16] But achievement in both subjects has steadily improved since 2004, when only about a third of students performed at grade level. As for minorities, fewer than half of African Americans and Latinos were at grade level in English and math, compared to three-fourths of Asians and more than two-thirds of whites. A less-than-mediocre academic performance at best.

14

COOPERATIVE LEARNING: COMMUNIST IDEOLOGY IN THE CLASSROOM

The reason why Americans do not understand this war is because it has been fought in secret—in the schools of our nation, targeting our children who are captive in classrooms.
—CHARLOTTE THOMSON ISERBYT, *THE DELIBERATE DUMBING DOWN OF AMERICA*

Several years ago a friend of mine in Kentucky, who had been keeping me abreast of how Outcome Education was being implemented in the public schools of that state, sent me a description of Cooperative Learning, written by a high school student who had experienced it in his classroom. Here is what the student wrote, uncorrected:

I am a freshman in Highschool and recently in Spanish class our teacher introduced us to a teaching method called "cooperative learning." In cooperating learning the teacher divides you into group[s] of four or five. He holds each and every student personally responsible for their group's learning. Anytime we do work he takes one of the students assignments for each group and gives each person in that group the same grade as the person's he took up.

When we take a quiz he gives each student the average grade for their group, therefore this could easily lower the "excelled" student's grade and improve the student's who slack off. My teacher believes that we should be responsible for teaching our fellow classmates in our group. My classmates and I feel as if this is unjust, and now we have spoken with our principal about this. As of now, we have not made any more progress toward finding a solution.

An example of this would be on a Spanish quiz out of 16 possible points. I scored a 15 and the other three grades were 13, 9, and 5. This lowered my 15 to a 10.5, which is a 66%. Cooperative learning lowered my 15 (94%) to a 10.5 (66%).[1]

For years, Charlotte Iserbyt has been warning us that public education has been taken over by small *c* communists. As a senior staff member of the US Department of Education, she had access to the correspondence and grant proposals of America's top educational operatives. She put all of that documentation in her book *The Deliberate Dumbing Down of America*, published in 1999. The book is available online.

Cooperative learning, as described by the student, is indeed a good example of communist ideology in the classroom. The student is not judged by his individual effort but as a member of a group. It was progressive social theorists such as Gordon Allport, George Herbert Mead, Clifford Shaw, and John B. Watson, who first began advancing the idea that working in a group was educationally more effective for students than working individually. But in actuality, group learning has never improved the work of the low achiever.

As the student pointed out, his score was 15 and the worst student's score was 5. The scores were then averaged so that everyone in the group earned the same score of 10.5. If everyone is given the same grade, how can we know who is the highest achiever and who is the lowest? Why did the lowest achiever get only 5 points originally? If cooperative learning is valid, shouldn't all the students in the group have achieved about the same score? The fact that the scores continued to vary so greatly is proof that cooperative learning didn't improve the learning of the low achievers. The average score simply camouflaged the reality of the disparate scores.

In the traditional classroom, each student is an individual responsible for his own achievement. And since each student is different in his learning abilities and the amount of effort he puts into his work, the outcome for each student would be different. But according to the socialists, individualism creates a competitive spirit that is opposed to a collectivist spirit, which is needed in a socialist society. Competition, of course, is the hallmark of a capitalist, individualistic society. Socialist philosophers from the 1930s and '40s believed in cooperative learning. Dewey thought students should learn social skills that would be helpful outside the classroom, in society. He and his colleagues wanted students to discuss information in groups rather than receive information by listening to a teacher.[2]

Is it any wonder that socialist societies lose their economic vitality and creativity because the individual is negated in favor of the group? When we look at the seventy-five years of communist rule in Russia, what did the Soviet Union contribute to world economic progress? Nothing. On the other hand, capitalist America produced an endless array of goods and products that made life better for everyone. Communist Russia had to borrow from America's achievements to maintain a semblance of modern progress.

Or look at Cuba, which once had the third-highest standard of living in the Western hemisphere. A half century of communism has turned it into an economic basket case, reducing everyone to poverty. Obama's socialist policies are calculated to lower the American standard of living as he tries to change America from a capitalist to a socialist society. And he is succeeding because most Americans don't know the difference between socialism and capitalism and are easily seduced by such concepts as "fairness" in income distribution, as if wealth were not earned by individuals but distributed from the poor to the rich—as if the poor have anything to give the rich. The absurd notion that we ought to give back to the poor what they never had is a form of socialist lunacy. It is totally irrational. But who among the left cares?

The truth that pure, unadulterated communist practice can be slipped into an American public school classroom with hardly a ripple from parents or anybody else is an indication of the depth of the public's ignorance.

But what about the teachers? Don't they know what's going on? As one teacher at the Hancock County High School in Kentucky wrote in 1993 in the *Hancock Clarion*, "For a 'dissident,' teaching in the public schools today is similar to living under a Stalinist 'Reign of Terror.' Many teachers submit their horror stories and misgivings to anonymous publications or ask legislators not to quote them—for fear of repercussions."[3]

All across America, more and more parents are opposed to what is going on in the public schools. But activist parents are labeled "extremists," "troublemakers," "censors," "religious bigots," "fanatics," "fascists," and so on. This is done to neutralize the vast majority of parents who don't want to get involved, who don't like controversy, or who go along to get along.

The good news is that the home-school movement continues to grow. Homeschooling is no longer considered an unusual and antisocial practice. It is now accepted as a legitimate and highly effective way of educating children. But lurking in the wings are those socialist educators who would like to outlaw homeschooling. They argue that the state has the right, if not the duty, to control the education of "its" children. Indeed, the socialists believe that the state owns all children and that the parents are mere caretakers.

Meanwhile, the Achilles' heel of the Democrats is the dysfunctional public schools. That's an arena of battle which conservatives must make the most of if we are to win this life-and-death struggle between freedom and tyranny.

15

THE GREAT AMERICAN MATH DISASTER

When Newton or Gauss explored mathematics that unlocked mysteries of their universe, their intent was to empower—and maybe inspire— humanity . . . not to create tools of torture for high school or college students.
—SALMAN KHAN, FOUNDER OF KHAN ACADEMY, *THE ONE WORLD SCHOOL HOUSE* (2012)

One of the reasons why so many Americans are confused about the large numbers being tossed around by our leaders in Washington these days is because of how poorly they were taught mathematics in the public schools. They find figures in the millions, billions, and trillions almost impossible to visualize as anything more than just strings of numbers. Most Americans can barely deal with thousands, let alone trillions.

The basic problem is that American children are no longer being taught arithmetic in public schools. They are taught math, which includes more than our simple counting system. Arithmetic deals with quantity. Math deals with relationships and uses complex symbols. When you submerge arithmetic in mathematics, without making sure that the children have mastered their counting skills, you get math failure. And this is nothing new. Back in 1991 Pat Wingert of *Newsweek* magazine reported: "How bad are eighth graders' math skills? So bad that half are scoring just above the proficiency level expected of fifth-grade students. Even the best students did miserably; at the top-scoring schools, the average was well below grade level. Hardly any students have the background to go beyond simple computation, most of those kids can add but they have serious trouble thinking through simple problems."[1]

What's really frightening about these results is that the alarm has been ringing since the 1983 publication of *A Nation at Risk*, the federally sponsored study that highlighted vast problems in the public schools. Yet despite years of talk about reform—and genuine efforts of change in a few places—American students are still not making the grade and remain behind their counterparts in other industrialized nations.

All those kids who did miserably in math in 1983 and 1991 are today's voting adults in their thirties and forties. And let us not forget the disaster called "new math," which swept through America's elementary schools like a hurricane during the 1960s and '70s, creating today's math illiterates among Boomers in their fifties and sixties. In the new math, set theory was supposed to be the way we look at the world. Everything in the world is made up of sets. Zero is an empty set. The theory was formulated by Georg Cantor, a German mathematician who wound up in an insane asylum.[2]

The highly entertaining *Straight Dope* blog has published its own take on how the teaching of math has evolved in the last few years:

The following examples may help to clarify the difference between the new and old math.

1960: A logger sells a truckload of lumber for $100. His cost of production is 4/5 of this price. What is his profit?

1970 (Traditional math): A logger sells a truckload of lumber for $100. His cost of production is $80. What is his profit?

1975 (New Math): A logger exchanges a set L of lumber for a set M of money. The cardinality of set M is 100 and each element is worth $1.
    (a) Make 100 dots representing the elements of the set M
    (b) The set C representing costs of production contains 20 fewer points than set M. Represent the set C as a subset of the set M.
    (c) What is the cardinality of the set P of profits?

1990 (Dumbed-down math): A logger sells a truckload of lumber for $100. His cost of production is $80 and his profit is $20. Underline the number 20.

1997 (Whole Math): By cutting down a forest full of beautiful trees, a logger makes $20.
    (a) What do you think of this way of making money?
    (b) How did the forest birds and squirrels feel?
    (c) Draw a picture of the forest as you'd like it to look.[3]

The educators blame students' low test scores on traditional arithmetic, which hasn't been taught in years but is a perfect scapegoat. They complain that too much time is wasted practicing adding, subtracting, multiplying, and dividing. The solution? More calculators and computers.

The real problem is that our educators really don't know the difference between arithmetic and mathematics, and if you don't know the difference, you won't know how to teach it either.

Our arithmetic system is an ingenious method of counting, keeping track of quantity. It uses ten symbols and place value for all of its operations and notations. As such, it is one of the greatest achievements of the human intellect, an invention that permits human beings to perform any counting feat with mere pencil and paper.

But the key to its proficient use is memorization of the basic arithmetic facts. If you don't memorize the facts, then you are stuck with unit counting and you might as well learn to use an abacus. Memorization requires rote drill, which is forbidden in today's schools, even though it is the easiest way for a child to learn anything. When educators think that children can learn to compute without memorizing the arithmetic facts, they are deluding themselves and cheating the children.

Why is it important for children to memorize the arithmetic facts? Because memorization will give them mastery of the system. And once the arithmetic facts are memorized through drill and practice with pencil and paper, kids will later be able to use calculators and computers with accuracy, spotting errors when they make them, always able to do the calculations on paper if necessary.

Why did eighth graders do so poorly even in wealthy suburban schools?[4] Because of bad teaching. Obviously, when even the richest and brightest fail, one cannot blame it on rote memorization when we are told that memorization is what makes the Japanese student so much better than the American. If teachers do not even know how to teach simple arithmetic effectively, how can we assume that they know how to teach algebra, geometry, trigonometry, or calculus effectively?

Besides, very few of us will need to use algebra, geometry, trigonometry, or calculus, but all of us will need to use arithmetic—in doing tax returns, figuring out mortgages, balancing our checking accounts, using credit cards, making change, and planning our retirement. So if everyone must use arithmetic in order to survive economically, why don't schools teach it?

Back in 1983 John Saxon, the celebrated author of superb mathematics textbooks used by homeschoolers and private schools, observed in the *National Review*:

For the last twenty years, these [mathematics] experts have worked unwittingly to bring matters to a point where only the brilliant can learn mathematics. They have tried to teach advanced concepts and a general overview before the student has learned the basics. . . . In an important sense, these authors are experts neither in mathematics nor in education. They do not know which mathematics topics must be mastered at which level and have no understanding of the capabilities of the average student. Their books are visible proof that they do not know how children learn and assimilate abstractions.[5]

Until rote learning is restored in our primary schools in the teaching of arithmetic, we can expect math failure to plague American public education for the foreseeable future. At no time in our history has knowledge of basic arithmetic been more important. Tax returns are more complicated than ever. City, state, and federal budgets can be understood only if one has a good knowledge of arithmetic. Comparative shopping in supermarkets requires an ability to make sense out of different prices. Setting up a small business requires the ability to figure out costs and profits. Buying stocks and bonds and borrowing money with interest require skill with numbers.

So why don't our schools teach everyone basic arithmetic? Because the dumbing-down agenda also covers math. It's easier for government and politicians to steal from the public when they can't add things up.

16

DRUG PUSHING: THE "CURE" FOR ADD AND ADHD

I took my son out of school in August 2006 in order to educate him at home. It has been the most amazing adventure of my life.
—ELISHEVA H. LEVIN, ONLINE REVIEW OF *DUMBING US DOWN* (2011)

Perhaps one of the greatest crimes currently being perpetrated by schools across America today is the heavy "medication" of literally millions of children with powerful psychotropic drugs. Like all psychiatric "diseases" and "disorders," which are invented and then voted on by psychiatrists, there is no way of objectively determining whether a child has so-called attention deficit disorder or attention deficit hyperactivity disorder. There is, however, plenty of evidence suggesting that the schools themselves are triggering these problems, and that the alleged "medicines" being forced on America's youth are causing grave, potentially irreversible harm.

Dr. Peter Breggin is the nation's leading authority on the negative and harmful effects of psychiatric drugs. In his book *Talking Back to Ritalin*, published in 1998, he wrote:

> A large segment of America's children are being subjected to drugs to control their minds and behavior. Nothing like this has ever happened in the history of any society or nation. Never before have so many parents been told that their children need psychiatric drug treatment for difficulties at school and in the home. Ritalin has become so ingrained in society that some parents have been forced by courts to give the drug to their children.[1]

According to the *Wall Street Journal*, in 2013 you could "walk into any American high school and nearly one in five boys in the hallways will have a diagnosis of attention deficit hyperactive disorder. According to the Centers for Disease Control and Prevention, 11% of all American children ages 4 to 17—over six million—have ADHD, a 16% increase since 2007."[2] *The Washington Post* reported a year earlier, "The number of doctor's visits by children being given a diagnosis of ADHD jumped to 10.4 million in 2010, a 66% increase over 2000."[3]

Why is there now such a horrendous epidemic of ADHD, a learning disorder that did not exist when I (Samuel) was attending public school in the 1930s and '40s? Younger parents and writers don't know why. But anyone who has studied the radical changes that have taken place in the schools since then knows that the schools themselves, with their gross educational malpractice, are the cause of the epidemic.

What are the symptoms of ADHD? A July 1994 *Time* cover story reported, "ADHD has three main hallmarks: extreme distractibility, an almost reckless impulsiveness and, in some but not all cases, a knee-jiggling, toe-tapping hyperactivity that makes sitting still all but impossible."[4]

And who decides that a child has ADHD? *Time* reported:

Diagnosing ADHD is a rather inexact proposition. In most cases, it is a teacher who initiates the process by informing parents that their child is daydreaming in class, failing to complete assignments or driving everyone crazy with thoughtless behavior. . . .

Diagnosing those with ADD without hyperactivity can be trickier. Such kids are often described as daydreamers, space cases. They are not disruptive or antsy.[5]

Is that teacher aware that her faulty teaching methods are causing increasing frustration among her students? Probably not. She was told by her professors that teaching children to read English as if it were Chinese is perfectly okay. And so she forces her students to look at each printed word as a picture that the student has to remember. She is forcing her students to use their right brains to perform a left-brain function, something she knows nothing about. She was also told in her college of education that 30 percent of all children would not be able to learn to read. So her job is to identify that 30 percent and give them the "help" they need. Incidentally, according to the *Washington Post,* the typical appointment for diagnosing ADHD takes all of fifteen minutes.[6] Everyone in the system works together: the teacher, the administrators, the school nurse, the pediatricians, the psychiatrists, and the drug companies. It's a diabolical machine designed to create a real mental disorder and enrich the pharmaceutical companies, all of which is a highly sophisticated form of child abuse.

And much of this is being taught the public by many well-meaning physicians who are ignorant of what goes on in the classroom because it's none of their business. In one of the most popular books on ADHD, *Driven to Distraction* by Drs. Edward M. Hallowell and John J. Ratey, the authors wrote, "ADD lives in the biology of the brain and the central nervous system. The exact mechanism underlying ADD remains unknown. There is no single lesion of the brain, no single neurotransmitter system, no single gene we have identified that triggers ADD. The precise workings of the brain that underlie ADD have so far escaped us, in part due to the extraordinary complexity of the attentional system."[7]

Actually, now that we have brain scans, it is not all that difficult to figure out what happens in the brain when a child is forced to use his right brain to perform the functions of the left brain. It creates brain impairment. Deliberately damaging a child's brain with a known faulty method of teaching reading is a crime.

The authors do admit that the cause of ADD may have something to do with the way schools teach reading, but they shy away from such controversy. They wrote, "Although a full discussion of learning and language problems, including dyslexia, is well beyond the scope of this book, we cannot discuss ADD without some mention of language problems—and learning disabilities in general—since they so often coexist with ADD, each usually making the other worse."[8]

In fact, virtually every ADD case history the authors discussed involves some traumatic experience in early education:

> Due to repeated failures, misunderstandings, mislabelings, and all manner of other emotional mishaps, children with ADD usually develop problems with their self-image and self-esteem. Throughout childhood, at home and at school they are told they are defective. They are called dumb, stupid, lazy, stubborn, willful, or obnoxious. . . . They are reprimanded for classroom disturbances of all sorts and are easily scapegoated at school. They are the subject of numerous parent-teacher conferences.[9]

In other words, to the primary symptoms of distractibility, impulsivity, and restlessness are added the secondary symptoms of cognitive confusion, academic failure, low self-esteem, depression, boredom and frustration with school, impaired peer relations, sometimes drug or alcohol abuse, stealing or even violent behavior due to mounting frustration, forgetfulness, disorganization, indifference, and unpredictability.

We wonder how many of today's adult ADD patients attended the once-controversial open classrooms in their primary school years in which they were subjected to wall-to-wall bedlam. Why should it have been expected that children under such conditions would be able to calmly concentrate on learning the abstractions of alphabetic writing and arithmetic being taught in a faulty, fragmentary, disorganized manner by an equally distracted, befuddled teacher with noises of all sorts coming from all directions? How could any child fail to be distracted and annoyed by the din of activities around him and by the constant interruptions inherent in such a learning-hostile environment?

Contrast that classroom bedlam with the quiet in a public library, where readers can concentrate on what they are reading without needless interruptions. Yet, apparently, none of the experts on ADD has bothered to investigate the possible school causes of attention deficit disorder. They might surmise that since many students have emerged from that classroom turmoil without ADD, those who were affected by the environment were biologically predisposed. And they might well have been. But the point is that schools are supposed to be healthy environments for all children, not just for those with nerves of steel.

As everyone knows, no two children are alike. Parents of more than one child recognize this phenomenon quite readily. Some children can tolerate loud noises; others can't. Some kids require silence in order to concentrate; others can listen to pop music while reading. A proper school provides an environment that makes it possible for all students to thrive, and you would think our educators would be aware of this. But American public schools have become increasingly chaotic—not only in curriculum and methodology, but also in classroom configuration.

Those of us who went to the traditional public schools of the 1930s and '40s remember the order and silence that prevailed. Our attention was focused on the teacher, who sat at the front of the room. There was no distractibility, no impulsive behavior, and no abnormal restlessness. And as a result, there was no ADD or ADHD.

But we are well into the twenty-first century, and the incidence of ADD and ADHD has increased significantly. Why? Because the Dewey-inspired plan to dumb down America is still in place, reinforced by progressive professors of education who train all the new teachers and are well funded by politicians who need the support of the teachers' unions.

Meanwhile, the drugging of millions of schoolchildren so that they will be able to sit zombie-like in their classrooms has made the pharmaceutical industry very rich. The authors of *Driven to Distraction* wrote: "Many people with ADD point to school as the first place they realized that anything was different about them."[10] And so they don't recommend changing anything in the classroom; they recommend drugging the child. They wrote:

> There are two main classes of medication for ADD: the stimulants [Ritalin, Dexedrine and Cylert] and the antidepressants. . . . Finding the right medication and the right dosage can take several months of trial and error, as we do not as yet have a way of predicting what medication in which dosage will help a given individual. . . . Often an increase in dosage or a change in medication will make a dramatic difference. . . .
>
> [The stimulants] act on neurotransmitters to activate or stimulate the central nervous system. . . . They do not "drug up" or cloud the sensorium of the individual taking them. They are not addictive in doses prescribed for ADD.[11]

However, a book by Dr. Peter Breggin, *Medication Madness*, warns us that medicating millions of children with psychiatric drugs not only harms the brains of these children, but is also having an enormously negative impact on our society:

> I was testifying before a committee of the Colorado State Legislature concerning why I thought the legislators should oppose the widespread drugging of schoolchildren. . . . The legislature

had a close-to-home example of both in Eric Harris, who was on Luvox at the time he slaughtered his classmates at Columbine and then committed suicide. . . .

The concept of medication spellbinding helps to explain medication-induced mayhem, murder, and suicide, and also why so many people take psychiatric drugs that are doing them more harm than good.

Put simply, psychiatric drugs are proven to cause bizarre, unwanted and dangerous mental states.. . . . Stimulants given to children often reduce all spontaneous behavior, and the antipsychotic drugs given to children and adults can utterly crush free will. . . . Free will and rational-choice making require an intact brain, and psychiatric drugs, one and all, always cause brain dysfunction. That's how they work.[12]

Dr. Breggin's book is full of horrendous human tragedies caused by psychiatric drugs. Yet our schools continue to produce ADD and ADHD, which then require drugging the students. The schools have no intention of changing the way they teach anything. In fact, they have become factories for creating learning disorders. In his earlier book, *Talking Back to Ritalin*, Dr. Breggin wrote:

The term "LD Child" is probably as commonplace as "ADHD Child." According to the *Diagnostic and Statistical Manual of Mental Disorders, IV* (1994), learning disorders are divided into three main categories: "Reading Disorder" (previously called dyslexia), "Mathematics Disorder," and "Disorder of Written Expression." The disorders are diagnosed "when the individual's achievement on individually administered, standardized tests in reading, mathematics, or written expression is substantially below that expected for age, schooling, and level of intelligence." In other words, the child isn't performing up to expectations. The everyday concept of the "underachiever" has been turned into a disorder.[13]

The concept of learning disabled (LD), like ADHD, puts the blame for the disorders on the child's brain. This discourages parents from looking at the true source of the problem, such as the way the child was taught to read in the primary grades. That, indeed, is the cause of the frustration, anger, acting out, and disruptive behavior that is then termed "ADD" or "ADHD." Parents are informed of their child's unacceptable behavior and told that he or she will have to be medicated in order to be able to sit quietly in the classroom.

It would be so easy to prove the truth of our assertions by taking two groups of students, one being taught to read by intensive phonics, the other by the sight method, and see how the children behave. But the educators won't accept the challenge. They prefer deceiving parents, destroying children's lives, and enriching drug companies. Many teachers may not know that this is what they are doing. But that is no reason for Americans to place the education of the greatest nation in history in the hands of the most ignorant, deceptive, and treasonous people on the planet.

17
CONTRIBUTING TO THE DELINQUENCY OF MINORS

I myself struggled with suicidal thoughts as a child and a teen. It is directly
related to the nightmare and torture of schooling.
—ANDREW PARODI, AMAZON REVIEWER, ONLINE REVIEW OF *DUMBING US DOWN*
(2011)

Public schools contribute to the delinquency of minors, which
is a crime. With the takeover by Dewey progressives, the
public schools have become a moral and academic detriment
to American youth by crippling their brains and destroying
their moral consciences. More recently they have become more
brazen in their corruption. They do so in four different ways:
(1) They promote semipornographic sex education that leads to premarital sex and all of the social and emotional problems associated
with it. (2) They promote teenage drug abuse by plying students
with stimulants like Ritalin and Adderall that lead many teenagers

to addiction to hard drugs that ruin their lives. (3) They commit blatant educational malpractice against children so that they never learn to read and become frustrated and angry at the society that turned them into illiterates. (4) They destroy the children's belief in religious morality by teaching moral relativism and values clarification that lead many children into immoral, antisocial behavior.

As we all know, parents who ply schoolchildren with liquor at parties can be hauled into court for contributing to the delinquency of minors. It's a serious crime to contribute to the delinquency of a minor. But that's what the public schools do every day. Some schools provide kids with condoms so they can engage in premarital sex, supposedly to guard them from getting a disease or impregnating another minor teenager. But apparently, the condoms are not being used or they fail because teenage girls are still getting pregnant and either getting abortions or having babies out of wedlock.

The schools teach everything wrong. Instead of teaching that love and marriage should precede sex, they teach that sex comes first without love or marriage. Indeed, probably the single most pressing moral issue facing youth today is premarital sex, which leads to widespread abortion, unwed motherhood, a life on welfare, fatherless families, venereal diseases that may lead to sterility and death, unhappy emotional entanglements, and the awakening of a sexual appetite, which may lead to promiscuity, prostitution, perversion, loss of self-esteem, abusive sexual partners, and nervous breakdowns.

But students have become so corrupted by our sex-obsessed culture that some of them clamor for more sex education, not less. They want more than just condoms. They want to know more about sexually transmitted diseases. The Boston Public Health Commission reported that "54 percent of city high school students have had sex, and half of them have had sex with more than three partners."[1] Thus, the likelihood of these students getting a sexually transmitted disease is high.

In 2007, 1,383 students between the ages of fifteen and nineteen in Boston were diagnosed with chlamydia—a disease that can cause infertility in women—a 70 percent increase since 1999.[2] Apparently there hasn't been enough discussion about the dangers of promiscuous, recreational sex. Many students are only dimly aware of the health risks that such sexual dalliance can lead to. Abstinence is not considered a realistic option by these students, although it's obvious that many students do practice abstinence out of good common sense and religious beliefs.

"I feel like they are focusing on 'Don't have sex or don't get pregnant.' There's more to it than that," one high school senior told the *Globe* reporter, "It was like, 'This is a condom. This is what males use to prevent pregnancy.' We didn't really talk about sexually transmitted diseases."[3]

Many high school students are now at the point of demanding sex education. At a 2011 Boston City Council hearing, for example, hundreds of students showed up to demand more sex education and better access to condoms, which kids can already receive from every government school in the city. "Sex education is important to me because sexual identity is part of our lives," high school sophomore Kimpsha Grant was quoted as saying. "And when we don't talk about it, people learn the wrong things about it or nothing at all. . . . It seems a shame that we aren't learning what we need to."[4]

It seems, then, that what American children in government schools have been taught to seek out is the "freedom" to have as much recreational sex as they please, but with guarantees from the state to protect them from the consequences of their actions. In other words, immorality with no personal responsibility is what is being drilled into their young minds. If the "safe sex" they teach at schools fails—resulting in pregnancy, disease, or emotional trauma— the students know the state will be there to bail them out, whether that be through abortion or taxpayer-funded medical care.

In a supposed response to student demands, school authorities announced action. The school system's "health education director" even promised the district would create new "health education frameworks" that would feature plenty of sex "education." The plan also included an overview of the district's existing "health education" schemes, a task force to review accessibility of condoms, comprehensive "health education benchmarks," and the training of school staff to implement it all.[5]

In other words, as is instantly apparent to anyone who understands public education "bureaucratese," the program director wanted a bigger budget for the task force to review condom access and to train staffs on how to implement all the new programs. Apparently, the school authorities as well as the liberal city councilors believed that taxpayers should be forced to pay for students' access to free condoms.

The notion that schools incapable of teaching proper reading would be able to properly teach students about sex is, of course, absurd on its face. Still, the Sexuality Information and Education Council of the United States provided the sex educators of America with their guidelines. Its 2009 report provided the following information on student sexual activity:

- 46 percent of students reported never having had sexual intercourse (47.8 percent in 2007)

- 5.9 percent of students reported having had sexual intercourse before age thirteen (7.1 percent in 2007)

- 13.8 percent of students reported having had sexual intercourse with four or more sexual partners in their lifetime (14.9 percent in 2007)

- 34.2 percent of students reported being currently sexually active, defined as having had sexual intercourse in the three months prior to the survey (35.0 percent in 2007)

- 61.1 percent of sexually active students reported that either they or their partner had used a condom during their last sexual encounter (62.5 percent in 2007)

- 87.0 percent of students reported having been taught about AIDS or HIV in school (89.5 percent in 2007).[6]

In essence, the data show that students were slightly less promiscuous in 2009 than they were in 2007. At the same time, however, fewer students reported knowing about AIDS and HIV in 2009 than two years earlier. It has become painfully obvious that so-called sex education has very little or nothing to do with education, but a lot to do with sex.

Of course, before the widespread implementation of "sex ed" in government schools, people somehow managed to fall in love, get married, and have families. Countless Americans lived happily ever after; some did not. So how did humanity manage to deal with sex before it became a subject to be taught to children at school? Simple: religious and cultural institutions, as well as parents, generally dealt with such matters—all of which have been shoved aside as the state increasingly seeks to usurp their roles. It is true that there has always been some titillating secrecy on the subject. However, adherents to biblical religion understood that premarital sex, also known as fornication, is a sin. Obviously, it was not a perfect world, but neither is the current sex-saturated environment in which high school students openly complain that their schools are not doing enough to protect them from the consequences of their own immoral and depraved behavior.

One piece of good news is that births to teen girls, ages fifteen to seventeen, have declined. In 2012, 86,423 infants were born out of wedlock to high school girls; in 2013 that number was down to 75,234 births. That's still a lot of children starting life in poverty.[7] In other words, humanistic sex ed reverses the normal sequence of love, marriage, and family to sex, child out of wedlock, poverty, and maybe, at some later date, love. What makes sense is no longer taught.

In Chicago, the public schools have decided to introduce a full sex education curriculum aligned with National Sexuality Education Standards. The groups involved in designing the standards include the radical Gay, Lesbian, and Straight Education Network (GLSEN); the equally radical liberal nonprofit dedicated to affirming one's sexual preference, Sexuality Information and Education Council of the United States (SIECUS); the abortion giant Planned Parenthood; and the National Education Association. For preschool and five-year-olds, the curriculum includes lessons about anatomy and physiology, reproduction, traditional families and gay families, healthy relationships, and personal safety. In fifth through twelfth grades they learn about abstinence (which SIECUS claims is ineffective); medically recommended contraceptives; how to prevent sexually transmitted diseases, including HIV; and healthy relationships, which includes informed decision making, sexual orientation, and personal safety. Here are some troubling statistics from the Centers for Disease Control and Prevention:

Many young people engage in sexual risk behaviors that can result in unintended health outcomes. For example, among United States high school students surveyed in 2013

46.8% had never had sexual intercourse

34.0% had had sexual intercourse during the previous three months, and, of these, 40.9% did not use a condom the last time they had sex

15.0% had had sex with four or more people during their lives

Sexual risk behaviors place adolescents at risk for HIV infection, other sexually transmitted diseases (STDs), and unintended pregnancy:

An estimated 8,300 young people aged 13–24 years in the 40 states reporting to CDC had HIV infection in 2009

Nearly half of the 19 million new STDs each year are among young people aged 15–24 years

More than 400,000 teen girls aged 15–19 years gave birth in 2009[8]

Many psychologists believe that children in primary schools are too young to be given elementary sex education. Peter Sprigg of the Family Research Council told the *Christian Post* that the notion of early-childhood sex education "is part of the legacy of Alfred Kinsey, and the belief that 'children are sexual from birth.' This is a false and pernicious idea that introduces words, thoughts, and concepts to children long before it is developmentally appropriate for them. This premature exposure may contribute to early sexual activity, when we should be working to prevent it."[9]

To sum it up, sex education as presently taught in the schools contributes to the delinquency of minors. Thus, it's a crime!

We also know that plying schoolchildren with highly potent psychiatric drugs can lead to drug abuse with other substances. How many lives are ruined by this kind of drug abuse? Here are some statistics from the website of Teen Rehab:

Almost 50 percent of high school seniors have abused a drug of some kind.

By eighth grade 15 percent of kids have used marijuana.

43 percent of high school seniors have used marijuana.

8.6 percent of twelfth graders have used hallucinogens—4 percent report using LSD specifically.

Over 60 percent of teens report that drugs of some kind are kept, sold, and used at their school.

One in every nine high school seniors has tried synthetic marijuana (also known as "spice" or "K2").

64 percent of teens say they have used prescription pain killers that they got from a friend or family member.

Of teens, 28 percent know at least one person who has tried ecstasy.

Among teens, 7.6 percent use the prescription drug Adderall.

Over 5 percent of twelfth graders have used cocaine and over 2 percent have used crack.

More teenagers die from taking prescription drugs than the use of cocaine *and* heroin combined.[10]

In other words, drug abuse among teenagers is a very serious problem. To what extent schools contribute to this problem is not known. But it can be assumed that when millions of schoolchildren are required to take highly potent mind-altering psychiatric drugs like Ritalin, Adderall, and others, it can lead to the delinquency of minors, who then experiment with more highly addictive drugs. The schools also teach drug education, which acquaints children with all of the drugs available and what they do to the body. These drugs include marijuana, pain relievers, cocaine, tranquilizers, hallucinogens, stimulants, heroin, inhalants, and sedatives. As for alcohol abuse, the statistics are alarming:

By eighth grade, almost 30 percent of kids have tried drinking alcohol.

58 percent of sophomores have abused alcohol.

71 percent of high school seniors have abused alcohol.

23 percent of twelfth graders reported on binge drinking—with over five drinks in a row.

8 percent of high school students admit to driving after drinking.

24 percent of high school students rode with a driver who had been drinking alcohol.

11 percent of all alcohol consumed in the United States is from underage drinkers.

The average age of a boy who tries alcohol is eleven; girls are on average thirteen.

Teens that started drinking before the age of fifteen are five times more likely to become addicted to alcohol later on, unlike those kids who waited until after they were twenty-one.

Teens that drink often are more than three times more likely to commit self-harm—such as cutting or suicide attempts—than teens that don't drink.

Alcohol is the leading factor in the top three causes for death in fifteen- to twenty-four-year-olds, which are auto crashes, homicides and suicides.[11]

Annually about five thousand youths under age twenty-one die from car crashes, homicides, and suicides that involve underage drinking.[12] In 2007, 1.4 million youths aged twelve to seventeen needed treatment for an alcohol use problem.[13]

In short, the pushing of drugs by educators in the schools does contribute to the delinquency of minors. That is a crime.

Depriving children of the ability to read through deliberate educational malpractice also contributes to the delinquency of minors. Michael S. Brunner, author of *Retarding America: The Imprisonment of Potential*, believes that there is a definite link between reading failure and delinquent, antisocial behavior. In 1991, he wrote, "Low reading levels tend to predict the likelihood of the onset of serious delinquency. Longitudinally, poor reading achievement and delinquency appear to mutually influence each other. Prior reading level predicted later subsequent delinquency . . . [moreover] poor reading achievement increased the chances of serious delinquency persisting over time."[14]

Researchers in 1990 wrote in the *Journal of Correctional Education*, "There is a disproportionate involvement in delinquency by those youth failing in school. Schools are apparently contributing to the delinquency problem by continuing to provide traditional programming, though it has failed repeatedly."[15]

E. E. Gagne wrote in the *Journal of Special Education*, "[The] compulsory school attendance law . . . facilitates delinquency by forcing youth to remain in what is sometimes a frustrating situation in which they are stigmatized as failures . . . . The longer learning-disabled students stay in school, the more likely they are to become involved with the police."[16]

A 1977 report to Congress by the comptroller general of the United States revealed:

> In our society, school is the only major legitimate activity for children between the ages of 6 and 18. If a child fails in school, generally there is little else in which he can be successful. . . . Delinquency and misbehavior become a way for the failing child to express his frustration at those who disapprove of his academic underachievement. This disapproval comes not only from parents and teachers, but also from other children who are keenly aware of the school status based on performance.[17]

Michael Brunner wrote in his study, Program of Research on the Causes and Correlates of Delinquency, "Urban Delinquency and Substance Abuse," issued in 1991 by the Justice Department:

> Continued failure in the most significant educational task challenging the child (reading) is a deeply frustrating experience when permitted to continue for several years . . . . Continued frustration over prolonged periods of time will result in aggressive behavior directed toward society (delinquency) or inward toward the self (neurosis).
>
> In investigating two groups of incarcerated delinquents, 48 in each group, in two different states, a significant correlation between reading underachievement and aggression for both groups was found. . . . Only reading failure was found to correlate with aggression in both populations of delinquent boys.[18]

It is quite conceivable that when functional illiterates in the form of gangs turn against society and burn down the community, as they did in South Los Angeles in 1992, they are directing their hatred at the very system that destroyed their minds. The government school represents the establishment as a whole, and these youths know that the schools did a job on them, for they remember the intelligence they had before they went to school, and the humiliating and frustrating experience of failure after they were in school.

In reality, the reading instruction methods were, in fact, devised to produce disability in the learner by way of a subtle, nonsurgical prefrontal lobotomy called the sight-word method. What the LA gang members saw in the Rodney King beating by the police was what had been done to them mentally and psychologically in the schools. The oppressive dumbing down turned them into walking time bombs waiting for the right moment to go off. And when several thousand walking time bombs organize into gangs, they can cause a social explosion of incredibly destructive force.

Destroying a child's belief in biblical religion is another school contribution to the delinquency of minors. Through values clarification and the philosophy of secular humanism, schools convince children that the morality of the Ten Commandments is old-fashioned and based on superstition and mythology. All those "Thou shalt nots" were born of an outdated religious dogma and have no place in modern society. The result is that children, no longer restrained by the absolute morals of the Bible, are free to construct their own moral codes based on their own concepts of right and wrong. Inevitably, they will justify their delinquent behavior on any grounds that will suit their egos. There is no heaven or hell. There is no sin. There is only the reality of one's individual emotions and desires. A dangerous way to live, but one encouraged by a morally dysfunctional education system. We will discuss this in greater detail in the next chapter.

18

DESTROYING A CHILD'S RELIGIOUS BELIEFS: A SPIRITUAL CRIME

That God rules in the affairs of men is as certain as any truth of physical
science. . . . Nothing is by chance, though men, in their ignorance of
causes may think so.
—GEORGE BANCROFT, HISTORIAN, MEMORIAL ORATION ON LINCOLN, FEBRUARY 12, 1866

ontrast George Bancroft's beliefs with those of the second
federal district court, which, in 1988, ruled against students
at Westside High School in Omaha, Nebraska, who sought to
form a Bible club under the Equal Access Law. The principal
denied the students' request, which was upheld by the school
board. They argued that a Bible club was not a curriculum-
related activity, unlike such organizations as Interact, the chess
club, and Subsurfers, which were. (Interact was related to Rotary
International; chess was related to logical thinking; and Subsurfers
was for students interested in SCUBA diving.)[1]

But what about Bible study? The Bible is the moral and spiritual foundation of the American system of government. It is related to early American history (the Puritans), ancient history, philosophy, the history of religion, comparative religion, literature, archaeology, geography, mathematics (BC and AD), psychology (human nature), the history of moral development, the development of Western law, ancient chronology, the history of Western civilization, Greek, Latin, Elizabethan English, the history of the Jews, early church history, biography, genealogy, early American education, the history of parochial education, and knowledge of such great biblical figures as Abraham, Moses, Joshua, Noah, Jesus, Paul, and many more.

The King James Version of the Bible is considered the greatest work of literature of the Elizabethan era. In fact, without knowledge of the Bible, one could hardly be considered educated. Biblical references are found throughout English and world literature, even in crossword puzzles. Not to know the Bible is to be ignorant of the single most important spiritual and moral influence in Western civilization. That so-called educators and a school board can claim that Bible study is not curriculum-related is glaring proof that American public education is morally and academically bankrupt.

Yet, while the Bible is not permitted in a public school, there has been a Bible on the moon since 1971, when Apollo 15 commander David Scott left a copy on the mission's lunar rover. Indeed, the Bible is so morally inspiring that schools that require students to study it would obviously produce better-educated children than those that don't.

These anti-Bible educators also ignore the vast amounts of research and evidence suggesting that virtually all children are born believers whether they or their parents know it or not. Indeed, according to Dr. Justin L. Barrett, author of *Born Believers: The Science of Children's Religious Belief,* published in 2012, children are born with an innate belief in the supernatural. "I have conducted numerous additional studies on religious belief, and colleagues in my field, the cognitive science of religion, have discovered more evidence that children have a natural affinity for thinking about and believing in gods. . . . People may practically be born believers," Dr. Barrett wrote. He added, "Regardless of culture and without need for coercive indoctrination, children develop with a propensity to seek meaning and understanding of their environments. Given the way their minds naturally develop, this search leads to beliefs in a purposeful and designed world, an intelligent designer behind the design, an assumption that the intentional designer is super-powerful, super knowing, super perceiving, and immortal."[2]

In other words, evidence shows that children, regardless of their parents' beliefs, arrive at school with a preexisting belief in the supernatural, providing knowledge and insight into God and their own purpose. The message conveyed to children by this innate supernatural force is that life has meaning, and this is affirmed by their parents' beliefs. However, when these children enter into atheistic public schools, teachers and books teach them to reject as superstitious nonsense the knowledge and beliefs they already possess. The impressionable young minds are told that there is no God, that life has no spiritual dimension with any transcendent meaning—that it's all a giant cosmic accident that rocks turned into soup that turned into cells that turned into humans. Basically, the children are taught to think of themselves as no better or more important than their pets.

Of course, a school does not need to be especially religious to be godly. It must, however, be a school that fully respects the God of creation and the children's preexisting beliefs in the supernatural. In the 1930s, I (Samuel) attended a public school in New York City. At every assembly, the principal read Psalm 23. It was always spiritually uplifting. The students came from all sorts of backgrounds—Catholics, Protestants, and Jews were all represented. All students, though, responded to the beautiful and poetic description of our most important relationship—the relationship with the loving God of the Bible.

The negative effects on children of schools' rejection of the supernatural and God—or even outright hostility toward Him—are easy to understand. Among other consequences is childhood depression, a condition that was virtually unheard-of when American education was still godly. The signs of these problems are becoming increasingly apparent. "Although for many years depression was considered a problem that afflicted only adults, in the last 30 years there has been an increasing recognition that this disorder can and does occur in children, particularly in adolescents," reads the introduction to the 818-page *Treating and Preventing Adolescent Mental Health Disorders.* "Fifty years ago its mean age was near 30, but now it is close to 15."[3]

With the previously inconceivable range of material wealth available to American adolescents today in the high-tech economy, how is it possible that they are becoming depressed? What could they possibly be lacking that in fact leads some to even commit suicide? Their parents love them. They generally have plenty of friends who love them as well. On top of that, they have more high-tech goodies and toys to enjoy than any generation in human history. Despite troubling trends, their country remains among the freest in the world, giving each American individual the opportunity to develop his or her own talents while pursuing happiness as a God-given right. Somehow, though, none of these advantages and good fortunes seem to be enough. How can this be?

It is my (Samuel's) conviction that what is missing in the lives of these troubled adolescents is God's love. Their teachers and books at their atheistic schools are constantly training them to believe that the Lord is a myth and that life, aside from the hedonistic pursuit of physical pleasure, has no meaning or purpose. Many even teach that humanity is essentially a plague on this earth, causing global warming, species loss, destruction of the environment, and on and on. That is why these youngsters, who should be happy, and in past generations were happy, are becoming depressed in such massive numbers. Put simply, the fundamental, deeply ingrained need to know God and have a sense of purpose in life is so powerful that, in attempting to fight it to please atheist and humanist teachers and "fit in," children and adolescents end up being condemned to depression or, in some cases, even suicide—to say nothing of the eternal consequences. John Taylor Gatto wrote in his essay *Education and the Western Spiritual Tradition*:

> Western spirituality granted every single individual a purpose for being alive, a purpose independent of mass behavior prescriptions, money, experts, governments. It conferred significance on every aspect of relationship and community. It carried inside its ideas the seeds of a self-activating curriculum which gives meaning to time.
>
> In Western spirituality, everyone counts. It offers a basic, matter-of-fact set of practical guidelines, street lamps for the village of your life. Nobody has to wander aimlessly in the universe of Western spirituality. What constitutes a meaningful life is clearly spelled out: self-knowledge, duty, responsibility, acceptance of aging and loss, preparation for death. In the neglected genius of the West, no teacher or guru does the work for you, you must do it for yourself.[4]

On the phenomenon of atheism, Dr. Justin L. Barrett wrote:

> Atheism is rarer than you might think. If you are one of those people who never recalls having believed in any kind of god . . . then the first thing you must understand is that you are very unusual.
>
> Atheists who only hear their colleagues affirm atheism are even more likely to think that everyone around them is an atheist. . . . [B]elief in gods is the norm and nonbelief has been very unusual indeed.[5]

What is even more interesting is that, while children become depressed by being forced to give up their innate belief in God, "committed theists," wrote Dr. Barrett, "are psychologically healthier and more equipped to cope with emotional and health problems than nonbelievers."[6]

In other words, if we want to improve the mental health of American children, the easiest and fastest way to do it is to convert our atheistic schools into godly schools. Barrett explains why:

[R]esearch does indicate that commitment to a religious belief system and participation in a religious community is associated with many positive outcomes. Actively religious people have been shown to enjoy more mental and emotional health, recover from trauma more quickly, have longer and happier lives, are more generous, volunteer more, and actively contribute to communities more than nominally religious or nonreligious people do.[7]

I would add that the author's comments apply mainly to believers in biblical religion. Obviously, Islamists, driven to violence by their interpretation of the Koran, are not committed to a happy life but to a love of death. Also, the mass suicide of the Kool-Aid drinkers led by a religious fraud was hardly based on biblical religion, in which love of life and love of God go hand in hand. In other words, if we want to improve the mental health of American children, the easiest and fastest way to do it is to convert our atheistic schools into godly schools, where the Bible is revered as America's spiritual foundation, as basic to the American creed as the Declaration of Independence and the US Constitution.

While today's public schools have no choice but to live with school shootings and student suicides, one thing they will not tolerate is the Holy Bible in their classrooms, for one simple reason: the entire progressive curriculum is based on the theory of evolution. Without evolution the students cannot be considered to be animals subject to the teaching methods the Skinnerian behaviorists use in training students. Also, belief in God teaches us that every human being has a soul destined to a life after death in eternity. With humanism—the anti-God philosophy that governs public education—there is only the here and now.

The schools and even the courts have gone so far as to forbid a fourth-grade student from conducting a Bible study class during recess. Cathy Summa, principal of the school in Knox County, Tennessee, stated, "I indicated to the students and the parents that I did not feel that an organized activity of this type was appropriate during the school day. . . . While we do not discourage students from reading at recess, I think that a daily planned activity that is stationary or physically static in nature defeats the real purpose of recess. The purpose is to give students an opportunity to have some physical activity during the school day."[8]

In other words, the school authorities will find any excuse to prevent students from Bible study inside a school building during school hours. But according to a local minister who had previously met with the principal about this issue, her concern was really about the so-called separation of church and state.

But if believers can't get the Bible back in the schools, there is another way of countering Darwinism: by getting the schools to include intelligent design, or scientific creationism, in the science curriculum. Indeed, during the past four years, two states have passed laws that protect teachers if they present the theory of scientific creationism in a course of learning.

Behind these two laws is the Discovery Institute, which evolutionists describe as "a non-science propaganda organization whose purpose is to attack Darwinism, and wedge intelligent design into the science curriculum." According to Jack Hassard, writing in *Education Week*:

> The academic freedom bills that have been passed in Louisiana (2008), and Tennessee (2012) disguise their intent of teaching creationism and intelligent design using clever and slick language that they are coming to the rescue of science teachers by passing a law that protects teachers' academic freedom to present lessons questioning and critiquing scientific theories being studied including but not limited to evolution, the origins of life, global warming, and human cloning. Kind of a poor "Trojan horse" scenario, don't you think? Where is the theory of gravity, plate tectonics, and atomic theory on their to-do list?[9]

While evolutionists insist that intelligent design or creation science is not science, the people at the Discovery Institute say that it is.

And it is the scientists, notably the physicists, who are proving that man is a spiritual being, for the deeper they probe into the nature of matter, the more they find less and less matter and more and more "spirit." That's what quantum theory is all about. It was Max Planck (1858–1947), the German physicist, who formulated the quantum theory, and his hypothesis has permitted man to move from exploration of visible matter to the exploration of invisible matter, which is really non-matter.

Planck wrote, "However much discussed and however promising this atomic theory might appear, it was, until recently, regarded merely as a brilliant hypothesis, since it appeared to many far-sighted workers too risky to take the enormous step from the visible and directly controllable to the invisible sphere, from the macrocosm to the microcosm."[10]

In his book *Microcosm*, George Gilder wrote, "The central event of the twentieth century is the overthrow of matter. In technology, economics, and the politics of nations, wealth in the form of physical resources is steadily declining in value and significance. The powers of mind are everywhere ascendant over the brute force of things. This change marks a great historic divide."[11]

But let us return to the subject of teen depression. Everything you ever wanted to know about teen depression is now on the Internet. Just type in the words "teen depression" and it's all there. In an article titled "Teen Depression" on the Teen Help website, I (Samuel) found the following:

> Depression is the most common mental health disorder in the United States among teens and adults, and can have a serious impact on the lives of the many teens who suffer from depression.
>
> Teen depression can affect a teen regardless of gender, social background, income level, race, or school or other achievements, though teenage girls report suffering from depression more often than teenage boys. Teenage boys are less likely to seek help or recognize that they suffer from depression, probably due to different social expectations for boys and girls— girls are encouraged to

express their feelings while boys are not. Teenage girls' somewhat stronger dependence on social ties, however, can increase the chances of teen depression being triggered by social factors, such as loss of friends.[12]

Note that the depression suffered by these teens is serious enough to require medical intervention, which generally includes psychiatric therapy and drugs to alleviate the mental pain caused by depression. Apparently there are also many depressed teens who manage to cope and don't seek medical treatment. Some of them commit suicide to alleviate the pain of being alive.

Here is a list of symptoms of teen depression as given on a website for the antipsychotic drug Abilify, which is widely prescribed to children and adolescents:

- Loss of interest in favorite activities

- Low energy or fatigue

- Difficulty concentrating

- Irritability, restlessness, or feeling slowed down

- Trouble sleeping or sleeping too much

- Significant weight change

- Sadness most of the day

- Feeling worthless or guilty

- Thoughts about suicide or dying[13]

"Thoughts about suicide or dying," it says. Indeed, teen suicide is a serious problem that is obviously influenced by the nihilistic overtones in the school system. But it is influenced even more obviously by what is called "death education," which is prevalent in many schools today.

(We will examine both teen suicide and death education in greater depth in the next chapter.) Basically, educators use the language of death (*bury, corpse, embalm,* and *morgue,* for example) for spelling tests, and they conduct exercises in which students ponder the best and worse ways to die.[14] Children are even forced to write their own obituaries in school. "It's an assignment teachers nationwide have been handing out for years," reported the *Bakersfield Californian* in 2006.[15] Students also visit cemeteries and funeral parlors. They are told there is no God and that life is purposeless. If a child is taught that his life is of no more significance than that of a cat or dog, that makes him feel pretty worthless.

Atheistic schools even destroy the joy of Christmas by banning any mention of it in the holiday season. The students are supposed to celebrate the "winter solstice," which is probably what the worshippers at Stonehenge celebrated.

The fact that neither parents, nor therapists, nor educators will even admit that removing God from education can produce depression is a sign of how spiritually perverse our society has become. Teachers of death education admit that teaching about death and dying and the writing of obituaries can cause student depression. But that doesn't seem to bother them. Indeed, tens of thousands American teenagers have committed suicide since the introduction of death education in America's public schools.

As far back as 1984, there were 12.4 suicides for every 100,000 people age fifteen to twenty-four, or about five thousand deaths, after reaching a peak of 13.2 in 1977.[16] A more recent statement, by the American Academy of Child and Adolescent Psychiatry, shows that "suicides among young people continue to be a serious problem":

Each year in the U.S., thousands of teenagers commit suicide. Suicide is the third leading cause of death for 15-to-24-year-olds, and the sixth leading cause of death for 5-to-14-year-olds.

Teenagers experience strong feelings of stress, confusion, self-doubt, pressure to succeed, financial uncertainty, and other fears while growing up. For some teenagers, divorce, the formation of a new family with step-parents and step-siblings, or moving to a new community can be very unsettling and can intensify self-doubts. For some teens, suicide may appear to be a solution to their problems and stress.

Depression and suicidal feelings are treatable mental disorders. The child or adolescent needs to have his or her illness recognized and diagnosed, and appropriate treatment plans developed. When parents are in doubt whether their child has a serious problem, a psychiatric examination can be very helpful.[17]

Note that suicide is the sixth leading cause of death for five-to fourteen-year-olds. The idea of child suicide was unheard-of before the schools became atheistic. It is true that family dysfunctions can depress a child, especially if that child has no recourse to God, because the school told him that there is no God, just as there is no Santa Claus.

Everybody wonders why there have been so many shootings and massacres in schools and elsewhere, so many teen suicides, so much self-destructive behavior among teens. But the obvious is too unbelievable to atheist-humanist America. Simply put, godless education leads to depression, suicide, and antisocial behavior.

Death educator Nina Ribak Rosenthal, in an article entitled "Death Education: Help or Hurt?" wrote:

> Death arouses emotions. Some students may get depressed; others may get angry; many will ask questions or make statements that can cause concern for the instructor. . . Students may discuss the fact that they are having nightmares or that the course is making them depressed or feeling morbid. . . . Others may have no reactions or feel a great sense of relief that someone finally is talking about the things they often felt they could not say. Others may become frightened. In fact, [Lawrence] Bailis and [William] Kennedy report that secondary students increased their fear of death and dying as a result of participating in a death education program.[18]

And according to *Western Journalism* blogger Joanne Saldiveri, death education "still is being taught today."[19]

Depression, fear, anger, nightmares, morbidity—these are the negative emotions and reactions stirred up in students by death education. Is this what parents want their children to experience? Is this why they send their children to school, so that they can learn about death rather than life? Of course not. And yet, according to the misguided Ms. Rosenthal, death education's causing such emotional turmoil and anxiety is no reason not to teach it. "Since death has been such a taboo topic, open and honest communication is essential. Such communication," she wrote, "helps to desensitize students to anxiety-arousing items."

Thus, the purpose of death education is to "desensitize" children to death—to remove or reduce that reasonable, rational, and useful antipathy toward death that helps us preserve our lives. It is when children begin to see death as "friendly" and nonthreatening that they begin to be drawn into death's orbit and lured to self-destruction. It's a phenomenon that might be called "death seduction" in which an individual is drawn irresistibly into a fascination and then obsession with death. The individual begins to disdain life and love death.

Atheistic schools play with fire. They play with the emotional lives of their students and are nonplussed when the students act up. Even as long ago as 1988, we were learning of alarming trends such as these:

A nationwide poll of 22,000 public-school teachers sponsored by the Carnegie Foundation for the Advancement of Teaching, has revealed a disturbing picture of the problems teachers encounter in their classrooms.

Nearly 90 percent reported disruptive behavior and student apathy to be serious problems in their classrooms. Almost 70 percent identified theft and vandalism as problems in their schools, and 50 percent said that alcohol and drugs were problems. Ninety percent complained about lack of parental support; 44 percent were concerned about violence against students; and 24 percent considered violence against teachers a problem.[20]

That's a perfect picture of what happens in a school without God. Violence, vandalism, theft, apathy, drugs—and add to that suicides, shootings and outright massacres, plus low test scores and children who can't read, and you get an idea of how serious the problem of godless education has become for this nation. None of the reform programs offered by the establishment addresses any of these problems because the establishment refuses to acknowledge the need for biblical religion in education.

Back in the 1930s and '40s, the public schools respected a child's religion. There was no effort to destroy religious belief. Also, the curriculum was a solid one based on traditional teaching methods. We learned to read with phonics, write in cursive, memorize the arithmetic facts, and study our history in chronological order.

All of that is gone today, and the educators refuse to go back to the methods that worked and the Bible-based morality that governed the schools. Thus, parents have no recourse but to refuse to put their children in atheistic schools and either teach them at home or enroll them in decent private schools where religion can be taught.

Computer technology has made homeschooling the most effective form of education in America today. But 49.8 million students (or 67 percent of all American children) will attend public elementary and secondary schools, sent by parents who have no idea what goes on in those classrooms.[21] The very decent parents of the two Columbine killers had no idea what the school was doing to their sons.

And when children come home from school depressed, parents have no idea why. The school is never blamed, so there must be something wrong with the children. If a child can't learn to read, it's not the fault of the school's teaching methods; it's obviously the fault of the child, who was born with a learning handicap. And if schools hand out condoms to teenagers, they are not contributing to the delinquency of minors; they are protecting them from a sexually transmitted disease and unwanted pregnancy. Thus saith the educators of the twenty-first century.

It's time for American parents to wake up. Atheistic schools are a danger to the health, safety, and emotional lives of their children. These schools should either be abolished or reconstituted as genuine institutions of learning where teachers are not forbidden to suggest that God created the universe and all of life in it.

19

THE UNSETTLING PHENOMENON OF TEEN SUICIDE

I am afraid that schools will prove to be the gates of hell unless they diligently labor in explaining the Holy Scriptures, engraving them in the hearts of youth. I advise no one to place his child where the Scriptures do not reign paramount.

—MARTIN LUTHER

On Wednesday, February 26, 2014, fifteen-year-old Jack Chen, a sophomore at Woodson High School in Fairfax, Virginia, walked to nearby railroad tracks and stepped in front of an oncoming commuter train, ending his life.

Jack, captain of his junior varsity football team, seemed to have everything to live for: a loving family, a 4.3 grade point average, and lots of friends. He had dreamed of becoming a computer science professor and having children. But at fifteen, according to the note he left behind, he "couldn't keep doing this." He wrote, "There is too much stress in my life from school and the environment it creates, expectations for sports, expectations from my friends and expectations from my family." He ended with a simple "Goodbye."[1]

Jack's death was one of six apparent suicides at Woodson High School during the past three years, including another student found dead the next day. Baffled, frustrated parents have asked the Woodson administration for answers while wondering if the school's high-pressure, high-achieving culture might be a cause.

Steve Stuban, whose son, a Woodson student, committed suicide in 2011, told a reporter, "I have no idea what causes this to occur with increased incidence." Ivy Kilby's fifteen-year-old son, Cameron, killed himself on August 4, 2012, a month before he would have returned to Woodson as a sophomore.[2]

The suicides have been especially baffling because the teens who killed themselves did not exhibit behaviors indicating that they were at risk. They had good grades, came from stable, loving families, and generally excelled in sports. So what could be the cause? Did Woodson High's curriculum contribute in any way to the suicide of its students?

We believe it did. Evolution teaches students that there is no God, no loving Creator, and that the sole purpose of living is to satisfy one's physical and emotional needs. This secular humanist philosophy (among others), which dominates not just Woodson but all public schools, produces unhappiness, depression, and a sense that a life without transcendent purpose is not worth living.

Most parents are unaware that American high schools no longer adhere to a traditional philosophy of education. The traditional approach is based on a Judeo-Christian worldview that sees education as a development of intellect and a personal morality based on the Ten Commandments. It sees the school as serving parents, who entrust the schools to teach their children the basic academic skills that will serve them in any future career they may pursue.

But all of that changed when progressive behaviorists created a new, humanistic curriculum based on Professor Benjamin Bloom's *Taxonomy of Educational Objectives*, published in 1956 and 1964.

The 1956 edition deals primarily with the "cognitive domain," which Bloom divided into six major classes: knowledge, comprehension, application, analysis, synthesis, and evaluation. That domain includes such subjects as evolution, environmentalism, and climate change. The volume published in 1964 deals with the "affective domain," those areas of the curriculum dealing with "interests, attitudes, appreciations, values, and emotional sets and biases."[3] That's where death education and suicide education fit in very nicely, as well as values clarification, sensitivity training, Eastern religion, and transcendental meditation. In fact, the teachers at Woodson offered their stressed-out students yoga exercises to relieve stress.

While the issue of teen suicide still shocks parents and students, that of death education seems to have faded into the background. But there is an interesting story from the past involving Columbine High School, the site of the April 1999 massacre. Back in 1985, Tara Becker, a student from Columbine High, went to a pro-family conference in Colorado to tell the attendees about death education at the school and the effect it had on her. Jayne Schindler, who heard Tara's testimony, reported, "For one of her classes Tara Becker helped compile a booklet entitled *Masquerade*. It was full of subliminal pictures and prose. She had been taught to use hidden, double-meaning subliminals. As a result, she devoted so much time and attention to the subject of death that she had even attempted suicide."[4]

A video was made of Tara's testimony and distributed nationwide by Eagle Forum. The video was aired on British television, and the *Atlantic Monthly* did a feature story based on it. The producers of the television show *20/20* saw the video and decided to do a segment on death education, which was aired in 1990.

Schindler wrote:

Tara explained that the subject of death was integrated into many of the courses at her high school. She said that death was made to look glamorous, that living was hard, and that reincarnation would solve their problems. Students were told that they would always return to a much better life form. They would return to the "Oversoul" and become like God.

After one of the students at her school committed suicide, a "suicide talking day" was held and every class was to talk about death. Class assignments were for students to write their own obituaries and suicide notes. They were told to trust their own judgment in choosing whether to live or die.[5]

So Tara began to think of suicide as a means of solving some of her problems. She thought of liberating her spirit from enslavement to her body. She says she also wanted to die to help relieve the planet of overpopulation. These were a few of the crazy thoughts put into her head by her "educators." God knows what kind of equally crazy thoughts were put into the heads of the two killers at Columbine. But if you read the diaries of the two killers, you will conclude that the idea of the "Oversoul" would have definitely appealed to them.

Fortunately, by embracing God's love Tara was able to survive death education and live to talk about it. But thousands of students have committed suicide all across America, and no one in Washington has even bothered to hold a hearing on the subject. It is now assumed that teenage suicide is as natural as burgers and fries. It's just one of those things that teenagers now do in America.

But what seems to be happening, as death education becomes more and more sophisticated, is that many of these teenagers with the suicidal urge now want to take some of their teachers and classmates with them. After all, reincarnation is an equal opportunity concept. It's for everybody. Fortunately for the other students at Woodson, their classmates' suicides were solitary acts.

Incidentally, the National Education Association played an active role in promoting death education. One death educator wrote in the March 1973 issue of the *NEA Journal*: "Death by its very nature involves science and medicine, social studies and sociology, psychology, history, art, literature, music, insurance, and law."[6] Thus, death education can easily be integrated into any subject and permits classroom discussion concerning "the moral and ethical issues of abortion and euthanasia, and the spiritual and religious aspects of death and afterlife."

The article ends with this justification for teaching about death, "Subject matter for today's education must have universality, must be intrinsically interesting, must be intellectually challenging, must have both personal and social relevance, and must prepare students for life. We believe that teaching about death meets these criteria."[7]

In short, teaching about death is supposed to prepare students for life. And so, the decision to introduce death education into the public school curriculum was made without consultation with parents, who are considered quite irrelevant in these matters.

Three years later, in another article in the *NEA Journal*, the author, an English teacher at a Wyoming high school, wrote, "The highlight of the course was our visit to a mortuary and cemetery. . . . Afterwards . . . a boy stated, 'The visit to the graveyard and funeral home really blew my head, and I had to talk and think about death.'" Another student commented, "After discussing it with others, death didn't seem like such a terrible happening." That's the mind change that can lead to death seduction.[8]

Not unexpectedly, the National Education Association played an important and active role in promoting death education. It pioneered in the development of sensitivity training and values clarification by sponsoring the National Training Laboratory, founded in 1948 at Bethel, Maine. It also sponsored the writing and publication of *Death and Dying Education* by Professor Richard O. Ulin of the University of Massachusetts. The book includes an eighteen-week syllabus for the death educator.

Death educators have long been aware that fear of the subject among teachers had to be overcome. An article in *Phi Delta Kappan* of March 1974 explained:

> It is considerably easier to know something about sex education as an adult than it is to have experience with one's own death.

But at least we do possess value-clarification precedents in approaching the subject of death. We have the rich experience now of sensitizing adults to racial and economic discrimination, sex stereotyping, and other human relations problems. It should be possible to apply some of the strategies used in those earlier inservice efforts to the topic of death and dying. No administrator should be surprised to find that his staff is afraid of handling this topic. When he considers that research studies reveal similar fears among medical practitioners and even prospective funeral directors. . . [s]urely the topic is too important to be kept in the morgue any longer.[9]

And so, out of the morgue and into the classroom! By now we've had about forty years of death education in the schools, and the subject has metastasized throughout the entire curriculum.

Thanatology, the study of death and dying, has become a subject of growing professional interest. You can earn a degree in thanatology at the National Center for Death Education. The Association of Death Education and Counseling (ADEC) also provides certification for teachers of death and dying. Its annual conferences have turned into extravaganzas of death and dying fellowship. This is their vision statement:

The Association for Death Education and Counseling® envisions a world in which dying, death and bereavement are recognized as fundamental and significant aspects of the human experience. Therefore, the Association, ever committed to being on the forefront of thanatology (the study of death and dying), will provide a home for professionals from diverse backgrounds to advance the body of knowledge and to promote practical applications of research and theory.[10]

Their thirty-fourth annual conference, which was held in Atlanta in March 2012, featured many speakers who waxed eloquent on the subject. Here are a few of the topics:

- Guided Imagery: Promoting Continuing Bonds with Children

- Teaching Death and Dying: Combating the Challenges of Two Pedagogies

- Soul Soothers: Psalms of Lament in a Hurting World

- Understanding the Needs of Grieving College Students

- Healing Presence: A Rural Child Bereavement Program

- Using Guided Imagery to Heal Traumatic Grief Reactions

- African-Centered Approach to Death Education

- When Youth of Color Lose a Peer

- Children and Grief: Theories, Skill and Interventions for the Grief Counselor

You can read the titles of all their conference sessions on their website.[11]

Now that death education has become a permanent part of the public school curriculum, it has taken a backseat to APEC's overall promotion of thanatology, which has become a respected subject of academic interest. Whenever there is a school shooting or a teen suicide, there is always a certified grief counselor ready and able to do his or her job. What can parents do? They've never been able to get rid of sex education, no matter how much they've tried, and they will never be able to get rid of death education. That's the simple, unvarnished truth.

But they still have the power to remove their children from death-oriented public schools and put them in life-oriented private schools or educate them with love and care at home.

20

THE MAKING OF THE BLACK UNDERCLASS

When they call you articulate, that's another way of saying "He talks good for a black guy."
—ICE-T, *INDEPENDENT* MAGAZINE, 1995

Why is there a black underclass in America? Why, after more than 150 years of freedom from slavery and with the benefits of compulsory, universal education, do we find in every large American city thousands of blacks who live in poverty, are functionally illiterate, and are engaged in drug trafficking, gang violence, and crime? Why does a phenomenon such as an "underclass" exist in today's technologically advanced America with so many people living without hope in this land of opportunity? Wasn't universal education supposed to lift up the African-American to the same standard of economic prosperity as the white? Theoretically, that is what should have happened. But it didn't. Why?

Census statistics on illiteracy provide some clues. In 1890 illiteracy among African-Americans over the age of ten was 57.1 percent. In 1900 it was 44.5 percent. In 1910 it was 30.4 percent. And by 1920 it was down to 22.9 percent. Among white Americans only 2 percent were found to be illiterate.

In other words, great strides in literacy were being made among African-Americans from 1890 to 1920. According to the 1920 census, the percentage of illiterates among African-Americans ranged from 38.5 percent in Louisiana to 2.9 percent in New York. The 1930 census showed an even greater improvement in literacy among African-Americans.

In 1930, illiteracy among African-Americans in the urban population was 9.2 percent; in the rural population, 23.2 percent; in the rural nonfarm population, 20.5 percent. That same 1930 census revealed that 4,283,753 of a total population of 122,774,046 Americans, or less than 4 percent, were considered illiterate.[1]

But if we fast-forward sixty-three years to 1993, we find a US government report revealing that 90 million American adults can barely read or write![2] Indeed, it is estimated that 50 percent of African-Americans today are functionally illiterate! What happened in the interim to produce this literacy catastrophe? Two things: (1) The progressives adopted the racial policies of the eugenics movement, which declared African-Americans racially inferior and relegated them to a nonacademic, manual education. And (2) the progressives denigrated high individualistic literacy created by intensive phonics in favor of collectivist social goals.

The tragedy is that African-Americans had made great educational advances in the first half of the twentieth century. But from 1950 onward the great slide into academic failure began for many African-Americans.

Indeed, the National Assessment of Educational Progress (NAEP) found in 2013 that 18 percent of New York City's white students scored at the Advanced Math level, as did 26 percent of the Asian students. Only 1 percent of the city's black and Latino eighth graders scored at Advanced levels. Is it because of stupidity or deliberate dumbing down?[3]

The acclaimed film *The Great Debaters* dramatically tells the story of black academic achievement in the racially segregated South of the 1930s. It reveals how education was stressed as the way out of poverty and ignorance. Indeed, the increase in African-American literacy and intellectual development during that period produced a vibrant culture of great writers and readers. But the film doesn't provide a clue as to why that process of educational advance was stopped and reversed.[4]

As we now know, it all started in 1898 when John Dewey, leader of the progressive education movement, advocated moving education away from individualistic high literacy in favor of social collectivism. He was able to get his fellow educators to accept a completely new educational philosophy based on collectivism and socialism. And it was understood among them that a decline in individual-centered literacy was essential in carrying out their plan for a new collectivist society in America.

Indeed, it was Professor G. Stanley Hall, a leading progressive educator and mentor to John Dewey, who wrote in defense of illiteracy in 1911:

> Very many men have lived and died and been great, even the leaders of their age, without any acquaintance with letters. The knowledge which illiterates acquire is probably on the whole more personal, direct, environmental and probably a much larger proportion of it practical. Moreover, they escape much eye-strain and mental excitement, and, other things being equal, are probably more active and less sedentary. . . . Perhaps we are prone to put too high a value both upon the ability required to attain this art and the discipline involved in doing so, as well as the culture value that comes to the citizen with his average of only six grades of schooling by the acquisition of this art.[5]

And seventy years later, in 1981, we find Harvard professor Anthony Oettinger asking an audience of communications executives, "Do we really have to have everybody literate—writing and reading in the traditional sense—when we have the means through our technology to achieve a new flowering of oral communication?"[6]

Of all Americans affected by this change in educational philosophy, African-Americans have suffered the most. They have had a much more difficult time adjusting to the new progressive curriculum and its teaching methods than any other group. As a result, a great negative gap has grown between the academic achievements of African-Americans and their white compatriots.

Frustrated and discouraged by their inability to learn to read, many African-American high schoolers drop out and wind up on the streets. They form gangs and angrily take their revenge on society by antisocial, criminal behavior, which lands them in jail. The "knockout game" is one very vicious manifestation of this pent-up frustration.

The simple truth is that American public education deliberately prevents many black students from succeeding academically. In an article titled "Black Education" in *FrontPage* magazine, Professor Walter Williams wrote:

> Detroit's (predominantly black) public schools are the worst in the nation and it takes some doing to be worse than Washington, D.C. Only 3 percent of Detroit's fourth-graders scored proficient on the most recent National Assessment of Education Progress (NAEP) test, sometimes called "The Nation's Report Card." Twenty-eight percent scored basic and 69 percent below basic. "Below basic" is the NAEP category when students are unable to demonstrate even partial mastery of knowledge and skills fundamental for proficient work at their grade level. It's the same story for Detroit's eighth-graders. Four percent scored proficient, 18 percent basic and 77 percent below basic.
>
> Michael Casserly, executive director of the D.C.-based Council on Great City Schools, in an article appearing in Crain's

Detroit Business, (12/8/09) titled, "Detroit's Public Schools Post Worst Scores on Record in National Assessment," said, "There is no jurisdiction of any kind, at any level, at any time in the 30-year history of NAEP that has ever registered such low numbers." The academic performance of black students in other large cities such as Philadelphia, Chicago, New York and Los Angeles is not much better than Detroit and Washington.[7]

Incidentally, according to the *Boston Globe*, black immigrants from Africa and the West Indies do much better in getting jobs than US-born blacks.[8] That's probably because they were not subject to mind-injuring primary education in their home countries. They are therefore much better readers than native blacks. SAT scores all reveal the inferior education black children get in the public schools. Williams wrote:

> SAT scores confirm the poor education received by blacks. In 2009, average SAT reading test scores were: whites (528), Asians (516) and blacks (429). In math it was whites (536), Asians (587) and blacks (426). Twelve years of fraudulent primary and secondary education received by most blacks are not erased by four or five years of college.
>
> This is evidenced by examination scores taken for admission to graduate schools. In 2007, Graduate Record Examination verbal scores were: whites (493), Asians (485) and blacks (395). The math portion scores were: whites (562), Asians (617) and blacks (419). Scores on the LSAT in 2006, for admission to law school, were: whites (152), Asians (152) and blacks (142). In 2010, MCAT scores for admission to medical schools were: whites (26), Asians (26) and blacks (21).[9]

Liberal black politicians, who generally do whatever the liberal-progressive utopians want, have not addressed the problem of declining black literacy. The few conservative blacks who know what is going on have little influence on the politically correct black leadership. Yet, films like *Waiting for Superman*, which movingly depicts the agony black parents go through in trying to get their children into charter schools, seem to have had little impact on the education establishment. Williams wrote:

> The education establishment's solution is always more money; however, according to a *Washington Post* article (4/6/2008), "The Real Cost of Public Schools," written by Andrew J. Coulson, if we include its total operating budget, teacher retirement, capital budget and federal funding, the D.C. public schools spend $24,600 per student.
>
> Washington's fraudulent black education is by no means unique; it's duplicated in one degree or another in most of our major cities. However, there is a glimmer of hope in the increasing demand for charter schools and educational vouchers. This movement is being fought tooth and nail by an education establishment that fears the competition and subsequent threats to their employment. . . .

The fact that black youngsters trail their white counterparts by three or four years becomes even more grim when we recognize that the education white youngsters receive is nothing to write home about.[10]

What is badly needed in the black community is for some leader to realize that the only way out of the underclass is through high literacy. And that can be achieved by teaching all black children to read by intensive, systematic phonics. It can be done if the will is there to do it.

Indeed, one black teacher in Chicago, the celebrated Marva Collins, proved that this idea was quite practical. She became a legend when she quit the failed Chicago schools in 1975 and created her own private school to prove that so-called uneducable, learning-disabled black children could become highly literate human beings if taught in the proper manner.

Her work was so successful that in 1981 Hallmark made a TV movie called *The Marva Collins Story*. It tells of the many difficulties she had to overcome to fulfill her dream of proving to the world that poor black children could achieve high academic success through inspired classical teaching. She also proved the importance of a devoted teacher in the life of a child who needs all the encouragement he can get. All of the children she taught achieved high academic success.[11]

Thus, Marva Collins also proved that Charles Murray's thesis outlined in *The Bell Curve: Intelligence and Class Structure in American Life*, published in 1994, was wrong because it ignored the fact that faulty education could actually dumb down a child by depriving that child of the use of his or her mind. Murray had assumed that low academic achievement was largely the result of genetically based low intelligence. That view originated with the progressives' belief in eugenics as proven science.

I (Samuel) had met Marva Collins during the 1970s at annual conferences of the Reading Reform Foundation, which had been founded in 1961 to promote the use of intensive, systematic phonics in reading instruction. Years later, whenever I went to Chicago, I visited her Westside Preparatory School and was always impressed by what I saw. Her students were becoming the leaders of tomorrow.

It was a report in the *Chicago Sun-Times* that made the world suddenly aware of what was taking place in Marva Collins's little private school: she had refused to accept any government money in order to maintain her school's independence. The CBS program *60 Minutes* first visited the school in 1979. Morley Safer interviewed the children. Sixteen years later, in 1996, he managed to bring these now-adult children back to Westside Prep for interviews. He found that they had graduated from some of the finest colleges and universities in the nation and had become physicians, lawyers, engineers, educators, and so forth. Those *60 Minutes* programs can also be viewed on YouTube.

In other words, there is no lack of information on how to conduct good education for all children. The key to success is in teaching children to read with intensive phonics. Once children learn to read, the sky's the limit. But the Chicago public schools were not interested in how Marva Collins's "uneducable" students had achieved high academic success. Meanwhile, the public schools in Illinois are as bad as, if not worse than, when Collins left them. Thus we read in the *Chicago Tribune*, "Illinois grade school test scores plunge—especially in poor communities: The push to toughen state exams for Illinois grade school students triggered widespread drops in 2013 scores, with hundreds of schools in some of the state's poorest communities seeing performances plunge, test results show."[12]

This means that the underclass will keep expanding as long as public education continues to dumb down the nation's children.

The existence of an underclass in highly advanced Western countries continues to be of great interest to sociologists who find it simply inconceivable that professional educators can be consciously involved in a conspiracy to dumb down a nation. That is why we decided to reprint the entire text of Dewey's article "The Primary-Education Fetich" in the appendix.

There is already in the United States a growing functionally illiterate white underclass. Charles Murray, in his book *Coming Apart: The State of White America 1960–2010*, wrote:

> [W]hite males of the 2000s were less industrious than they had been twenty, thirty, or fifty years ago, and . . . the decay in industriousness occurred overwhelmingly in Fishtown [Murray's prototype of a white, working-class town]. . . .
>
> In the 1960 census, about 9 percent of all Fishtown men ages 20–64 were not in the labor force. In the 2000 census, about 30 percent of Fishtown men in the same age range were not in the labor force. . . . They talked about men who just couldn't seem to cope with the process of getting and holding a job.[13]

What Murray described in his book is the making of a white underclass. He wrote, "Our nation is coming apart at the seams—not ethnic seams, but the seams of class. . . . The American project is disintegrating." He continued, "A significant and growing portion of the American population is losing the virtues required to be functioning members of a free society. On the other side of the spectrum, the people who run the country are doing just fine. . . . In the absence of some outside intervention, the new lower class will continue to grow."[14]

But the idea that the planned dumbing down of America by our educators has something to do with this cultural and moral disintegration is simply too inconceivable to a professional sociologist. But idleness among the dependent poor creates dangerous cultural dysfunction. John Taylor Gatto wrote in "Education and the Western Spiritual Tradition":

> Work produces a spiritual reward unknown to the reinforcement schedules of behavioral psychologists like B.F. Skinner. . . . If the secular aversion to work is a thing to be rationalized, as schools do rationalize minimal effort, a horrifying problem is created for our entire society, one which has proven so far to be incurable. I refer to the psychological, social, and spiritual anxieties that arise when you have no useful work to do.[15]

Concerning the "cultural causes" of the underclass in England, British former prison doctor and psychiatrist Theodore Dalrymple wrote in his book *Life at the Bottom:*

> I have little hesitation in saying that the mental, cultural, emotional, and spiritual impoverishment of the Western underclass is the greatest of any large group of people I have ever encountered anywhere. . . . [P]atterns of behavior emerge—in the case of the underclass, almost entirely self-destructive ones. Day after day I hear of the same violence, the same neglect and abuse of children, the same broken relationships, the same victimization by crime, the same nihilism, the same dumb despair. . . .
>
> It will come as a surprise to American readers, perhaps, to learn that the majority of the British underclass is white, and that it demonstrates all the same social pathology as the black underclass in America—for very similar reasons, of course.[16]

Dalrymple places the blame for the moral depravity of the underclass on the intellectual elite, the intelligentsia, who promoted among themselves the tantalizing idea of free love and moral relativism. These ideas have filtered down to average Americans mainly through their secularized culture and education. He wrote, "But intellectuals in the twentieth century sought to free our sexual relations of all social, contractual, or moral obligation and meaning whatsoever, so that henceforth only raw sexual desire itself would count in our decision making."[17]

That's why kids in the public schools need condoms! He commented, "Where fashion in clothes, bodily adornment, and music are concerned, it is the underclass that increasingly sets the pace. Never before has there been so much downward cultural aspiration. . . . Each day my faith in the ability of human beings comprehensively to ruin their lives is renewed. . . . Truly, the ways of human misery are infinite."[18]

Words of wisdom from a close observer of the underclass. Their nihilism comes from the schools they attended. Without religious guidance from their educators to imbue their existence with transcendent significance, their lives have become void of any spiritual meaning. If anyone believes that there are no evil consequences to removing God and biblical morality from the schools, there is more than enough misery in the underclass to prove otherwise.

Functional illiterates become violent because they can't use their brains. The inability to read creates boredom and resentment against the society that dumbed them down. They were intelligent when they entered school at age five or six. But in a few short years they were told that they were learning disabled or just plain dumb and could not learn to read. They became functional illiterates.

According to Michigan prison psychologist Martin Newburn, who has spent thirty years in the criminal justice system learning about the motives behind racial violence and hatred, the violence is about hate. And the hate is about race. He wrote:

To people who practice this type of racial violence, all non-blacks are the enemy since they were weaned on the idea that whites/Asians/Hispanics/Martians were "keeping my people down."

They may be functionally illiterate, and I have yet to meet one that wasn't, but their older family members or people in their neighborhood along with the popular culture drove that early message into their skulls.

They believe that they have some black toxic-tribal license to attack, and the more brutal, the more "down with the struggle" they are. The degree of viciousness also demonstrates just how manly (or womanly) they are. In other words, the more sadistic, the higher the social and personal power status.

It's also great street cred for them, the sacred status for assaulting the all-pervasive and imaginary white power structure, and in regard to Asians and Hispanics, those people are just "takin' jobs" from them.

The people who practice this kind of racial violence—like the Knockout Game—have imaginary, social injustice tags as legitimate reasons to assault all non-blacks.

To say the black assaults on non-blacks isn't racist is a blatant lie. Black predators are racist to the bone. Most all live the part in prison.[19]

It is obvious that Dr. Newburn is unaware of how our schools deliberately injure the brains of millions of children, black and white, by using teaching methods intended to do just that. It was Dewey's plan to use the look-say method of teaching reading as the means to dumb down the nation.

As a result, growing functional illiteracy in America has produced a lethal time-bomb: a race war. A literate society is a less violent society. Until the American people understand the evil consequences of educational malpractice, they will be forced to tolerate increasing violence among those who have been deliberately deprived of the use of their brains.

The solution? Teach every child in kindergarten and first grade to read with intensive, systematic phonics. That will turn them all into superb readers and enhance their brainpower by enabling them to master language. A simple idea, but one that works. High literacy is the road out of the underclass.

21
EUGENICS AND THE CREATION OF THE BLACK UNDERCLASS

The right of the state to safeguard the character and integrity of the race or races [is] incontestable.
—HENRY FAIRFIELD OSBORN BEFORE THE 1923 SECOND INTERNATIONAL CONGRESS OF EUGENICS

One of the evil fruits of the tree of evolution is the idea of eugenics, the notion that human beings can be bred to perfection by the same methods used to breed perfect cattle. Since evolution itself reduces man to the level of animal, it is not surprising that eugenics was adopted by many in the educational elite as the means of solving man's social problems. But eugenics in itself poses a problem: what do we mean by human perfection, and whose definition of perfection shall be adopted?

The founder of the eugenics movement, Sir Francis Galton (1822–1911), cousin of Charles Darwin, found his model of perfection in the British elite. But he was painfully aware that the birthrate of the elite was far lower than that of the inferior classes. In this he saw a great danger to civilization. He concluded that ways had to be found to encourage the fertility of the superior stock and to discourage the fertility of the inferior stock.

To determine which individuals had superior traits, Galton created an anthropometric laboratory in 1884 for the measurement of man, with the hope that by means of tests he could single out those individuals who should survive. However, Galton realized that physical measurements alone were not enough to determine the criteria he needed. He began searching for ways to investigate psychological differences.

In 1886, he was introduced to James McKeen Cattell, a young American who had just completed two years of study in the laboratories of Professor Wilhelm Wundt, the world's leading experimental psychologist, at Leipzig University in Germany. It was there that Cattell conducted his reaction-time experiments, which became the "scientific" basis for teaching children to read by the whole-word or sight method. Cattell spent the next two years working in Galton's lab at Cambridge University, where he used experimental techniques to investigate the mental differences among normal individuals. He coined the term "mental test." Cattell used Galton's framework of physical and physiological anthropometry to conduct his experiments on individual differences.

Born in 1860, Cattell graduated in 1880 from Lafayette College (Easton, Pennsylvania), where his father, a Presbyterian minister, was president. While at college, Cattell studied the ideas of Auguste Comte, the French philosopher who stressed the authority of scientific knowledge over religious or metaphysical forms of thought. This philosophy, known as *positivism*, led Cattell to adopt a new "religion" of science.

In 1882–83 Cattell studied at Johns Hopkins University, where his classmate was John Dewey and their professor was psychologist G. Stanley Hall. Hall was the first American to study at Leipzig under Professor Wundt, and he encouraged Cattell to get his doctorate under Wundt at Leipzig.

After completing his studies in Germany and his experiments at Cambridge, Cattell returned to the United States, where he became professor of psychology at the University of Pennsylvania. In 1891, Cattell moved to Teachers College, Columbia University, where as professor of experimental psychology he built the nation's leading psychology department. He trained many young psychologists who then fanned out across American academia to teach the new gospel of psychology. In 1904, Cattell arranged for his friend John Dewey to come to Columbia as professor of philosophy.

At Teachers College, Cattell's star pupil was Edward L. Thorndike, who espoused the principles of eugenics and became America's leading educational psychologist. He devised a new theory of learning based on conditioning techniques used in animal training. His book *Animal Intelligence* (1898) laid the groundwork for the school of behaviorism.

Both Cattell and Thorndike were active in applying the principles of eugenics to education. Like Dewey, they held an organic view of society. Socialist Dewey wrote in his famous *My Pedogogic Creed*, "I believe that the individual who is to be educated is a social individual and that society is an organic union of individuals. . . . Examinations are of use only so far as they test the child's fitness for social life and reveal the place in which he can be of most service and where he can receive the most help."[1]

Inherent in Dewey's creed is the notion that individual human worth is determined by social usefulness, a concept taught today in such values-clarification exercises as the lifeboat and fallout shelter survival games.

This was clearly the educational philosophy of a collectivist state, not a constitutional republic in which the purpose of government is to secure the God-given rights of individuals to life, liberty, and the pursuit of happiness. The purpose of education in a free society is to provide the individual with the basic intellectual skills needed to make his way in the world as a free adult, not to determine where he can be "of most service."

It was inevitable that those who believed in eugenics would see society in racial terms and impose racist ideas on American education. The veneer of science made racism respectable among the social-radical progressives who were supposedly only interested in the future good of mankind.

Eugenics conferences were held in the United States to spread the new spirit of scientific racism within academia. G. Stanley Hall, who had become president of Clark University (Worcester, Massachusetts) in 1889, encouraged his students to develop tests to assess mental capacity. One of his students, Lewis Terman, devised a mental test that was to become the most famous of them all, one that measured the IQ, or intelligence quotient. The IQ expressed the ratio of a child's mental age to his chronological age, multiplied by one hundred. Terman believed that intelligence was a matter of genetic inheritance and that genetic superiority could therefore be determined by this test.

One of the earliest tests to determine racial differences was conducted by R. Meade Bache and published in *Psychological Review* in 1895. It was a reaction-time test, using three groups of males: twelve Caucasians, twelve American Indians, and eleven African-Americans. They were tested for the speed with which they reacted to the sight of a pendulum, a particular sound, and a slight electric shock.

The American Indians reacted fastest, the Caucasians slowest, and the blacks fell in the middle. On the basis of these flimsy results, Bache determined that the smarter and more intellectually developed the individual, the slower his reaction time to ordinary physiological stimuli. From this, he concluded: "Pride of race obscures the view of the white with reference to the relative automatic quickness of the negro. That the negro is, in the truest sense, a race inferior to that of the white can be proved by many facts, and among these by the quickness of his automatic movements as compared with those of the white."[2]

In other words, a superior physical trait was now a sure sign of mental inferiority!

The Anglo-American eugenics movement grew in influence on both sides of the Atlantic. In England it was embraced by Fabian socialists because they believed that an ideal utopian society could be produced only by "superior" people. In America, it drew such progressives as Margaret Sanger, Gifford Pinchot, David Starr Jordan, Charles W. Eliot, Emma Goldman, and such conservatives as Herbert Hoover and Charles Davenport. Sanger was motivated by her belief in eugenics to start the birth-control movement.

The eugenics movement persuaded Congress to pass new immigration laws to curtail the influx of "inferior" peoples from eastern and southern Europe. In 1921, the Second International Congress of Eugenics was held at New York's Museum of Natural History. Its president was Henry Fairfield Osborn, who wrote in the program:

> The right of the state to safeguard the character and integrity of the race or races on which its future depends is, to my mind, as incontestable as the right of the state to safeguard the health and morals of its people. As science has enlightened government in the prevention and spread of disease, it must also enlighten government in the prevention of the spread and multiplication of worthless members of society, the spread of feeble-mindedness, of idiocy, and of all moral and intellectual as well as physical diseases.[3]

It was this philosophy of government that enabled Congress to pass Prohibition, which made it illegal to drink alcoholic beverages—and we all know what a social disaster Prohibition turned out to be. Likewise, in the twenty-first century, Mayor Bloomberg of New York believed that it is government's highest duty to determine what people should be allowed to eat. Sounds benign and sensible to a statist. But nothing in our Constitution gives government such powers to interfere with an individual's eating habits.

Among the members of the Eugenics General Committee were Herbert Hoover, Gifford Pinchot, Robert M. Yerkes, and Edward L.

Thorndike, who was then chairman of the Psychology Department at Teachers College, Columbia.

Thorndike taught the principles of eugenics in his books on teacher training, which were widely read in the profession. In *Elementary Principles of Education*, which he authored with his protégé Arthur I. Gates and published in 1929, he wrote:

> Education, then, cannot improve the racial stock by the direct means of biological heredity, but it may do so, indirectly, by means of social inheritance. It may improve the race by teaching prospective parents to breed men, as they do plants and animals, by discovering the nature of the best stocks and by seeking to increase their fertility while decreasing the productivity of the poorest strains. To achieve this end, ideas and mores different from those now prevailing must be established since most persons still feel superstitious dread of tampering with the question of who shall be born, though no other question so deeply affects the welfare of man.[4]

To Thorndike, blacks were inferior and had to be treated differently in education. Thorndike's colleagues were in agreement on this issue, for the eugenics-inspired tests always seemed to provide "scientific proof" that blacks were inferior to whites. Cattell's weekly publication, *School and Society*, often reported the results of these tests. For example, the March 6, 1915, issue published an account of tests conducted by W. H. Pyle of the University of Missouri, titled "The Mind of the Negro Child." When some of the Negroes turned out to be more intelligent than expected, Pyle commented, "It may be that the negroes living under better social conditions are of better stock. They may have more white blood in them." The March 20, 1915, issue carried an advertisement for "The Mental Capacity of the American Negro" by Marion J. Mayo. And at the National Education Association convention in August 1915, Lewis Terman spoke on "Education and Race Improvement."

The practical result of all of this was the relegation of blacks to an education in keeping with their inferior status. In a speech Thorndike gave to his colleagues in 1928, he said:

I am commissioned to describe and discuss scientific researches concerning the curriculum. . . . Teachers in the course of their work observe certain facts about the results which certain courses of study have upon certain pupils and make up their minds that this, that and the other features of the course of study have such and such advantages or weaknesses. They then proceed to change the curriculum in so far as they have the zeal and power to do so. Many improvements have had such an origin, of example the change in certain schools for Negroes from a predominantly literary to a predominantly realistic and industrial curriculum. . . .

Researches concerning individual differences have also exposed the fallacies of judging curricula by their products without allowances for the selection of the human material upon which the curriculum worked. . . . The differences in gain due to studied English, history, mathematics and Latin rather than English, history, typewriting and cooking is less than the differences in the gains made by very intellectual pupils . . . and average pupils taking identical programs, and is less than the difference in gains made by white pupils and colored pupils taking identical programs.[5]

In other words, as a result of "scientific research," pupils were now no longer being judged as individuals, but as members of different racial groups. Scientific racism had become an integral part of progressive education policy.

The rise of National Socialism (Nazism) in Germany, with its evil racial policies, brought the whole eugenics movement into disrepute. Many scientists had rejected it as pseudoscience, in the same category as phrenology. But Nazi racism indicated dramatically how eugenics would work in practice. In 1933, the Nazi government passed a eugenic sterilization law that resulted in the compulsory sterilization, within three years, of 275,000 people judged "unfit" by the Hereditary Health Court. In 1939, the Nazi regime inaugurated a policy of euthanasia for the mentally diseased or disabled. Some 70,000 patients were shot and gassed to death. All of this was a prelude to the mass extermination of Jews that would take place during the war years.

Despite the growing revulsion to eugenics after 1933, Edward L. Thorndike continued to believe in it right up to his death in 1949. In his last book, *Human Nature and the Social Order*, published in 1940, he wrote, in a section titled "Eugenics and the Good Life," "Improvement of the human genes . . . is the surest means of fostering the good life; it operates at the source by producing better people."[6]

In other words, there was no hope of improvement for people who started out with bad genes, like blacks. Therefore, they should be trained with a "realistic and industrial curriculum." These are the monstrous ideas that those who reject the benign influence of God in the lives of human beings substitute for so-called educational purposes.

While Thorndike is barely remembered today, his impact while he lived was enormous. Lawrence Cremin, in his history of Teachers College, wrote:

Coming to Teachers College in 1899 at the age of 25, [Thorndike] rose within five years from instructor to full professor and head of the Department of Educational Psychology. For 40 years he served Teachers College and his chosen field, becoming in every sense the outstanding educational psychologist of his era. . . . Thus, the schoolroom was for Thorndike a "great laboratory" in which the modification of instincts and capacities into habits and powers was the central and unending subject of educational research. . . .

Like all pioneers, Thorndike inspired innumerable disciples and leaders to carry on his revolutionary work in education . . . . Indeed, it may well be stated that two thinkers, Thorndike and Dewey, supplied the two great formative influences of the twentieth-century educational theory and together established the frame of references in which their contemporaries and successors were to work.[7]

In other words, the two most important influences in modern American education were a eugenicist and a socialist, two radical utopians, and today's public schools reflect their influences. They were the educators who deliberately engineered the decline of literacy in America. Their colleagues in crime included James McKeen Cattell, G. Stanley Hall, Arthur I. Gates, Charles Judd, William Scott Gray, and Edmund Burke Huey—a combination of eugenicists and progressive socialists.

John Dewey provided the educational philosophy and the dumbing-down plan that justified the shift from intellectual training to socialization. Cattell's reaction-time experiments in Wundt's Leipzig laboratories provided the supposedly scientific basis for the change from phonics to look-say. He was also Francis Galton's prize disciple. Edmund Burke Huey, a pupil of G. Stanley Hall's, wrote the "authoritative" book advocating the change in reading instruction (*The Psychology and Pedagogy of Reading*, 1908). Thorndike provided the new stimulus-response technique of conditioning as the new classroom methodology. His protégé, Arthur Gates, actually edited the new primary readers for the Macmillan Company. Charles Judd of the University of Chicago, another Wundtian PhD, organized the wholesale reform of the public school curriculum, and his protégé, William Scott Gray, supervised the writing, editing, and publication of the Dick and Jane reading program.

These are the men whose utopian ideas have ruined American public education. They have led to the creation of millions of functional illiterates and a nation of dummies. Unfortunately, the system cannot be returned to what it was before the progressives took control of it. Neither the public nor the politicians have the knowledge or the will needed to reform the system. Thus it is up to parents to either homeschool their children or provide them with the kind of education they want in a private school. Charter schools are public schools, and to what degree they are free to create an academic curriculum that produces high literacy is still questionable. Those who issue the charters have the power to determine curriculum.

But there is no doubt that liberal utopians have done a job on the black community. They adhere to the Democratic Party, which keeps the whole criminal enterprise in place. Ignorance of political reality, progressive racism, and educational malpractice will keep blacks in the underclass for the foreseeable future.

One of the educational gurus who has written several books promoting whole language, the philosophy behind the current progressive concept of literacy, is Frank Smith, author of *Reading Without Nonsense*. He wrote, "Readers don't need the alphabet. . . . [L]earning the alphabet is not a prerequisite for learning to distinguish words . . . . [T]rying to teach children to read by teaching them the sounds of the letters is literally a meaningless activity."[8]

Since the alphabet is the basis of our written word, to deliberately deprive a child of the knowledge and use of the alphabet is a crime. The key to the development of Western civilization is the alphabet, first used by the ancient Hebrews to record the Word of God. Famous composer and conductor Leonard Bernstein, recalling his early learning of Hebrew, told an interviewer in 1989:

> In the Jewish tradition, the one gift that God gave to man in his travail and *tsuris* [aggravating trouble] under the curse of having been expelled from the garden was something called the alphabet. And those twenty-two Hebrew letters are said to have been presented in fire . . . and that's why those letters, with their strokes and serifs, seem to be like flames. They *burn*. And you can also point to the Pentecostal manner of speaking in tongues with the flames coming down from heaven. So you could say that Christianity is Judaism tidied up a little bit.
>
> Though I can't prove it, deep in my heart I know that every person is born with the love of learning. Without exception.[9]

Yet there are among our utopian educators those who believe that there is a large group of children who can't learn. They are taught by the sight method. And so they become the functional illiterates who sit in the back of the classroom and are considered uneducable. Their lives, for all practical purposes, have been ruined—at the cost of billions of dollars.

22

THE ROLE OF BEHAVIORAL PSYCHOLOGY IN THE DEWEY PLAN

It is the business of behavioristic psychology to be able to predict and control human activity.
—JOHN B. WATSON, FROM *THE WAYS OF BEHAVIORISM*, 1928

Another key tool used by the radical utopians in their war on education is known as "behavioral psychology." The name sounds innocent enough. As we shall see, however, hidden behind this scheme is a scientific effort to literally mold an individual into the type of person desired by the education establishment.

In John Dewey's 1898 plan to dumb down America, he wrote, "Change must come gradually. To force it unduly would compromise its final success by favoring a violent reaction. What is needed in the first place is that there should be a full and frank statement of conviction with regard to the matter from physiologists and psychologists and from those school administrators who are conscious of the evils of the present regime."[1]

In other words the full collaboration of experimental psychologists would be needed to help make the plan succeed. That was no problem since all of his academic colleagues were involved in promoting the new Wundtian experimental psychology, which concentrated on the physical behavior of the organism rather than on its mental attributes. G. Stanley Hall got his doctoral student Edmund Burke Huey to write the needed authoritarian book, *The Psychology of Reading*, which quoted Dewey's 1898 article and promoted his radical views on the need to change the curriculum of primary education.

Dewey's colleague, James McKeen Cattell, who had spent the 1880s in Leipzig, became professor of experimental psychology at Columbia College in 1890. Among his many graduate students was Edward L. Thorndike, who reduced learning to simple stimulus-response behaviorism. He formulated the conditioning techniques that Pavlov was to use in his famous experiments with salivating dogs in Russia. Indeed, a Russian translation of *Principles of Learning Based upon Psychology* by E. L. Thorndike was published in Moscow in 1926 with a foreword by Lev Vygotsky, one of Pavlov's colleagues.

Thorndike's claim to fame was his discovery that you could train children like animals. He wrote in 1928, "Our experiments on learning in the lower animals have probably contributed more to knowledge of education per hour or per unit of intellect spent, than experiments on children. . . . The best way with children may often be, in the pompous words of an animal trainer, 'to arrange everything in connection with the trick so that the animal will be compelled by the laws of his own nature to perform it.'"[2]

But it was John B. Watson, the most arrogant behaviorist of them all, who revealed the true contempt that he and his fellow behaviorists had toward their fellow human beings. In his book *Behaviorism,* a textbook for his students, he wrote:

Human beings do not want to class themselves with other animals. They are willing to admit that they are animals but "something else in addition." It is this "something else" that causes the trouble. In this "something else" is bound up everything that is classed as religion, the life hereafter, morals, love of children, parents, country, and the like. The raw fact that you, as a psychologist, if you are to remain scientific, must describe the behavior of man in no other terms than those you would use in describing the behavior of the ox you slaughter, drove and still drives many timid souls away from behaviorism.[3]

Watson meant to be shocking, because he had to convince his students that they had to treat human beings coldly and callously as animals. He wrote further, "The interest of the behaviorist in man's doings is more than the interest of the spectator—he wants to control man's reactions, as physical scientists want to control and manipulate other natural phenomena. It is the business of behavioristic psychology to be able to predict and control human activity."[4]

However, the most influential behavioral psychologist in matters of education was B. F. Skinner, who reduced all of learning to conditioning. Skinner believed that, like animals, humans acted only in response to consequences, good or bad, of the same action performed previously. An action that resulted in an unfavorable or painful outcome was not likely to be repeated. But actions that produced a pleasant outcome were repeated over and over, a law he referred to as the *principle of reinforcement*. Hence, there was no such thing as "free will," but only mechanical repetition of what was seen to bring positive effects to an individual.[5]

Skinner was born in Susquehanna, Pennsylvania, in 1904. Although his parents were Christians, he became an atheist at an early age. He attended Hamilton College in New York and then Harvard, where he received his BA in English literature in 1926.

During his time at Harvard, Skinner invented the prototype for his so-called Skinner Box, a sort of animal-experimentation cage, in which he raised his infant daughter in accordance with his theory of learning. This apparatus contained a lever that afforded its occupant the prospect of gaining a reward by pushing the lever. Skinner's reading of John B. Watson's *Behaviorism* led him into graduate study in psychology and to the development of his own operant behaviorism. Skinner got his PhD from Harvard in 1931 and remained there as a researcher until 1936. After that, he went to teach at the University of Minnesota at Minneapolis and later at Indiana University, where he served as chairman of the Psychology Department in 1946 and 1947. The next year, Skinner went back to Harvard as a tenured professor, staying for the rest of his life. Skinner was also among the signers of the controversial *Humanist Manifesto II*, written in 1973.

Skinner called his particular brand of behaviorism "radical" behaviorism. Unlike less austere behaviorism, it does not accept private events such as thinking, perceptions, and unobservable emotions in a causal account of an organism's behavior. Skinner wrote:

> The position can be stated as follows: what is felt or introspectively observed is not some nonphysical world of consciousness, mind, or mental life but the observer's own body. This does not mean, as I shall show later, that introspection is a kind of psychological research, nor does it mean (and this is the heart of the argument) that what are felt or introspectively observed are the causes of the behavior. An organism behaves as it does because of its current structure, but most of this is out of reach of introspection. At the moment we must content ourselves, as the methodological behaviorist insists, with a person's genetic and environment histories. What are introspectively observed are certain collateral products of those histories.
>
> In this way we repair the major damage wrought by mentalism. When what a person does [is] attributed to what is going on inside him, investigation is brought to an end. Why explain the explanation? For twenty five hundred years people have been preoccupied with feelings and mental life, but only recently has any interest been shown in a more precise analysis of the role of the environment. Ignorance of that role led in the first place to

mental fictions, and it has been perpetuated by the explanatory practices to which they gave rise.[6]

In other words, Skinner was about as pure a behaviorist as a psychologist could be. The life of the mind was of no interest to the behaviorist. He also opposed humanistic psychology and disdained such human concepts as freedom and dignity. Much of this self-observed theory stemmed from Thorndike's puzzle boxes, from which he got the idea for his own Skinner Box. He further expanded on Thorndike's earlier work by introducing the concept of reinforcement to Thorndike's law of effect. Skinner advocated behavioral engineering and the notion that people should be controlled through the systematic allocation of external rewards. Thus he shared the liberal utopian dream of a controlled society. Indeed, his political philosophy was summed up by the following statement: "Control of the population as a whole must be delegated to specialists—to police, priests, owners, teachers, therapists, and so on, with their specialized reinforcers and their codified contingencies."[7]

Skinner's theories of education removed any last vestige of spirit from the student, who is now totally deprived of any spiritual life or soul. All of this fitted in nicely with Dewey's plan to change America. Skinner also became an active member of the Pavlovian Society, devoted to the further study of Pavlovian conditioning. He attended meetings of the Society in Moscow, where he collaborated with Soviet psychologists.

In the 1920s, behavioral psychologists in the Soviet Union were conducting experiments on predicting and controlling human activity. Ivan Pavlov was experimenting on dogs to produce conditioned reflexes. He and his helpers were also experimenting on ways to artificially create behavioral disorganization, which we discussed in an earlier chapter.

Incidentally, there are two kinds of reflexes: unconditioned and conditioned. An unconditioned reflex is a natural immediate response to stimuli. For example, when you are driving a car in daylight and enter a tunnel, your eyes automatically adjust to the darkness of the tunnel. A conditioned reflex is simply a learned habit. For example, when the traffic light ahead turns red, your foot automatically steps on the brake, even though your mind is on other things. When you learn to drive on the right, you develop all kinds of learned habits or conditioned reflexes. But when you rent a car in England, where they drive on the left, your right-driving reflexes may kill you. So now you have to think about every move you make. If you live in England long enough, you may develop a left-drive reflex.

Now, getting back to Pavlov and his experiments on artificially creating behavioral disorganization, why would anyone want to do that? Well, the communists were out to conquer the world, and the power to create behavioral disorganization among their enemies could be quite helpful.

In 1932, Alexander Luria, one of Pavlov's colleagues, described those experiments in great detail in his book *The Nature of Human Conflicts.* The book was translated into English by American W. Horsley Gantt, who had spent six years working in Pavlov's laboratory in Russia, after which he joined the staff of the Phipps Psychiatric Clinic at Johns Hopkins University. Luria wrote:

> We are not the first of those who have artificially created disorganisations of human behaviour. . . .
>
> I. P. Pavlov was the first investigator who, with the help of exceedingly bold workers, succeeded experimentally in creating neuroses with experimental animals. Working with conditioned reflexes in dogs, Pavlov came to the conclusion that every time an elaborated reflex came into conflict with the unconditioned reflex, the behaviour of the dog markedly changed. . . . Although, in the experiments with the collision of the conditioned reflexes in animals, it is fairly easy to obtain acute forms of artificial affect, it is much more difficult to get these results in human experiments.
>
> K. Lewin, in our opinion, has been one of the most prominent psychologists to elucidate this question of the artificial

production of affect and of the experimental disorganisation of behaviour. . . . Here the fundamental conception of Lewin is very close to ours.[8]

Now, who is this K. Lewin, whom Luria praised so highly as being a master at creating behavioral disorganization? He is none other than the Kurt Lewin who came to America in 1933, set up the Research Center for Group Dynamics at MIT, and invented "sensitivity training." Shortly before his death in 1947, Lewin founded the National Training Lab at Bethel, Maine, under the sponsorship of the National Education Association.

Think about it. Here you have a communist behavioral psychologist who is an expert at artificially creating behavioral disorganization—that is, driving people crazy—being sponsored by the National Education Association.

The importance of Lewin in this story is that he represented the collectivist or communist mentality in the psychological community, which had its own sociopolitical agenda. Lewin's biographer, Alfred J. Marrow, wrote, "Students of progressive education also saw the need for studies of group behavior. This was stimulated by the educational philosophy of John Dewey. . . . This called for the development of leadership skills and collective setting of group goals."[9]

Note how the philosophy of John Dewey justifies everything. And of course, that is what we have in today's classrooms: group learning, groupthink, and outcome-based education. So we have destroyed the ability of children to learn to read and instead forced them to be indoctrinated by collectivist means. That's not education. That's a program to destroy the individual, independent mind. Charlotte Iserbyt summed up the process in her book *Back to Basics Reform*:

The radical transformation of America's classrooms from places of traditional cognitive/academic learning, where intellectual and academic freedom flourish, into experimental laboratories for psychological (attitude and value) change, using modern technology (the computer for individualized instruction and for administrative management systems) in conjunction with the totalitarian theories of Professor B. F. Skinner and other less well-known social engineers is the goal.[10]

We know that one of the reasons children become frustrated in the classroom and act up is because of the way they are being taught. They enter school at age five or six feeling very confident that they are intelligent enough to be able to learn to read. After all, they taught themselves to speak their own language on their own without the help of a certified teacher. So their confidence in their learning ability is quite justified. But once in school they discover that they can't learn to read in the manner they are being taught. So they become angry and frustrated, doubting their own intelligence. And soon they join the ranks of the reading disabled, the dyslexic, and the ADD or ADHD sufferers and are given a drug to solve their learning and behavioral problems and make the teacher happy.

It should not surprise you to learn that one of Kurt Lewin's most significant experiments was aimed at determining the behavioral effects of frustration on children and how these effects are produced. Marrow wrote, "The experiment indicated that in frustration the children tended to regress to a surprising degree. They tended to become babyish. Intellectually, children of four and a half years tended toward the behavior of a three-year-old. The degree of intellectual regression varied directly with the strength of the frustration. . . . Aggressiveness also increased and some children went so far as to hit, kick, and break objects."[11]

So what do you do with kids like that? You drug them! And what does this do to the American brain? It destroys it.

23

WHY JOHNNY CAN'T TELL RIGHT FROM WRONG

Humanistic education is the institutionalized love of death.
—REV. R. J. RUSHDOONY, FROM A 2010 SERMON

Back in the 1930s and '40s, when I (Samuel) was attending public school in New York City, school shootings, let alone massacres, were unheard-of. Yes, there was an occasional tragedy in a school in some far-off place, but in general, we all loved our schools because they were not doing us any harm. In fact, they were really educating us: teaching us to read with traditional phonics; teaching us how to hold a pen or pencil correctly and to write in a neat cursive script; teaching us basic arithmetic, grammar, history, and geography; and teaching us how to be good, patriotic Americans. We respected our teachers and obeyed them.

And at assemblies, the principal read from the Bible. But all of that is gone. It has vanished. What we have now can hardly be understood.

The horrendous massacre at the Sandy Hook primary school in Newtown, Connecticut, in which twenty children and six adults were brutally murdered, indicates that an evil force has been let loose that no one knows what to do about. This is the same evil force that turned two normal teenagers at Columbine High School in Colorado into nihilist murderers. What the two Columbine killers and Adam Lanza, the twenty-year-old Sandy Hook killer, had in common was unusually high intelligence combined with hatred of God. The *Telegraph*, a British newspaper, reported online:

> Lanza was said by classmates to be fiercely intelligent.
> "You could tell he was, I would say, a genius," said Miss Israel. "There was something that was above the rest of us."
> He'd correct people's Latin homework, when they were aged around 14, and at 16 was among the list of top students in his English class, studying "Of Mice and Men" and "Catcher in the Rye"—the classic tale of troubled youth.
> "It was almost painful to have a conversation with him, because he felt so uncomfortable," said Olivia DeVivo, who sat behind him in English. "I spent so much time in my English class wondering what he was thinking."
> "He didn't have any friends, but he was a nice kid if you got to know him," said Kyle Kromberg, now studying business administration at Endicott College in Massachusetts. He studied Latin with Lanza.
> "He didn't fit in with the other kids," he said. "He was very, very shy. He wouldn't look you in the eyes when he talked. He didn't really want to lock eyes with you for very long."
> He was also a technical whizz kid, keen on computers and video games, and part of a group who would meet up for computer programming get-togethers.[1]

Obviously, Lanza was also exposed to the entire secular-humanist curriculum of our atheist public schools: evolution, values clarification, sex education, and other programs that served to wrest children away from traditional biblical religion. What's interesting to note is that the Columbine shooting took place on April 20, 1999, when Lanza was seven. Had Dylan Klebold and Eric Harris, the Columbine killers, become his heroes?

The *Telegraph* article continues:

> "My brother has always been a nerd," Ryan Lanza said, according to Gloria Milas, whose son was a club member along with Adam Lanza.
>
> Catherine Urso, who was attending a vigil on Friday evening in Newtown, said her college-age son knew the killer and remembered him for his alternative style.
>
> "He just said he was very thin, very remote and was one of the goths," she said.[2]

The so-called goth subculture is said to have started in England during the early 1980s as part of the gothic rock scene, an offshoot of the post-punk genre. The imagery and ethos of the subculture suggests it was influenced, at least to some extent, by nineteenth-century gothic literature—hence the name—as well as by horror movies. It also includes an obsession with death, which may be influenced by the death education taught in our public schools. Nihilism, too, played a major role in shaping this shadowy subculture.

Adam's parents divorced in 2009, when he was seventeen. Peter Lanza, his father, an academic and vice president of an energy investment firm, remarried in 2011. According to the *Telegraph*, "Mr. Lanza agreed to pay $240,000 (£148,400) annually to his ex-wife, and Mrs. Lanza appeared to live in comfort with Adam. There were also suggestions that she was unable to work. 'She needed to be home with Adam,' one family insider said."[3]

In other words, this was an upper middle-class family, living very comfortably in a lovely Connecticut town. Both brother Ryan and father were well educated and well employed in finance and earning good money. As for Nancy Lanza, Adam's mother, whom he killed just before driving to Sandy Hook:

> Marsha Lanza, aunt to the boys, described Mrs Lanza as a good mother and kind-hearted. Mrs Lanza would host games of dice, or else venture out to visit her neighbours for a glass of wine. The home was immaculate; the swimming pool behind the house well maintained.
>
> But Mrs Lanza was also, according to friends, an avid gun collector.
>
> Dan Holmes, owner of a Connecticut landscaping firm, said Mrs Lanza once showed him a "high-end rifle" that she had purchased, adding, "She said she would often go target shooting with her kids."
>
> The gun used to shoot Mrs Lanza was her own.[4]

And the guns used to murder the children and adults at the Sandy Hook school also belonged to Mrs. Lanza.

Though we know nothing of the Lanza family's spiritual life, we do know that public schools, where Adam was educated, have eliminated every trace of biblical religion from their curriculum. They have adopted a secular-humanist philosophy that leads many children, perhaps even Adam Lanza, to reject their family's religion. The steep decline of Christianity in America can be directly attributed to the public schools, which have become the parochial schools of atheism.

But the Sandy Hook shooting is not the only school shooting that followed the Columbine massacre. There have been a number of school shootings across this country since that fateful day in 1999. Though the following list is not exhaustive, it will give you a snapshot of what is happening in today's schools.[5]

- On April 28, 1999, in Taber, Alberta, Canada: fourteen-year-old Todd Cameron Smith walked into W. R. Myers High School and began firing at three students, killing one and wounding another. It was the first fatal high school shooting in Canada in more than two decades.

- On May 20, 1999, at Heritage High School, Conyers, Georgia, six students were injured by fifteen-year-old shooter Thomas Solomon, who was reportedly depressed after breaking up with his girlfriend. Solomon was quickly taken into custody.

- On November 19, 1999, in Deming, New Mexico, Victor Cordova Jr., twelve, shot and killed thirteen-year-old Araceli Tena in the lobby of Deming Middle School. On December 6, at Fort Gibson, Oklahoma, Seth Trickey, thirteen, opened fire with a 9mm semiautomatic handgun at Fort Gibson Middle School, wounding four students.

- On February 29, 2000, at the Mount Morris Township, Michigan, near Flint, six-year-old Kayla Rolland was shot dead at Buell Elementary School by six-year-old Dedric Owens with a .32-caliber handgun. Owens had allegedly told Kayla, just before pulling the trigger, "I don't like you." At a tender six years of age, Kayla Rolland is reportedly the youngest school shooting victim in US history. Owens is the youngest school shooter.

  Due to the legal claim that at age six he would lack the ability to form intent, Owens was not charged with murder. In fact, the US Supreme Court had ruled in 1893 that "children under the age of seven years could not be guilty of felony, or punished for any capital offense, for within that age the child is conclusively presumed incapable of committing a crime." However, back in colonial days, five- and six-year-olds were taught: "In Adam's fall we sinned all." That was the first line of the *New England Primer*.

- On March 10, 2000, in Savannah, Georgia, two teenagers were killed by nineteen-year-old Darrell Ingram, while leaving a dance sponsored by Beach High School, in celebration of the school's basketball championship. Stacy Smalls, nineteen, died from gunshot wounds at Savannah Hospital. Ramone Kimble, a sixteen-year-old student at Savannah High School, was shot in the head and died shortly thereafter.

- On May 26, 2000, Lake Worth Middle School English teacher Barry Grunow was shot and killed by Nathaniel Brazill, thirteen, with a .25-caliber semiautomatic pistol on the last day of classes. Brazill was convicted of second degree murder and aggravated assault, and sentenced to twenty-eight years in state prison followed by seven years of felony probation. His release date is May 18, 2028.

- On March 5, 2001, two students were killed and thirteen wounded by Charles Andrew Williams, fifteen, at Santana High School in Santee, California. Two days later, fourteen-year-old Elizabeth Catherine Bush wounded student Kimberly Marchese in the cafeteria of Bishop Neumann High School in Williamsport, Pennsylvania. Cause of the shooting? Envy.

- On March 22, 2001, Jason Hoffman, eighteen, wounded a teacher and three students at Granite Hills High School, in California. A policeman shot and wounded Hoffman. On March 30, a student at Lew Wallace High School in Gary, Indiana, was killed by Donald R. Burt Jr., a seventeen-year-old who had been expelled from the school. Six months later, on November 12, Chris Buschbacher, seventeen, took two hostages at the Caro Learning Center in Caro, Michigan, before killing himself.

- On April 24, 2003, James Sheets, fourteen, killed principal Eugene Segro of Red Lion Junior High School, Red Lion, Pennsylvania, before killing himself.

- On September 24, 2003, at Rocori High School in Cold Spring, Minnesota, two students were killed by John Jason McLaughlin, fifteen. The killer was diagnosed as schizophrenic.

- There were no school shootings reported in 2004, but in 2005, the Red Lake reservation in Red Lake, Minnesota, was the scene of a gruesome murder that then turned into a school massacre. It began at noon on March 21, when sixteen-year-old Jeffrey Weise killed his police sergeant grandfather and his grandfather's girlfriend, then later drove his grandfather's police vehicle to Red Lake Senior High School, where, at 2:45 p.m. he began shooting, killing five students, one teacher, and an unarmed security guard. Five others were wounded. The shooting ended with Weise's suicide.

Witnesses say Weise smiled as he was shooting at people. One witness said that he asked a student if he believed in God, which chillingly resembled events that took place during the Columbine High School massacre.

- On September 27, 2006, an adult held six students hostage at Platte Canyon High School, Bailey, Colorado, then shot and killed Emily Keyes, sixteen, and himself. Two days later, in Cazenovia, Wisconsin, a fifteen-year-old student shot and killed Weston School principal John Klang.

- On October 3, 2006, in Nickel Mines, Pennsylvania, a thirty-two-year-old milk-truck driver, Carl Charles Roberts, entered the one-room West Nickel Mines Amish School and shot ten schoolgirls, ranging in age from six to thirteen, and then himself. Five of the girls and Roberts died.

- On January 3, 2007, Douglas Chanthabouly, eighteen, shot fellow student Samnang Kok, seventeen, in the hallway of Henry Foss High School in Tacoma, Washington. On April 16, 2007, in Blacksburg, Virginia, a twenty-three-year-old Virginia Tech student, Cho Seung-Hui, killed two students in a dorm, then killed thirty more just two hours later in a classroom building. His suicide brought the death toll to thirty-three, making that shooting rampage the deadliest in US history. Fifteen others were wounded.

- On September 21, 2007, at Delaware State University, Dover, freshman Loyer D. Brandon shot and wounded two other freshmen students on the university campus. He was charged with attempted murder and assault. Then on October 10, fourteen-year-old Asa H. Coon shot and injured two students and two teachers before killing himself at Cleveland High School, Cleveland, Ohio. The victims survived the shooting.

- The United States is not the only country afflicted with school shootings. On November 7, 2007, an eighteen-year-old student in Tuusula, Finland, shot and killed five boys, two girls, and the female principal at Jokela High School. At least ten others were injured. The gunman then shot himself and died of his wounds in the hospital.

- On February 8, 2008, a nursing student at Louisiana Technical College, in Baton Rouge, shot and killed two women and then herself in a classroom. Three days later, in Memphis, Tennessee, a seventeen-year-old student at Mitchell High School shot and wounded a classmate in gym class. A day after that, on February 12, in Oxnard, California, a fourteen-year-old boy shot a student at E. O. Green Junior High School, causing the fifteen-year-old victim to become brain-dead. Two days later, a gunman at Northern Illinois University killed five students, wounded seventeen others, and then killed himself. The gunman, Stephen P. Kazmierczak, was identified as a former graduate student at the university in 2007.

- On September 23, 2008, there was another massacre at a school in Finland. A twenty-year-old male student shot and killed nine students and himself at a vocational college in Kauhajok, two hundred miles north of the nation's capital.

- On November 12, 2008, a fifteen-year-old female student was shot and killed by a classmate at Dillard High School in Fort Lauderdale, Florida.

- On February 5, 2010, at Discovery Middle School in Madison, Alabama, a boy pulled out a gun and shot ninth grader Todd Brown in the head while walking in the hallway. Brown later died at the hospital. A week later, February

12, at the University of Alabama in Huntsville, during a meeting on campus, biology professor Amy Bishop shot her colleagues, killing three and wounding three others. A year earlier, she had been denied tenure.

- On May 10, 2011, in San Jose, California, three people were killed in a parking garage at San Jose State University. Two former students were found dead on the fifth floor of the garage. A third, the suspected shooter, died later at the hospital. On December 8, 2011, at Blacksburg, Virginia, a Virginia Tech police officer was shot and killed by a twenty-two-year-old student from Radford University. The shooting took place in a parking lot on Virginia Tech's campus.

- On February 10, 2012, in Walpole, New Hampshire, a fourteen-year-old student shot himself in front of seventy fellow students. Seven days later, at Chardon High School, in Chardon, Ohio, a former student entered the school cafeteria and shot into a group of students, killing one and wounding four. Several days later two of the wounded also died, bringing the total dead to three.

    The shooter, identified as seventeen-year-old T. J. Lane, was described by classmates as an outcast who had been bullied and who had gotten into the "goth" phase. He also came from a divorced family with a history of domestic violence. In late December he had posted a poem on his Facebook page that read, "He longed for only one thing, the world to bow at his feet," and ended ominously: "Die, all of you." Apparently he had learned to hate life and love death.

- On March 6, 2012, in Jacksonville, Florida, Shane Schumerth, a twenty-eight-year-old teacher at Episcopal High School, returned to the campus after being fired and shot and killed the headmistress, Dale Regan, with an assault rifle.

- On June 7, 2013, at the campus of Santa Monica College, California, a gunman shot wildly into cars and people, killing five people and wounding four others. Shooter John Zawahri was killed by responding police officers.

- On December 13, 2013, at Arapahoe High School, Centennial, Colorado, a student entered the school, looking for a particular teacher, who had left the building. The shooter shot several students before killing himself.

- On Friday night, May 23, 2014, Elliot Rodger, twenty-two, a student at Santa Barbara City College, went on a killing rampage, stabbing his three roommates in his apartment, then driving his black BMW to shoot two women outside a sorority house and a man in a deli in Isla Vista near the University of California–Santa Barbara. Several other people were hospitalized as a result of the gunfire sprayed at the sorority and the deli. Rodger was also involved in a gun battle with sheriff's deputies before crashing into a parked car. He then shot himself in the head. He had left a YouTube video titled "Elliot Rodger's Retribution," in which he sits in a car, looking at the camera, and promises gruesome violence against humanity while periodically laughing. He also left a 140-page manifesto in which he complained of being constantly rejected by women, saying, "If I can't have you girls, I will destroy you."

- On June 6, 2014, twenty-six-year-old Aaron R. Ybarra began firing a shotgun in the lobby of Otto Miller Hall on the Seattle Pacific University Campus, killing one person and wounding three others. When he paused to reload, he was taken down by a student guard, who pepper-sprayed him. Once on the ground, other students piled on and kept the shooter pinned down until police arrived. Ybarra, obsessed with school shootings, was not a student at the university.

- Four days later, in Troutdale, Oregon, fifteen-year-old Jared Michael Padgett arrived at Reynolds High School, carrying a guitar case and a duffel bag. Inside them were an AR15 rifle, a semiautomatic handgun, nine loaded magazines, and a large knife. He wore a vest used to carry bullets and a sporting helmet in a camouflage design. Once inside the school, he shot and killed fourteen-year-old Emilio Hoffman. Minutes later he shot himself.

What can we conclude from this gruesome record of horrors? One thing I know. When I was going to public school in the days when belief in God was still the norm and school principals could quote the Bible at assemblies, there were no school massacres. Take God out of the schools, and you get mayhem and hatred of life. Children do not enter their public schools hating life. Some children may have miserable childhoods, but a public school should be a benign place where hope and possibilities inspire us. Instead, educators tell children that they are animals with no special purpose in life and that there is no God who cares for them. No wonder so many children begin to hate life. As the famous Christian Reconstructionist Reverend R. J. Rushdoony said, "Humanistic education is the institutionalized love of death."

24

BIG BROTHER'S DATA-COLLECTION SYSTEM AND THE ROAD TO TOTALITARIANISM

To be effective, however, these systems must record data accurately and comparably for all students, in all places, and at all times.
—STUDENT DATA HANDBOOK

Big Brother wants to know just about everything on you and your kids. Soon, it will. If there is any doubt in your mind that lurking in the bowels of the US Department of Education (DOE) there are liberal utopian bureaucrats intent on changing free America into a totalitarian state, all you have to do is study and follow closely the inception and continued growth of the DOE's data-gathering system on students and faculty. You will be convinced that what they are doing has nothing to do with education.

First, why is all of this highly personal information being

gathered? Who will own this information, and how will it be used? The department tells us that all of this is being done so that the educators can make appropriate decisions for the students. What kind of decisions? When I (Samuel) attended public school in New York City in the 1930s and '40s, the only information the school had about me was my name, date of birth, address, and maybe my parents' names. That was it.

But to begin with, does the federal government have the right to collect all of this private information about every student and teacher in the public schools of America and house that data in perpetuity in a Washington data bank? Is that not a violation of the privacy rights of every American citizen? Why would the federal government want that information?

Indeed, of all the troubling developments taking shape at the Department of Education, one of the most alarming is the bureaucracy's voracious appetite for data on students. In all, it is seeking to collect four hundred data points on each child—often in intimately private fields that have essentially nothing to do with education. The National Center for Education Statistics has been selected by the psycho-educators to receive massive dossiers on every student and teacher in the nation. It would all seem to be strange, at the very least. However, when viewed from the perspective of the totalitarians seeking to use behavioral psychology to modify, mold, and control Americans, suddenly everything makes sense.

In *Educating for the New World Order*, author and educational whistle-blower Beverly Eakman, who has held numerous prominent positions in the federal government, explains that the Orwellian database has been around for quite some time. Known as the Elementary and Secondary Integrated Data System, the scheme is linked with all of the other federal computer networks collecting data on American citizens.[1]

The fact that the feds' ongoing efforts to vacuum up data on US students have been under way for decades is illustrated by a 1974 "Handbook" on State Educational Records and Reports produced by the US National Center for Education Statistics. The publication is very revealing. In the "Student/Pupil Accounting" section, for instance, is a list of the major categories of student information, organized around a three-digit system used to categorize all of the data. "Personal Identification" falls under 1 00; "Name," 1 01; "Student Number," 1 02; "Sex," 1 03; "Racial/Ethnic Group," 1 04 and so on. Note the use of an identification number that will probably be the individual's Social Security number, which has become the American citizen's all-purpose ID number.

"Family and Residence" data fall under 2 00, "Family Economic Information" under 2 40, and "Family Social/Cultural Information," 2 50. "Physical Health, Sensory, and Related Conditions" fall under 3 00, starting with the Student Medical Record Number, 3 01, and then covering every aspect of the student's physical health and medical life. For example, under "Oral Health" (2 30), Big Brother wants to know the following details: number of teeth, number of permanent teeth lost, number of teeth decayed, number of teeth restored, occlusion condition, gingival (gum) condition, oral soft tissue condition, dental prosthetics, orthodontic appliances.[2]

Why all this interest in teeth? What does any of this have to do with education?

Perhaps even more troubling: "Mental, Psychological and Proficiency Test Results and Related Student Characteristics" fall under 4 00. All data collected through psychological testing will be placed under that category, with Specific Mental and Psychological Characteristics under 4 30.

Under Assessment, we find the following types: 01 Achievement Test, 02 Advanced Placement Test, 03 Aptitude Test, and 04 Attitudinal Test, described as "an assessment to measure the mental and emotional set or pattern of likes and dislikes or opinions held by a student or a group of students. This is often used in relation to considerations such as controversial issues or personal adjustments."[3] What kind of personal adjustments? Is that the proper concern of the federal government? Is this something you want the government knowing about your children? What happens if the child's views on, say, marriage, are politically incorrect? Next, 05 deals with cognitive and perceptual skills test, 06 with developmental observation, 07 with interest inventory, 08 with language proficiency test, 09 is manual dexterity test, 10 is the mental ability (intelligence) test, 11 performance assessment, 12 personality test, 13 portfolio assessment, 14 psychological test, 15 psychomotor test, and 16 reading readiness test. Never before in human history has a government had the means to gather so much data on so many people, and the feds show no signs of letting up. More recent versions of the handbooks have been released, and they are even more troubling than previous ones.

Of course, America's Founding Fathers didn't believe that the new federal government should be interested in citizens' teeth or in tests of students' attitudes. The Constitution never provided that sort of authority, either. However, using bribes to state governments, the Department of Education has created what amounts to one of the most detailed databases of personal information on the public that has perhaps ever been created or even dreamed of.

As the old cliché goes, "Knowledge is power." The feds already have plenty of knowledge about the citizenry—and as Common Core and related data-mining schemes go into effect, they will soon have a lot more. So, the next troubling questions that must be raised include: Who will control all of that data? What will it be used for? Could the information be shared with potential employers and law enforcement? If the information is released and leads to emotional harm, who will be responsible? The government insists it will keep the data private. However, if the Department of Education is not going to make the private information available, why are bureaucrats spending billions on collecting it? The government of a free people does not collect massive dossiers of personal, private information on all of its citizens. A police state does. Has America become a police state? In the Declaration of Independence, the Founding Fathers wrote that the purpose of government is to secure the God-given, unalienable rights of citizens. Privacy is one of the most fundamental rights, and the Founders explicitly protected privacy in the Fourth Amendment to the US Constitution. Instead of protecting that right today, however, government has become its chief abuser in everything from its data-collection schemes against students to Obamacare, the IRS, and the NSA. The implications of these trends should be deeply disturbing to anyone who values liberty or even their children's privacy.

In fact, the situation has become so dire that the federal government even touts its violations of those rights as if it were a positive development. The 2001 edition of the *Data Handbook*, for example, proudly explains its intrusive purpose:

> To make appropriate, cost-effective and timely decisions about students, educators must have accurate and complete information. Recognizing this need, most education systems have moved from paper documents in filing cabinets to automated student information systems. These systems provide teachers and others concerned with effective program design with day-to-day access to information about the students' background, learning experiences, and performance. They also provide the flexibility necessary to supply aggregate data to school boards, state and federal governments, and other interested parties; and to conduct program evaluations. To be effective, however, these systems must record data accurately and comparably for all students, in all places, and at all times.
>
> The Student Data Handbook for Elementary, Secondary, and Early Childhood Education was developed by the U.S. Department of Education's National Center for Education Statistics (NCES) to provide guidance concerning the consistent maintenance of student information. This handbook is useful to public and private education agencies, schools, early childhood centers, and other educational institutions, as well as to researchers involved in the collection of student data. In addition, the Handbook may be useful to elected officials and members of the public interested in student information. This handbook is not, however, a data collection instrument; nor does it reflect any type of federal data maintenance requirements. It is presented as

a tool to help the public and the American school system make information about students more useful and effective in meeting student needs.[4]

While exposing their mind-set for all to see, the writers of the handbook also appear to have contradicted their own statements. What else could the document be besides a data-collection instrument? After all, every individual is identified with a personal number to connect the data collected to the individual to whom it belongs. Proponents of Big Brother defend the system, saying it could also be used for general information-gathering purposes. For instance, the fact that a child's religion is among the data collected would allow bureaucrats to analyze and release information showing how many Catholics, Baptists, Mormons, and others are in government schools. However, there is no doubt that they can also identify the religious beliefs of any children in the system—and their families by extension.

As with virtually all abusive government programs, the seeds of the data-gathering Leviathan were plated under the guise of innocent-sounding excuses. The federal government's original justification for vacuuming up all this data was that it was "needed" to see if American students were reaching the national educational goals established under the Clinton-era Goals 2000 scheme. Again, as with virtually all government programs, Goals 2000 has come and gone. The program was a failure. However, the feds continue to collect ever-greater quantities of data on students and teachers with no end in sight.

Understanding the Orwellian data-mining apparatus erected by the feds over a period of decades is made easier by exploring the inner workings of Washington's mammoth educational bureaucracy. The National Center for Education Statistics (NCES), for instance, is the grand overseer of all of this nationwide data collection. In 1991, it awarded a three-year contract to the Council of Chief State School Officers (CCSSO), one of the primary entities behind Common Core, "to facilitate the implementation of a national education data system." The project was called the Education Data System Implementation Project (EDSIP). Two years before EDSIP, the NCES began constructing "an interstate student records transfer system currently called ExPRESS," an acronym for Exchange of Permanent Records Electronically for Students and Schools. The function of ExPRESS is as follows:

> The activity has included the development of standard data elements for inclusion in an electronic student transcript and a pilot exchange of student records across school districts and from districts to institutions of higher education. The system is now ready for further development, including the appointment of a Governing Board, making formal arrangements with a communications network for exchanging the records, and expansion to more sites.[5]

EDSIP also included implementing a Personnel Exchange System for sharing state expertise in solving education data problems, the development of an Information Referral System for sharing information to improve data systems across states, and the development of student and staff data handbooks.

Before that, the CCSSO had already worked on two other projects for the NCES related to Big Brother. The first, the Education Data Improvement Project (1985–88), "analyzed each state's capacity to provide standard, comparable and timely data to NCES on public elementary and secondary school and school district, staff, students, revenues and expenditures." The second project, known as the New Education Data Improvement Project (1988–91), was supposed to provide technical assistance plans to each state government, which addressed the states' problems in responding to Common Core data-gathering mandates from the feds.

The technology involved is also raising alarm bells. A report by the Department of Education, dubbed *Promoting Grit, Tenacity, and Perseverance: Critical Factors for Success in the 21st Century*, provided a vision of the future if this continues.[6] If you thought the databases were bad, advances in technology exploited by DC "educrats" are creating a nightmarish situation that sounds like something out of a bad fiction movie. Included in the hundred-plus-page report, for example, is information about technology *already* in use as part of an Education Department–funded tutoring program. "Researchers are exploring how to gather complex affective data and generate meaningful and usable information to feed back to learners, teachers, researchers, and the technology itself," the report explains. "Connections to neuroscience are also beginning to emerge." The report describes several technological tools already being used by federally funded education schemes to get inside students' minds and "measure" the children using "four parallel streams of affective sensors." Among the devices is a facial expression camera used to "detect emotion" and "capture facial expressions." The report explains that the camera is connected to software that "extracts geometric properties on faces." There is also a "posture analysis seat" and a "pressure mouse." Finally, the report describes a "wireless skin conductance sensor" strapped to students' wrists. According to the report, the sensors collect "physiological response data from a biofeedback apparatus that measures blood volume, pulse, and galvanic skin response to examine student frustration."

A separate Education Department report, *Enhancing, Teaching and Learning through Educational Data Mining and Learning Analytics*, suggests that DC education bureaucrats even hope to predict the *future* behavior of students based on the data they collect. "A student learning database (or other big data repository) stores time-stamped student input and behaviors captured as students work within the system," the report states. "A predictive model combines demographic data (from an external student information system) and learning/behavior data from the student learning database to track a student's progress and make predictions about his or her future behaviors or performance."[7]

By now, it should be obvious that one of the end goals of linking all states' education data systems into a centralized system in Washington, DC, is to further nationalize American education. Now, this brings up a new issue. Government schools have traditionally relied on local property taxes for support under the pretext that the community was in control of its local schools and was concerned with their performance. The building of this mammoth national Big Brother data system, though, is merely a prelude to the type of control DC totalitarians hope to exercise over all schools and students in America. When combined with Common Core, which will be explored in more depth in the upcoming chapters, it ought to be abundantly clear by now that tyranny in America is not just lurking; it is waiting for the right time to take off the mask. This is Big Brother on steroids, plain and simple, but with the rapid dumbing down of America's youth, it remains to be seen whether anyone will even notice or care.

A handful of lawmakers have expressed concerns. "As part of what you described as a 'cradle to career agenda,' the Department of Education is aggressively moving to expand data systems that collect information on our nation's students," complained Rep. John Kline (R-MN), chairman of the House Education and Workforce Committee, in an early 2010 letter to Obama education secretary Arne Duncan. "The Department's effort to shepherd states toward the creation of a de facto national student database raises serious legal and prudential questions." Kline pointed out in the letter that it appears the Obama administration is even violating the law in its efforts to expand the scheme. "Congress has never authorized the Department of Education to facilitate the creation of a national student database," he explained. "To the contrary, Congress explicitly prohibited the 'development of a nationwide database of personally identifiable information' . . . and barred the 'development, implementation, or maintenance of a Federal database.'"[8] The Obama administration paid no attention.

Still, beyond merely expressing concerns, the emergence of Big Brother's would-be omnipotent data systems represents yet another excellent reason for abolishing the US Department of Education entirely—a longtime staple of conservative thought that was recommended by Ronald Reagan and countless others. Schools should then be returned to local control, where they belong. Not only is there no need or constitutional authority for Washington to possess these godlike powers; it has become painfully obvious that such control has been counterproductive from the standpoint of improving education. Neither Goals 2000 nor No Child Left Behind improved American education, even by their own metrics. For example, Goal 6 of Goals 2000 stated, "By the year 2000, every adult American will be literate and will possess the knowledge and skills necessary to compete in a global economy and exercise the rights and responsibilities of citizenship."[9] That didn't happen.

In fact, in 2007, the National Endowment for the Arts released a grim survey of the decline of literacy in America. According to the survey, entitled *Reading at Risk*, more and more young Americans are reading less and less. The report's Executive Summary concluded:

> *Reading at Risk* presents a distressing but objective overview of national trends. The accelerating declines in literary reading among all demographic groups of American adults indicate an imminent cultural crisis. The trends among younger adults warrant special concern, suggesting that—unless some effective solution is found—literary culture, and literacy in general, will continue to worsen. Indeed, at the current rate of loss, literary reading as a leisure activity will virtually disappear in half a century.
>
> *Reading at Risk* is testimony that a cultural legacy is disappearing, especially among younger people. Twenty years ago, just after the NEA 1982 survey, the landmark study *A Nation at Risk* warned that "a rising tide of mediocrity" had overtaken the school system and threatened a generation of students. The report sparked a massive reform effort whose consequences are still evolving today. *Reading at Risk* reveals an equally dire situation, a culture at risk. The National Endowment for the Arts calls upon public agencies, cultural organizations, the press, and educators to take stock of the sliding literary condition of our

country. It is time to inspire a nationwide renaissance of literary reading and bring the transformative power of literature into the lives of all citizens.[10]

As we now know, the decline of literacy in America was no accident. Instead, it is the result of a carefully planned program by John Dewey and his progressive colleagues to dumb down America. And what we also now know is that the ultimate aim of all of this centralized activity is a nationalized public education system in which schools are no longer controlled by local communities. Nobody in the federal education bureaucracy will acknowledge this, of course. But it is happening. In other words, the only way to truly address America's ongoing education "crisis" is for the American people to get the federal government out of the education business. The House of Representatives, controlled by Republicans as this is being written, could simply refuse to appropriate another dime for the Education Department. Once the federal Leviathan is out of the way, local communities can begin to address the problems of their local schools in conformity with the principles of individual freedom and the rights of parents to control their children's education.

Only then will American education begin to improve.

25

WHEN UTOPIANS ARE IN POWER, EXPECT TYRANNY

A universal peace, it's to be feared, is the catalogue of events which will never exist but in the imaginations of visionary philosophers or in the breasts of benevolent enthusiasts.
—JAMES MADISON, 1792

There are three kinds of organizations that must be dictatorships in order to function successfully: governments, utopias, and criminal empires. Because the Founding Fathers understood the coercive power of government, they crafted a Constitution that gave the federal government limited powers so Americans could exercise and enjoy maximum individual freedom. Thus, for most of our history, Americans have considered their government to be a benign force, securing the God-given unalienable rights of the American individual.

But our system has been under the assault of socialists for over a century. Socialists, by definition, are utopians. But voluntary utopianism has always failed, because human nature is incompatible with the utopian ideals, which require self-abnegation to the extreme. The only utopian societies that survive for any length of time are those that are imposed by force. When people are able to escape from the utopian paradise, they flee by the millions. One-third of the total population of Cuba has left the island in any way they could. Many died in the effort. In Russia, Lenin and Stalin were able to maintain their workers' paradise only by terror and dictatorship. But even that failed after seventy-five years of unadulterated tyranny.

What the socialist thugs in Washington are now trying to do is pass as many laws as possible to impose a coercive system of government that will end individual freedom and create the infrastructure of a socialist system. This is being done speedily so the new system will be in place before the American people can reverse the process. That is why the members of Congress were not given time to read the two-thousand-page Obama health care bill, because if they actually knew what was in it, they would have voted against it. But that is hardly the kind of government the Founding Fathers created.

Criminals and utopians are attracted to governments because they know that is where the power to coerce lies. Criminals may kidnap one or several people in order to gain ransom money, but utopian socialists must kidnap an entire nation to succeed in their quest for total power. Since we know that communists and socialists cannot create a productive economy, they must deceive the electorate into believing that what they will produce is equality in paradise, such as they have in Cuba: free medical care, free education, and equality of poverty and enslavement. Only a dumbed-down people would fall for that sham.

While the liberals and socialists are celebrating their power to impose crippling restrictions on free-market capitalism, the world knows that socialist societies produce economic stagnation, unemployment, and food shortages. Governments do not create wealth. They confiscate it from those who produce it. But a generation of young Americans, educated to believe that socialism is good and capitalism is evil, will be easily convinced that poverty is good and wealth immoral, just as they believe that man is causing global warming even though we are experiencing some of the coolest springs and summers on record.

This is simply mass hypnosis in action, in which people prefer to believe a celebrated authority like Al Gore rather than their own senses. And there is no doubt that the liberal mass media have succumbed to the same mass hypnosis and are on their knees, worshipping the new messiah in the White House.

John Dewey knew that socialist change had to come slowly, bit by bit, piece by piece. That is why it took a hundred years to bring America to its present state. Dewey knew that gradualism was the only way to deceive Americans into giving up their individual freedoms. The Fabians had stressed the need for patience while they undermined the free-market system. Fabian Tract No. 1 described that strategy in these words: "For the right moment you must wait, as Fabius did most patiently when warring against Hannibal, though many censured his delays; but when the time comes, you must strike hard, as Fabius did, or your waiting will be in vain and fruitless."[1]

And that is why the Obama administration has been "striking hard," while Obama had the power to move Congress in the direction he wanted it to go. But in 2010, he lost that precious Democratic majority in the House of Representatives, just as he did in 2014 in the Senate, thus creating constitutional obstacles to any further socialist advance. As a result, the president is resorting to the use of unconstitutional means to advance his agenda.

Meanwhile, the liberals have made it clear that they intend to use executive agencies such as the corrupt Internal Revenue Service to advance their political agenda. Utopians feel they have the moral imperative to use whatever power they have to reach their goals, even if it means corrupting the nonpolitical agencies of government.

And in case you've forgotten what socialists really want, in 1887 the Fabian Society openly published its credo, to which every member was obliged to subscribe:

The Fabian Society consists of Socialists. . . . It aims at the reorganization of society by the emancipation of land and Industrial Capital from individual and class ownership, and the vesting of them in the community for the general benefit. . . . The Society accordingly works for the extinction of private property in land. The Society further works for the transfer to the Community of such Industrial Capital as can conveniently be handled socially. For the attainment of these ends the Fabian Society looks to the spread of Socialist opinions, and the social and political consequent thereon.[2]

American communists are generally Marxists who prefer violent revolution to the gradualism of the Fabians, but they have realized over the years that such a revolution is impossible in America and thus have followed Dewey's educational strategy, which Saul Alinsky translated into a political strategy in a book, *Rules for Radicals*. Alinsky wrote: "Lest we forget at least an over-the-shoulder acknowledgment to the very first radical: from all our legends, mythology, and history . . . the first radical known to man who rebelled against the establishment and did it so effectively that he at least won his own kingdom—Lucifer." The election of 2008 finally gave them the victory they had wanted for more than a century.

Today, the American people are in a state of mass confusion. Economic turmoil has thrown them off balance. Our medical system is in disarray. Gas prices go up and down. There is confusion of apparent inflation and deflation at the same time. Credit card debt is at an all-time high. Home foreclosures are taking their toll on thousands of families. Meanwhile, the Obama administration is piling up debt in the trillions of dollars. And a sclerotic socialist system will only make things worse.

Americans still believe that elections are the way to change political reality in America. That is why the Tea Party movement got started. Also, many state governments are much more conservative than the US Congress and the White House. And that is why the federal bureaucracies are doing all in their power to expand their control over every aspect of an American citizen's life. Between the IRS, NSA, ED, and Obamacare, the totalitarians are convinced that they've already conquered America. The next few elections will tell us if they are right.

26

MULTICULTURALISM: THE NEW CULTURAL GENOCIDE

The term "Americanization" is no longer to be found in encyclopedias
of the social sciences.
—NATHAN GLAZER, *WE ARE ALL MULTICULTURALISTS NOW*

One of the main tenets of multiculturalism is that all cultures
are equally valid in that there are no superior or inferior cultures, and that all deserve equally serious respect and study.
This, when put into practice in schools, means that children
from immigrant families should be proud of the cultures
they came from and that these cultures should be celebrated
in the classroom.

For example, in an article titled "Developing a Multicultural
Curriculum," authors Carolyn Brush and Judie Haynes cited a
successful multicultural curriculum being used in a second-grade

classroom in River Edge, New Jersey. The authors wrote, "This program combines teaching students about world cultures with the talents of the diverse student population." They explained:

> High student achievement is fostered by this program. Students from diverse backgrounds develop pride in their heritage. When they see their home cultures and languages being studied in the mainstream classroom, they feel that their culture has been validated. This helps to develop positive self-esteem in culturally and linguistically diverse children. All students in the class develop pride in their origins and are encouraged to study and share them. They gain a greater understanding of world cultures and world geography.[1]

This is not what I was taught in the New York City public schools back in the 1930s and '40s. I was the American-born child of immigrants who had come from Poland in the 1920s. They sent me and my siblings to public school to become Americans. They had left behind a culture of poverty and discrimination, and the last thing they wanted was for their children to take pride in that depressing country. Indeed, when I entered the public school, I was awed by the large picture of George Washington on the classroom wall, and the American flag. We sang "My Country 'Tis of Thee" in a land of liberty. I was in love with my country from the very beginning. I even wrote a poem about that love, which the school's principal read at an assembly, much to my embarrassment. I was proud to be an American and proud to be an adherent to the ideology of Americanism, which Yale professor David Gelernter calls "the Fourth Great Western Religion. . . . a militant creed dedicated to spreading freedom around the world."

But multicultural education considers Americanism to simply be a form of American "ethnocentrism," a worldview that promotes American patriotism at the expense of an immigrant child's adherence to the country and culture from which he or she came. To the multiculturists, the reason why these immigrants came here was not because American culture and values are superior to those of their mother countries, but because America is richer and can provide them with more economic benefits.

But despite what the schools have tried to do, there is an inherent patriotism in most Americans. And this is often exhibited at international sports events, where the chant "USA! USA! USA!" resonates loudly in the stadium. The fact that thousands of young Americans join our military forces each year is indicative of an inherent love of country instilled by their parents or knowledge of our history, the land of the free and the home of the brave.

To Professor Gelernter, Americanism is much more than mindless patriotism. He wrote in his book, *Americanism*, "I will argue that America is no secular republic; it's a biblical republic. Americanism doesn't merely announce the nation's ideals on its own authority; it speaks on behalf of the Bible and the Bible's God, as Lincoln did in his Second Inaugural Address. Its goal is for America to move forward 'with firmness in the right, as God gives us to see the right,' as Lincoln said in that same speech."[2]

In other words, there is a deeply spiritual aspect to the concept of Americanism, which our secular, anti-God education system rejects.

The concept of multiculturalism has been around since the 1970s, and it now infects every aspect of American life. Its latest manifestation is in airport security, where the notion that all ethnic groups must be equally valued and respected has made ethnic profiling a no-no. Just because all of the suicide bombers have been Islamic jihadists doesn't mean that young Muslim men should be singled out for greater scrutiny than anyone else.

That is why everyone who wants to travel by air must be subjected to the same intensive security inspection as a would-be suicide bomber, because it would be unfair to single out young male Muslims as the only people capable of blowing themselves up in a plane. Under multiculturalism everyone is capable of doing just that.

And that's why the United States government is willing to waste billions of dollars a year scrutinizing everyone—grandmothers in wheelchairs and little children—so it can maintain the fiction that everyone is potentially willing and capable of committing suicide on an airplane by blowing it up.

As for multicultural education, back in July 1982 the National Council for Accreditation of Teacher Education (NCATE) decided that multiculturalism had to become an integral part of teacher training. Its manual states:

> *Multicultural Education* . . . is preparation for the social, political, and economic realities that individuals experience in culturally diverse and complex human encounters. . . . Multicultural education could include, but would not be limited to experiences which: (1) promote analytical and evaluative abilities to confront issues such as participatory democracy, racism and sexism, and the parity of power; (2) develop skills for values clarification including the study of the manifest and latent transmission of values; (3) examine the dynamics of diverse cultures and the implications for developing teaching strategies; and (4) examine linguistic variations and diverse learning styles for the development of appropriate teaching strategies.[3]

Since then, the NCATE has adopted the Common Core Standards. Its 2008 standard on multiculturalism reads:

> One of the goals of this standard is the development of educators who can help all students learn or support their learning through their professional roles in schools. This goal requires educators who can reflect multicultural and global perspectives that draw on the histories, experiences, and representations of students and families from diverse populations. Therefore, the unit has the responsibility to provide opportunities for candidates to understand diversity and equity in the teaching and learning process. Coursework, field experiences, and clinical practice must be designed to help candidates understand the influence of culture on education and acquire the ability to develop meaningful learning experiences for all students. Candidates learn about

exceptionalities and inclusion, English language learners and language acquisition, ethnic/racial cultural and linguistic differences, and gender differences, and the impact of these factors on learning. Proficiencies, including those related to professional dispositions and diversity, are drawn from the standards of the profession, state, and institution. Candidates are helped to understand the potential impact of discrimination based on race, class, gender, disability, sexual orientation, and language on students and their learning. Proficiencies related to diversity are identified in the unit's conceptual framework. They are clear to candidates and are assessed as part of the unit's assessment system.[4]

In other words, the Common Core standard on multiculturalism does not call for the Americanization of all these diverse students from different countries and cultures. What it also means is that the traditional Judeo-Christian model of American values is no longer to be upheld as the model for children to adopt in the public schools. A multicultural society is made up of many equally valid ideals that could serve as equally valid models for young Americans. No one is required any longer to conform to the once-dominant Judeo-Christian patriotic ideal. That culture is to be virtually erased from the minds of American students. The need to implement multiculturalism in the classroom was spelled out in a series of articles printed in *Theory into Practice*. According to Charles A. Tesconi, dean of the College of Education at the University of Vermont, "As a descriptor, multiculturalism points to a condition of numerous lifestyles, values, and belief systems. By treating diverse cultural groups and ways of life as equally legitimate, and by teaching about them in positive ways, legitimizing differences through various education policies and practices, self-understanding, self-esteem, intergroup understanding and harmony, and equal opportunity are promoted."[5]

Thus, multicultural education embraces much more than mere cultural pluralism or ethnic diversity. It legitimizes different lifestyles and values systems, thereby legitimizing moral diversity—which is simply moral anarchy. The concept of moral diversity directly contradicts the biblical concept of moral absolutes based on the Ten Commandments, on which this nation was founded.

How is multicultural education taught? It is not a course that is taught separately from the rest of the subject matter. It is, in reality, a worldview that, in the words of Theresa E. McCormick, a multicultural specialist at Emporia State University, "must permeate the total educational environment."[6]

Indeed, according to associate professor Sandra B. DeCosta at West Virginia University, multicultural education "must be carefully planned, organized, and integrated into all the subject areas. But most emphatically it must begin when children first enter school." She explains: "Through this process teachers and students should more fully comprehend the extent to which Americans genuinely represent a cultural mosaic—a culture which reflects the colors, textures, shapes, and influences of people from throughout the world."[7]

But it was assumed in the old days when all of these diverse people came to America that their aim was to become Americans. Yes, they may have retained some of the values of their cultural heritage, as in culinary tastes, but that did not stop any new immigrant or his or her second-generation children from embracing Americanism as a unique culture based on individual freedom and biblical morality. All one has to do is read the inaugural addresses of our presidents to capture the essence of Americanism, the state of mind inherited from our Founding Fathers.

But the idea that there exists a common value system known as Americanism no longer prevails in American public schools. Yet we know that Americanism does exist and does constitute the basis of American consciousness: the conviction that this nation was created with God's help and blessings to demonstrate to the world that with the true God all good things are possible, and that without Him we will be consigned to the same tyranny and misery that now afflict the millions of people who live under paganism, atheism, and communism.

During the celebration of the one hundredth anniversary of

the Statue of Liberty, that concept of Americanism was expressed over and over again in song and speech in three simple words: *God bless America*. Those three words acknowledge the existence, power, and sovereignty of the God of the Bible. They express the essence of Americanism, the peculiar consciousness that makes us different from other peoples.

While that American consciousness was given to us by our Founding Fathers, who, for the most part, were indeed white, Anglo-Saxon Protestants, one does not have to be white, Anglo-Saxon, or even Protestant to accept it. There are many African-Americans, Hispanics, Germans, Armenians, Russians, Catholics, and Jews who accept it.

Becoming an American does not mean aping WASPs. It means accepting the essence of what the Founding Fathers stood and died for. That essence is founded on biblical principles, which include the concept of moral absolutes. To deprive schoolchildren of that knowledge is to rob them of their common American heritage.

Multiculturalism is also an important stepping-stone to globalism, that concept of a future world government that the public schools are promoting as aggressively as ever. In an article entitled "Multicultural Education and Global Education: A Possible Merger," Donna J. Cole of Wittenberg University wrote, "A multicultural-ized global education would address the basic concern of where the individual fits into the mosaic of humanity and where others fit in the same mosaic. . . . [It] would aid students in understanding that our membership in groups affects our values and attitudes. . . . [It] would assist students in recognizing the need to be flexible and adjustable citizens in a rapidly changing world."[8]

The National Education Association (NEA), of course, endorses multicultural-global education as "a way of helping every student perceive the cultural diversity of the US citizenry so that children of many races may develop pride in their own cultural legacy, awaken to the ideas embodied in the cultures of their neighbors, and develop an appreciation of the common humanity shared by all people of the earth."

That was written in 1986, before Islamist jihadists, those fanatic adherents to a system of values based on the Koran, declared war on the United States. But apparently that hasn't changed anything. Note that the NEA recognizes no American culture that the student may take pride in. He is to appreciate the cultures of others, and learn about them, at the expense of learning about his own.

The ultimate purpose of multicultural-globalist education is to prepare young Americans to accept as inevitable and desirable a world socialist government in which American national sovereignty will be surrendered for the greater good of "world peace and brotherhood." Social studies professors have rewritten American history to play down patriotism and national pride. They advocate a kind of cultural genocide. Patriotism leads to an ethnocentric mind-set not conducive to world government.

The only way parents can safeguard their children from such socialist brainwashing is to educate them at home or place them in private schools where traditional subject matter is taught in the traditional way. Patriotism is alive and well in the home-school movement, where biblical principles prevail. And while we must all live in a society where multiculturalism has run amok, the greatest gift parents can give their children is the knowledge that moral sanity is far more important and necessary for our national survival than conforming to secular humanist cultural standards that reject God's law.

In 1904, the State of New York published a *Manual of Patriotism* for use in its public schools. It was compiled, arranged, and edited under the direction of Charles R. Skinner, state superintendent of public instruction. The manual emphasized the importance of the American flag and what it stands for. It contained many great patriotic poems by Henry Wadsworth Longfellow, John Greenleaf Whittier, Oliver Wendell Holmes, and James Russell Lowell, poets who are hardly read in today's public schools. No public educator would dare use that manual in today's public schools. It is not only out-of-date. It is dead and buried. But you may be able to find a copy for your own homeschool library at an antiquarian bookshop.

27

COMMON CORE: CONSUMER EXTORTION ON STEROIDS

It would be great if our education stuff worked, but we won't know for probably a decade.
—BILL GATES

Governor Jeb Bush, president of the Foundation for Excellence in Education, in speaking at the 2013 meeting of the American Legislative Exchange Council in Chicago, drew attention to the skyrocketing costs of public education and the lousy product it delivers. He said, "Look at Detroit. As the city descended into bankruptcy, its public school system was mired in corruption and mismanagement, prompting Education Secretary Arne Duncan to call it a 'national disgrace.' The city spends more than $19,000 a year per pupil, and for that investment it produces some of the worst academic outcomes in the nation."[1]

Multiply $19,000 by twelve, the number of years a child spends in public school, and we get a mind-boggling cost of $228,000 to create a functional illiterate. In other words, the taxpayer is being taken to the cleaners by educators who know how to featherbed their pensions but haven't the faintest idea how to create a literate human being. Governor Bush further stated:

> Since 1950, the number of adults in public education has increased at four times the rate of students. The increase in administrators and other non-teaching personnel has been sevenfold.
>
> Big Government turned the one-room schoolhouse into a massive jobs program. Kids were FTEs—full time equivalents, good for a guaranteed payment regardless of outcome. FTEs also are the lynchpins for funding outsized pensions at the expense of current spending in the classroom.

If schools don't do a good job, we are told it is because they aren't getting enough money. If spending increases and they still aren't performing, it is because it isn't enough money.[2]

In other words, the more the taxpayer pays for education, the worse it gets. This is as bad as any scam concocted by a professional extortionist. The simple truth is that the educators are highly skilled at getting taxpayers to cough up billions of dollars for less-than-worthless "education." Extortion, of course, is a crime.

Along comes Bill Gates, the richest man in America, highly critical of American public education and determined to improve it. He believes that what we need are better teachers and higher academic standards. And that is why he decided to throw over $2 billion at the Common Core State Standards initiative. Indeed, the Bill and Melinda Gates Foundation has already awarded 161 grants to a plethora of think tanks that are in the process of developing Common Core curricula and implementation.[3]

For example, in order to improve literacy standards, Gates has financed the creation of the Literacy Design Collaborative with a grant of $12 million. Its mission? "LDC seeks to ensure that every student in America graduates from high school with the Common Core literacy skills necessary for success in college and career." If you log onto the LDC's website, you will find more complexity and vagueness about what literacy is than you could dream of.[4]

Yet, the solution to our literacy problem is ridiculously simple: just teach every child to read by intensive systematic phonics in kindergarten and first grade and you will have a rebirth of high literacy in America reminiscent of the high literacy we had in the early days of the republic with Noah Webster's *Blue-Backed Speller*. You would have a much larger pool of literate Americans to fill all of the high-tech jobs now available.

Had Bill Gates come to me (Samuel), the inventor of *Alpha-Phonics*, for advice, I would have urged him to put a copy of *Alpha-Phonics* in every primary classroom in America. When children acquire high literacy, the world opens up before them. We would not have fifty million functional illiterates, produced by the faulty teaching methods in our schools, unable to perform the jobs Gates wants young Americans to fill.

Indeed, Gates could have saved a lot of money by conferring with E. D. Hirsch Jr., founder of the Core Knowledge Foundation. Created in 1986, the CKF has provided 888 K–8 schools and 523 preschools with a content-rich curriculum, far better than what is being offered by the Common Core. Hirsch has published a series of books that outline what every child needs to know in each grade. In other words, he recognized what had happened to the public schools and organized a way of getting schools back into academic shape. He had already done the work the governors said needed to be done. So why didn't the governors go to Hirsch? Because the CKF was not politically correct. It didn't create worker robots for the new world order. It didn't create a monster project for degreed educationists to work in. It merely created educated individuals.

A major reason why Common Core is provoking so much opposition is that it will deprive the American people of the freedom to control their children's education and create a national schooling system no longer controlled by local communities. And all of this has been planned without any input from American parents. Most Americans don't want a nationalized education system.

Actually, the Common Core State Standards originated with the National Governors Association and its Center for Best Practices (NGA Center). According to its website, the center develops "innovative solutions to today's most pressing public policy challenges and is the only research and development firm that directly serves the nation's governors."[5] It also helps shape federal policy. The NGA is also the copyright owner of the Common Core Standards. Here is how it all started.

The initiative for the Common Core State Standards seems to have arisen from a speech NGA chairman Governor Paul Patton (D-KY) gave at the NGA meeting on June 12, 2002, in which he said:

> Governors are constantly searching for solutions that will help all schools succeed, but some schools require more help than others. The long-term goal for states is to improve overall system performance while closing persistent gaps in achievement between minority and non-minority students. Fortunately, there are places to look for guidance. Although some schools continue to struggle, some have responded successfully to state reform efforts and others have gone far in improving student performance and closing the achievement gap. Current research also suggests there are ways state policies can effectively stimulate and support school improvement.[6]

Somehow, the governor's speech was translated into a need for a new set of educational standards rigorous enough to lift American public schoolers out of the academic doldrums. But who was to write the new standards? No problem. Jim Wilhoit, former Kentucky education commissioner and executive director of the Council of Chief State School Officers (CCSSO), approached David Coleman, head of a new nonprofit educational think tank, Student

Achievement Partners. It had been founded in 2007 by two liberal Rhodes Scholar entrepreneurs, Coleman and Jason Zimba. Coleman and Wilhoit discussed the idea of creating the new Common Core set of standards for the schools. But the project required a lot of money. So in the summer of 2008 they approached Bill Gates to see if he would be willing to finance the project. After much discussion with his foundation staff, Gates agreed. Student Achievement Partners was chosen to write the standards, and they were given a grant of $6.5 million to start the process. They were also given the job of implementing the CCSS in all the school districts in America. They got off to a great start with financial inducements from the Department of Education's Race to the Top program. The sales pitch described the CCSS in these glowing terms:

> The Common Core is a set of high-quality academic standards in mathematics and English language arts/literacy (ELA). These learning goals outline what a student should know and be able to do at the end of each grade. The standards were created to ensure that all students graduate from high school with the skills and knowledge necessary to succeed in college, career, and life, regardless of where they live. Forty-three states, the District of Columbia, four territories, and the Department of Defense Education Activity (DoDEA) have voluntarily adopted and are moving forward with the Common Core.[7]

The first state to adopt the standards unseen was Kentucky. A well-financed promotional campaign was launched to get the Common Core accepted by everyone in the state. The legislature adopted it unanimously.

But why does America need to spend billions on a new set of standards when we had great standards before the Dewey conspirators decided to destroy them? Why are we reinventing the wheel? Back in the 1930s and '40s, our public schools provided the kind of education that permitted those students to become America's "Greatest Generation." That generation not only learned enough to win World War II but also enough to create the scientific foundation of our high-tech society. What happened to those standards? Indeed, there are plenty of private schools in America with similar exacting standards. Why have our public schools not copied those standards?

But luckily for our educationists, Bill Gates has money to burn. For example, in 2013 CCSS got $4 million; in 2012, $1,100,000; and in 2011, $9,388,911.[8] All 161 Common Core grants are listed on the Core Knowledge Foundation's website, which can be perused by anyone with a computer.

Despite this lavish private funding, the CCSS adds nothing to what we know about how to teach reading and writing. It adds nothing to how we teach arithmetic and mathematics. It adds nothing to how we teach history, geography, and the "social studies." In short, its aim is to get the American taxpayer to shell out billions for something that we already know how to do. Yes, science has greatly advanced, but it also advanced from 1850 to 1950 and didn't require a different methodology from the scientific method developed by the great scientists of the past. We now have computers and the Internet, but the scientific method has not changed.

And of course, the Common Core Standards have turned out to be as complicated and obtuse as possible so that no parent can possibly understand them. They were actually written by Coleman's cadre of young masters of education—full of great intentions, but little, if any, teaching experience. In other words, when highly credentialed liberal educationists try to reform public education, they inevitably create a monster. For example, there is something called "Common Core State Standards Official Identifiers and XML Representation," which describes the complexity of trying to implement the Core Standards. It states:

As states, territories, the District of Columbia, and the Department of Defense Education Activity move from widespread adoption of the Common Core State Standards (CCSS) to implementation, there is a need to appropriately identify and link assets using a shared system of identifiers and a common XML representation. The Council of Chief State School Officers (CCSSO) and National Governors Association Center for Best Practices (NGA Center), working closely with the standards authors, have released an official, viable approach for publishing identifiers and XML designation to represent the standards, consistent with their adopted format, as outlined below.[9]

"The standards authors" are the Student Achievement Partners who work closely with the Council of Chief State School Officers (CCSSO) and the NGA Center. Since everything is now done by computer, participants in this mammoth program are provided with the following information:

De-referenceable Uniform Resource Identifier (URIs) at the corestandards.org domain, e.g. http://corestandards.org/2010/ math/content/6/EE/1 or http://corestandards.org/2010/math/ practice/MP7. Matching the published identifiers, these dereferenceable URIs allow individuals and technology systems to validate the content of a standard by viewing the web page at the identifier's uniform resource locator (URL). The NGA Center and CCSSO strongly recommend that www.corestandards.org remain the address of record for referring to standards.[10]

None of this means anything to the average parent who wants to speak to a live teacher or superintendent. But these Gates-endowed educationists know how to make everything so complicated that only they are capable of understanding their own complexity. Here's more:

Globally unique identifiers (GUIDs), e.g. A7D3275BC52147618D-6CFEE43FB1A47E. These allow, when needed, to refer to standards in both disciplines in a common format without removing the differences in the published identifiers. GUIDs are unwieldy for human use, but they are necessarily complex to guarantee uniqueness, an important characteristic for databases, and are intended for use by computer systems. There is no need for educators to decode GUIDs.[11]

Not only does the Common Core remove control of education away from local school districts, but it makes it impossible for parents to speak to any of those who are writing the standards. David Coleman and Jason Zimba do a lot of speaking around the country, and you may have a chance to confront either of them if he happens to be speaking in your town. But they can be watched on YouTube if that's any help.

In any case, the NGA is staffed by professional policy wonks. The head man was director of the Congressional Budget Office from 1999 to 2002. The director of the NGA Center for Best Practices is also from the Congressional Budget Office. The director of the Education Division is in charge of research, policy analysis, technical assistance, and resource development for early childhood, K–12, and postsecondary education. I doubt that any of these policy makers have read Rudolf Flesch's *Why Johnny Can't Read*, published in 1955, or my (Samuel's) book *The New Illiterates*, published in 1973.

We are told that the "Education Division is working on a number of key policy issues relevant to governors' efforts to develop and support the implementation of policy, including: birth to 3rd grade access, readiness and quality."[12]

Are they really serious about "educating" newborn infants when they don't know how to teach six-year-olds to read?

Note this interest in "birth to 3rd grade" education, which is the kind of interest that totalitarians dream of. Besides, what sane parent would entrust his or her newborn child to government educators? The family, humanity's oldest social institution, is still in charge of bringing up its children. The idea that the government should take over the family's God-given rights and responsibilities is so foreign to the American way of life that one wonders what kind of Americans would even entertain such ideas.

In other words, the Common Core State Standards have no more legitimacy than the plans of your local village idiot to reform education. They are the thought emanations of those who are paid enough to write "standards" whether or not they have knowledge and wisdom for such a task. Yet, even with Bill Gates's help, they will still cost the American taxpayer billions of dollars and make American public education even more confusing than ever.

In short, the CCSS movement is basically a jobs program for bureaucrats, masters and doctors of education, and newly created think-tank staffs and "experts." It is also a make-work program for educators, administrators, career counselors, assorted federal bureaucrats, and textbook writers and publishers, who will rake in millions.

And why does anyone think that this reform is any more likely to succeed than any of the previous ones enacted by Congress? Experience has shown that education "reform" is simply the educators' way of getting the taxpayer to shell out more for our failing public schools. We are told that the CCSS is needed to help more high school students get a college education. But according to a *New York Times* editorial of June 8, 2014, "44 percent of young college graduates in 2012 were working in jobs that didn't require a college degree. . . . In 2000, half of college-educated workers in jobs that didn't require a degree were in generally well-paid professions, working as electricians, for example, or dental hygienists. Now they are more likely to be waiters, bartenders or cashiers."[13]

And the mediocre beat goes on. According to Phyllis Schlafly's *Education Reporter* (January 2012):

> The California Department of Education estimates that Common Core will cost the state about $760 million. Outside estimates place California's fiscal commitment at up to $1.6 billion. California already expects a $3 billion deficit at the end of fiscal year 2011, and a $10 billion deficit in 2012–13. . . . "Adding up to a billion-and-a-half-dollar expenditure to implement national standards under these circumstances is fiscal madness," said Lance Izumi, senior director of education studies at the Pacific Research Institute.[14]

But educational madness is not new to California. This is the same state that implemented whole language as the way to teach its precious children to read, with disastrous results, from which most functionally illiterate California children will never recover.

According to Liv Finne, director of the Washington Policy Center's education initiative, the total nationwide costs of implementing Common Core will be $30 billion.[15]

Some states are already seeking an exit strategy from Common Core, which they hastily agreed to adopt before it was fully analyzed by its critics. In December 2013 the Education Task Force of the American Legislative Exchange Council (ALEC) drafted model legislation that will provide states with a lawful way of getting out of Common Core.

There are thousands of private schools in America that don't have access to the federal gravy train and manage to educate their students a lot better than the public schools. What is the secret of their success? The freedom to use teaching methods and a curriculum that work. They don't need national standards or a Common Core because they have a philosophy of education generally based on four hundred years of successful experience.

In the year 2000, there were 27,223 private schools in America with more than five million students and over 400,000 teachers. In contrast, there were 84,735 public schools with a student population of 45,366,000 and 2,905,000 teachers. There must be among those 27,000 private schools excellent curricula that could be used by the public schools at very low cost.[16] But I have never heard of a public school ever adopting a successful private school curriculum. Private school catalogs are generally available free of charge. Why don't the educationists read some of them?

We haven't even considered the home-school movement and the plethora of educational materials available at homeschool conventions and on the Internet. Think of it. Parents are able to educate their children at home without a principal, administrator, or state bureaucrat breathing down their necks. They choose the best educational materials they can find at much lower cost than what the state pays to indoctrinate a child in the public school. Homeschooling usually costs parents about $900 a year, at no expense to the taxpayer. However, the cost of educating a child, for example, in a New Jersey public school is $13,800; in the District of Columbia, $12,979; and in Vermont, $11,835. And none of these public schools can provide the kind of quality education that homeschooling parents provide for their own children. Indeed, New York State spent $14,119 per student in 2005—more than any other state in the nation—and its students are hardly well educated.[17]

And despite all this money spent by states on their public schools, they are still turning out thousands of poorly educated young adults who, if they haven't already dropped out, can barely read their diplomas.

The simple truth is that public education represents the largest river of government cash flow in the United States, and the educationists get the money no matter how much failure they produce. What makes the Common Core program so tantalizing is the sheer amount of money required to feed it.

It isn't all that difficult to figure out what to teach in a school. What requires real ingenuity is figuring out a way of extorting billions of dollars from a long-suffering public that is becoming more and more disenchanted with the public schools but is still susceptible to educators' deception.

As for Bill Gates, who has poured billions into CCSS, he said in an interview in September 2013 at Harvard University, "It would be great if our education stuff worked, but we won't know for probably a decade."[18] Are we supposed to hold our breath for ten years?

As for David Coleman, architect of the Common Core, in 2012 he was appointed to head the College Board, producers of the SATs. According to *Atlantic* magazine:

> Coleman's most radical idea is to redesign the SAT, transforming it from an aptitude test intended to control for varying levels of school quality, to a knowledge test aligned with the Common Core. He describes this change as a way to put applicants on an

equal playing field, a message to "poor children and all children that their finest practice will be rewarded." . . .

Not to mention that with almost 54 percent of recent college graduates jobless or underemployed, and with total student debt surpassing $1 trillion, college has become a much riskier investment than it once was.[19]

But none of this will bother Common Core advocates. As long as Bill Gates is willing to pick up the tab, why worry? Things will change and everyone will adjust. After all, forty-five million children will need to be educated regardless of whether the educators know how to do it or not.

28

COMMON CORE STANDARDS: AN EDUCATIONAL FRAUD

The children belong to all of us.
— PAUL REVILLE, FORMER MASSACHUSETTS EDUCATION SECRETARY WHILE ON A
PANEL PROMOTING COMMON CORE

Growing levels of illiteracy, plunging international rankings, the decline of critical-thinking skills, mushrooming decadence, mass shootings, and companies that can't find the skilled workers they need—those have become some of the atrocious hallmarks of US public schools. The fact that government education in America has become a failure is plain to see—even to many parents who subject their children to it. The reasons for the failure, though, are obscured by special interests. Teachers' unions and educational bureaucrats always claim the need for more taxpayer money, which is simple extortion. But now the totalitarian-minded establishment claims that what are truly needed are national standards beyond the reach of pesky parents and voters.

However, Common Core schemers are engaged in what can only be described as consumer fraud with monumental implications for education and the future of America. In fact, virtually every element of the marketing plan for the national standards is steeped in lies, deception, and fraud. Common Core backers, for instance, claim the standards will improve education and prepare students for college and careers. They also claim that it is a "state-led" scheme and that the federal government has nothing to do with it.

While the statistics and numbers are not yet available, all of that is patently untrue, as we shall show. In fact, if a businessman were selling a product with such brazen whoppers, he would likely be jailed for fraud. In the world of education, alas, not only are scam artists not punished; they are rewarded big-time. As this is being written, more than forty states are still marching toward Common Core implementation, with billions of private and public dollars being showered on the education establishment, major publishing houses, and Common Core propagandists.

Will these new national standards, as their proponents claim, improve education? There are only two real ways to answer that question honestly. The first is that nobody really knows because the scheme was never field-tested before being foisted on America. It is, in fact, at the very least, a giant experiment being perpetrated against unwitting American parents and their captive students in Common Core schools.

Despite the lack of real testing before implementation, however, there is now plenty of evidence available to show what might happen. Let us first consider the English and Language Arts component of Common Core. Among the most oft-heard criticisms surrounding the scheme, aside from failing to teach children how to read properly, is what the students will be reading. At least 50 percent of the reading under Common Core will be what is described as "informational" texts.

So, instead of reading the literary classics, American children will read government documents, technical manuals, and similarly boring writing. Among the "suggested" texts are, for example, "Recommended Levels of Insulation" by the US Environmental Protection Agency/US Department of Energy, or "Executive Order 13423: Strengthening Federal Environmental, Energy, and Transportation Management."[1] In other words, as many education experts have testified, students will be taught what to think rather than how to think.

The absurdity of such a scheme was obvious even to experts selected by the developers of Common Core. Consider Dr. Sandra Stotsky, the twenty-first-century chair in teacher quality at the University of Arkansas's Department of Education Reform. As part of the largely for-show "Common Core Validation Committee," Stotsky refused to sign off on the standards, noting that they were of poor quality, not "internationally benchmarked" or "research based," and would fail to teach children to think critically.[2] Four other members of the committee—members have described their role as that of a "rubber stamp"—also refused to approve them.

Stotsky has testified about the controversial standards in state legislatures across the nation and is widely regarded as one of the leading experts on the scheme. In addition to serving as senior associate commissioner in the Massachusetts Department of Education, where she was in charge of developing or revising all of the state's K–12 standards, she has also conducted extensive research in the field. Among her specialties are the deficiencies in the K–12 reading curriculum and teacher preparation programs. She serves on multiple high-profile boards and committees dealing with education, has written numerous academic papers on education topics and standards, and is widely respected even among the education establishment.

In testimony before Texas lawmakers, Stotsky demolished many of the untruths being used to justify the nationalization of education via Common Core. "Common Core's 'college readiness' standards for English language arts and reading do not aim for a level of achievement that signifies readiness for authentic college-level work," she said. "They point to no more than readiness for a high school diploma (and possibly not even that, depending on where the cut score on tests based on these standards is set). Despite claims to the contrary, they are not internationally benchmarked."[3]

States that adopt the standards, Stotsky continued, "will damage the academic integrity of both their post-secondary institutions and their high schools precisely because Common Core's standards do not strengthen the high school curriculum and cannot reduce the current amount of post-secondary remedial coursework in a legitimate way." Eventually, in response to many charges of lack of transparency, the names of those on the Standards Development Work Group were released in the summer of 2009. "The vast majority, it appeared, work for testing companies," she added.[4]

In an issue brief for the Heritage Foundation, Stotsky explained the long-term consequences of Common Core's approach to English and Language Arts—essentially shifting from reading literature to reading manual-type, technical writing. "A diminished emphasis on literature in the secondary grades makes it unlikely that American students will study a meaningful range of culturally and historically significant literary works before graduation," Stotsky warned. "It also prevents students from acquiring a rich understanding and use of the English language. Perhaps of greatest concern, it may lead to a decreased capacity for analytical thinking."[5]

Indeed, this appears to be among the goals of the architects of Common Core, as dumbing down the population reduces the probability of a citizenry that questions authority.

Stotsky went on to say that it is "more than likely that college readiness will decrease" when secondary English teachers start reducing the study of complex literature and literary traditions to prioritize informational and nonfiction texts. "By reducing literary study, Common Core decreases students' opportunity to develop the analytical thinking once developed in just an elite group by the vocabulary, structure, style, ambiguity, point of view, figurative language, and irony in classic literary texts," she warned. "An

English curriculum overloaded with advocacy journalism or with 'informational' articles chosen for their topical and/or political nature should raise serious concerns among parents, school leaders, and policymakers."[6]

It gets even worse, though, according to Stotsky. "Common Core's standards not only present a serious threat to state and local education authority, but also put academic quality at risk," she concluded. "Pushing fatally flawed education standards into America's schools is not the way to improve education for America's students."[7]

In other words, it appears that the Common Core architects of education are plotting to make sure that—even among those students who do manage to learn to read properly despite being taught using faulty methods—critical thinking skills are reduced. Yes, the children might become good at reading "informational" text, but that will just contribute to making them better at following orders and instructions. Why would the Obama administration and billionaire Bill Gates want drones that can follow instructions and take standardized tests but not think critically? We shall return to that question later.

What about the math standards? As with English, the criticism has been loud and harsh. The standards are so poor, in fact, that another member of the Common Core Validation Committee, Stanford professor Dr. James Milgram, who was responsible for the mathematics component, refused to sign off on them as well. "The Core Mathematics Standards are written to reflect very low expectations," he said, calling them "as non-challenging as possible" with "extremely serious failings."[8] Indeed, as error-riddled Common Core-linked "modules" in math have been created and posted online, parents and teachers alike have been left scratching their heads. Even comedians like Stephen Colbert and Louis C. K. have ridiculed the Common Core math.

Again, as with the English standards, some state governments have had to lower their expectations to fall in line with Common Core math. In Minnesota, officials refused to adopt the math standards because "ours were more rigorous and matched where kids were mastering those [skills] in their content areas," according to state education commissioner Brenda Cassellius.[9] Because of Common Core in California, students will no longer be required to take Algebra I by eighth grade. Massachusetts will also soon have students taking Algebra I in ninth grade or later rather than eighth, as currently required. Indiana has also been cited as another state with mathematics standards that were stronger than the Common Core scheme.

In a letter outlining some of his concerns, Dr. Milgram even pointed to "actual errors" in the standards—"they are neither mathematically correct nor especially clear." He did allow that the Common Core standards might be an improvement in some states, but only because the existing standards there were so atrocious to begin with that just about anything else would be better. In his letter declining to approve the standards, Dr. Milgram, an actual expert charged with reviewing and approving Common Core's mathematics elements, said "there is no real research base for including any of these standards in the document." Despite multiple requests for references to justify the standards, which he said contained "many serious flaws," none were provided.[10]

"Also among these difficulties are that a large number of the arithmetic and operations, as well as the place value standards are one, two or even more years behind the corresponding standards for many if not all the high achieving countries," Milgram continued, demolishing the notion that Common Core would raise US standards to the level of better-performing nations. "Consequently, I was not able to certify that the Core Mathematics Standards are benchmarked at the same level as the standards of the high achieving countries in mathematics."[11]

Among the myriad problems he found were approaches such as the "visual fraction model" that represent "all that is wrong" in standard approaches, which have "seldom" actually worked. "It is as though the authors had a master-list of topics and felt free to sprinkle them wherever there might have been room," he said. "I feel that we are dealing with an experiment on a national scale. . . . Before we dare to challenge teachers and students with standards like these, we absolutely have to test the approach in a more limited environment."[12] Of course, testing Common Core on a small number of students has been suggested by countless experts, but the education establishment decided to make the entire nation its laboratory instead.

As if the preceding criticism of the math standards was not enough, Milgram also uncovered mathematics that was simply incorrect. "In any case there are now actual errors in the sixth and seventh grade discussions of ratios and rates," he explained. "They had been clear and mathematically correct presentations of material that is typically very badly done in most state standards in this country. Now they are neither mathematically correct nor especially clear."[13]

Milgram and Stotsky were the only two subject matter experts on the validation committee, and both refused to sign off. Beyond Common Core's troublesome English and math components, the same forces working to nationalize education in those subjects are also advancing a plot to do the same with other subjects, including history, science, sex education, and more. All of the schemes have been sharply criticized.

The history standards, for example, have been attacked for leaving out the true study of history in favor of "process"—extracting meaning from a text as opposed to knowing history. Many of the "suggested" textbooks that go along with the standards are also packed with inaccurate information and blatant "progressive" bias. One representative example is *A History of US*, by Joy Hakim, a purportedly "comprehensive" textbook series on US history that is widely viewed as extremely liberal and packed with factual problems. "Examination of Hakim's material discloses many errors (including errors of fact, of chronology and of terminology) as well as unjustified assertions and some displays of bias," noted author and historian Alice Whealey in a scathing analysis of the book series for the Textbook League, which reviews educational material for accuracy. "Joy Hakim should not attempt to write about Western history, particularly the history of Europe, because she obviously hasn't had enough training in these subjects. It is a shame that Oxford University Press has let her get away with so many falsehoods and with such extreme exhibitions of bias." With Common Core, though, children in more than forty states will be reading similarly inaccurate, biased material.[14]

The national science standards, produced by the same elements of the education establishment and known as the "Next Generation Science Standards," are even more controversial. Instead of teaching children about science—real science—the standards will offer students a steady stream of controversial propaganda presented as unchallengeable fact.[15]

On increasingly discredited and controversial "global warming" theories cited by the United Nations as the justification for a planetary climate regime and carbon taxes, for example, students will be required to learn that human activities are mostly to blame, even though this notion is disputed by countless scientists and a vast, growing body of actual scientific observational evidence. "Human activities, such as the release of greenhouse gases from burning fossil fuels, are major factors in the current rise in Earth's mean surface temperature (global warming)," the elementary school standards claim, despite the fact that even climate alarmists admit there has been no "global warming" in some seventeen years and that CO_2 released from fossil fuels represents a fraction of a percent of the greenhouse gases present naturally in the atmosphere.[16]

On evolution, widely regarded by the secular educational establishment as a key dogma of its anti-Christian faith, the standards claim that believing man evolved from rocks that turned into soup that turned into life that eventually became apes is "fundamental." About half of Americans reject the evolution theory in polls—more than eight out of ten Americans reject the atheistic version of it—yet it will still be taught to their children as fact.[17]

The new "National Sexuality Education Standards," which aim

to begin the sexualizing of children in kindergarten, might be even more alarming to parents. Developed by a coalition of radical "sex-ed" outfits including tax-funded abortion behemoth Planned Parenthood and its allies, the standards seek to nationalize the teaching of extreme sexual education across America. "The goal of the National Sexuality Education Standards: Core Content and Skills, K–12 is to provide clear, consistent and straightforward guidance on the essential minimum, core content for sexuality education that is developmentally and age-appropriate for students in grades K–12," Planned Parenthood and other organizations involved in the standards claim on their websites.

The content would shock most American parents. Among the topics to be introduced to kindergartners and set to be mastered by second grade, for example: "Identify different kinds of family structures" and "Demonstrate ways to show respect for different types of families." Is learning about "homosexual marriage" before first grade in government schools really "age-appropriate" or necessary? You decide. It only gets more and more radical from there, with graphic lessons promoting everything from masturbation and fornication to transgenderism and homosexuality. Parents hoping to shelter their children from this anti-Christian propaganda are being left with increasingly few options. And it is only going to get more extreme from here.

If you thought that was all bad enough, the centralization of national education in unaccountable hands virtually guarantees that it will get worse. For obvious reasons, totalitarian leaders have always sought to centralize and control education. National Socialist (Nazi) leader Adolf Hitler, for example, noted in his book *Mein Kampf* that "whoever has the youth has the future." With a fanatical devotion, his regime ensured that *it* had the youth. Communist dictators from Mao to Lenin and Stalin did the same. After all, it is only logical that whoever molds the minds of the youth can eventually dominate the population, even if it takes a generation or two. Whereas government-school standards were once largely the responsibility of state and local government—communities, parents, and so on—that is all changing at warp speed as Common Core moves ahead.

While parents, teachers, and school boards will not have a chance to revise or change the standards, they will be changed down the line. In fact, the organizations behind Common Core admit that explicitly: "The Standards are intended to be a living work: as new and better evidence emerges, the Standards will be revised accordingly."[18] Who will do the revising? Not you or your community. Instead, complete control over what your children learn, now and in the future, will be in the hands of the same organizations and forces that produced them in the first place.

As government schools have met the Common Core steamroller, the results have been an unmitigated disaster. Even some of its most ardent proponents, including many on the Common Core gravy train, have admitted as much. In fact, the rollout has been so bad in New York that after listening to an outraged public in a series of eleven forums held across the state, assemblyman Al Graf, a member of the Assembly Education Committee, who has a degree in elementary education, called the imposition of the standards "state-sponsored child abuse."[19] We will return to the ongoing uprising against Common Core in the next chapter.

In other words, we are dealing with outright consumer fraud on a national scale. Consumer fraud is a crime. Contrary to the claims of proponents, the standards will not "improve" education or make American students truly ready for college and career— at least not in the traditional sense, where critical thinking is viewed as a good thing. (Even the notion of standards that could make a student simultaneously ready for both "college" and "career" has been ridiculed, as the two are inherently different.) Instead, the standards will centralize control over young people's minds and hence the future of this nation—while at the same time dumbing them down, tracking everything about them, and socially engineering them for an Orwellian future. Even homeschoolers and private schools are in the crosshairs already.

All of that brings us to the next big lie used by the Common Core masters to fraudulently foist the scheme on America: the notion that the standards are "state-led." The ploy is so crucial to the broader agenda that the whole order was even named "Common Core State Standards." That particular fraud, however, is so easy to debunk it is hard to believe that Common Core proponents continue to employ it.

The reality is that the deeply controversial standards had almost nothing to do with the "states." They were, in fact, almost entirely the product of progressive billionaires and their foundations, the education establishment, Obama administration machinations, massive international companies hoping to profit, and an assortment of front groups and trade associations funded by Bill Gates and the federal government. It helps to look at the organizations that are, on the surface at least, behind Common Core: the National Governors Association, the Council of Chief State School Officers, and Achieve, Inc.

Of course, despite their names, none of those organizations are actually "states." The NGA and the CCSSO are in fact "trade organizations" based in Washington, DC. Neither lobbying/policy group features a great deal of involvement from state officials; and both outfits receive massive amounts of taxpayer funding from the federal government. Is a federally funded trade organization really a "state"? You decide.

Separately, the two DC-based groups have received well over $100 million over the last decade from the Bill and Melinda Gates Foundation, which has spent upwards of $150 million ($2.3 billion by some estimates) on developing and promoting Common Core—including huge grants to supposedly "conservative" organizations to help push the standards on the right. Even the *Huffington Post* had to point out the obvious: "CCSS is not 'state led.' It is 'Gates led.'"[20] Gates's foundation, of course, is also infamous for supporting the United Nations, Planned Parenthood, population control, and more—offering a very good indication of the sort of values the controversial billionaire hopes to instill in your children.

Gates's money is more deeply involved than one might think. On March 17, 2014, the *North Denver News* revealed that Gates spending on the Common Core is not mere millions, but billions: "Research by Jack Hassard, Professor Emeritus at Georgia State, shows compelling evidence that Gates has spent $2.3 billion pushing the Common Core. More than eighteen hundred grants to organizations running from teachers unions to state departments of education to political groups like the National Governor's Association have pushed the Common Core into forty-five states, with little transparency and next to no public review."[21]

In terms of foisting the non-state-led standards on states, the federal government—and the Obama administration in particular—was the main player. In all, American taxpayers were forced to pay for tens of billions of dollars in "grants" aimed at coercing their state officials into accepting Common Core and related schemes.

Much of the bribe money came through the "Race to the Top" scheme in the so-called stimulus bill, which would be awarded only to state governments that approved Common Core. That created a built-in incentive for state education officials and government-school employees to support the standards—especially because the unconstitutional bribes were marketed as a way to ensure that they could keep their jobs amid the economic crisis and supposedly declining state budgets. The other primary tool the Obama administration used to impose Common Core on states was offering "waivers" to mandates from the failed Bush-era "No Child Left Behind" scheme to state governments that complied. Congress never approved, but Obama's Department of Education did it anyway.

Perhaps even more incredible, despite "state-led" claims, most state officials had not even seen the final "Common Core" product before agreeing to impose it on the students of their states. Even the Common Core–aligned testing regimes—a crucial component of the broader effort—are being developed with taxpayer money extracted from Americans by the federal government. Federal law

and the Constitution both prohibit any federal involvement in school curricula, but neither has represented a serious obstacle to the administration's designs. Even the Orwellian data mining of students was the work of the federal government.

The primary role of state and local officials, then, has merely been to serve as enforcers—shoving the standards onto a skeptical public in exchange for bribes and waivers. State and local governments are also expected to pay for much of the imposition of the multibillion-dollar "federal-led" boondoggle by borrowing and taxing more.

The next fraud: Proponents of the standards also continually claim that the standards will not dictate the curriculum. Well, that fraudulent bit of marketing propaganda was exposed by Mr. Common Core himself, Bill Gates, during a speech at the 2009 National Conference of State Legislators. "Last month, 46 Governors and Chief State School Officers made a public commitment to embrace these common standards," Gates said. "This is encouraging—but identifying common standards is not enough. We'll know we've succeeded when the *curriculum and the tests are aligned to these standards.*"[22]

Bill Gates is still lying about it all, most recently contradicting his 2009 comments in a *USA Today* column purporting to address "myths" about his scheme. "These are standards, just like the ones schools have always had; they are not a curriculum," he claimed. "It's still up to local educators to select the curriculum."[23] With the federally funded tests, all curriculums will, of course, have to conform to Common Core, exactly as Gates correctly suggested in 2009.

Gates is hardly the only architect behind Common Core to have let the cat out of the bag, so to speak. The overarching agenda was summarized neatly in a 2008 column on "education reform" for the *Wall Street Journal* (WSJ) by former IBM CEO and current "Achieve" chairman emeritus Louis Gerstner Jr. Achieve, Inc. is the organization that developed the standards. Gerstner, a prominent member of the Council on Foreign Relations and a Bilderberg summit attendee,

cochaired Achieve until 2002, when he formed the Teaching Commission with a list of prominent establishment figures.

In his *Wall Street Journal* column, Gerstner offered what he described as a "prescription for leadership from the Obama administration." Among the myriad recommendations: "abolish all local school districts" and "establish a set of national standards for a core curriculum."[24]

The fraud continues to this day, with Common Core proponents continually claiming that only "right-wing extremists" and "left-wing extremists" oppose the machinations. Obama's education secretary even argued that it was "white suburban moms" who are upset because they did not realize how dumb their kids are. As we shall see in the next chapter, the uprising against Common Core transcends the political spectrum, race, class, gender, and all of the other divide-and-conquer categories defined by collectivists. It is, in fact, an American rebellion.

29

REBELLION AGAINST "OBAMACORE" MAKES STRANGE BEDFELLOWS

It's fascinating to me that some of the pushback is coming from white
suburban moms who—all of a sudden—realize their child isn't as brilliant
as they thought they were.
— ARNE DUNCAN, SECRETARY OF EDUCATION

The controversial Common Core standards—also known as
ObamaCore—were put in place across America almost entirely
under the radar. In all, some forty-five state governments
and the District of Columbia quietly accepted the Obama
administration's "Race to the Top" bribes and "No Child Left
Behind" waivers in exchange for surrendering control over
education. Once proponents of the scheme thought it was a done
deal, news reports began to emerge, with many essentially claiming
that Common Core was, in fact, a done deal—basically irreversible.

However, once the public began finding out—and learning

the details—an unprecedented backlash from activists across the political spectrum shocked the political establishment. In Texas, which never joined to begin with, state lawmakers passed a bill with a vote of 140 to 2 in the state House of Representatives banning Common Core in the Lone Star State. Governor Rick Perry signed it into law in June 2013.

Several states, meanwhile, had officially retreated from Common Core as of early 2014. Indiana became the first to "officially" back out in March 2014. Oklahoma, South Carolina, and Louisiana soon followed. There was no state—liberal or conservative—where policymakers were not feeling the intensifying heat. Even in the US Congress, lawmakers have also pursued various sheepish efforts to slam the brakes on the Obama administration's scheming, or at least pretended to be doing something to quiet down their base.

The uprising against Common Core received a powerful shot in the arm when the Republican National Committee (RNC) unanimously adopted a resolution in early 2013 calling on the GOP and its members to stand firm against the centralization plot. Among other key points, the RNC measure blasts the "one size fits all" educational scheme as "an inappropriate overreach to standardize and control the education of our children so they will conform to a preconceived 'normal.'"[1]

Instead of the "Common Core State Standards," the RNC, echoing the 2012 Republican Party Platform, said it believed in providing "broad education choices" to parents and children at the state and local level. A free market–based approach to education is best, the resolution continues, adding that it would help students to achieve individual excellence.

Among the many complaints against Common Core outlined by the GOP is the fact that the (federally funded) organizations responsible for developing the deeply controversial standards did so through a secretive process that was not subject to Freedom of Information laws. Also on the list of grievances were the scheme's federally funded testing regimes and the unprecedented federally funded data collection on children and their families, as well as the sharing of "massive amounts of personal student and teacher data."

The centralization of education and the accompanying loss of choices is one of the most common themes found throughout the strongly worded RNC resolution. "The CCSS effectively removes educational choice and competition since all schools and all districts must use Common Core 'assessments' based on the Common Core standards to allow all students to advance in the school system and to advance to higher education pursuits," the document explains.

Federal law, the resolution goes on, prohibits federalizing school curricula. Despite that clear prohibition, however, the Obama administration accepted Common Core and even used so-called stimulus money to reward state governments that were most committed to advancing the president's controversial education agenda, the measure says. According to the resolution, the executive branch also failed to give states, legislatures, and citizens enough time to review the national standards before having to commit to them.

"The 2012 Republican Party Platform specifically states the need to repeal the numerous federal regulations which interfere with State and local control of public schools . . . and therefore, the Republican National Committee rejects this CCSS plan which creates and fits the country with a nationwide straitjacket on academic freedom and achievement," it adds.

However, the RNC resolution hardly came about in a vacuum. In fact, the measure represents a culmination of the Herculean efforts of grassroots Republicans and conservatives all across the country, including Tea Party groups, the Eagle Forum, the Heritage Foundation, the Cato Institute, FreedomWorks, the Heartland Institute, Americans for Prosperity, the Pioneer Institute, the American Principles Project, the Independence Institute, the Home School Legal Defense Association, and countless others.

In the media, more than a few conservative heavyweights, such as Glenn Beck and Michelle Malkin, among many others, have been building opposition to the educational fraud as well. In the increasingly influential right-leaning press—WND, the *Daily Caller,* the *American Thinker,* the *New American, Infowars,* the Blaze, and similar operations—strong criticism of Common Core has become something of a staple.

State and local organizations dedicated primarily to stopping Common Core have also been sprouting up across America. Often in collaboration with other organizations—FreedomWorks, which says it has millions of grassroots activists, for example—these anti–Common Core groups have been holding rallies, seminars, local meetings, protests, and even online activism in virtually every state, pushing politicians to stop the national standards. Physical protests against Common Core have been growing steadily larger from coast to coast as well.

On the other side of the supposed political spectrum, the battle against Common Core has been gaining grassroots momentum quickly as well. While the Democrat Party continues clinging to its latest Big Government centralization plan, among grassroots liberals and progressives opposition to the standards is escalating. The attacks on Common Core often come from other angles—claiming it is some sort of corporate plot to hurt government schooling and teachers—but the passion is real.

Consider as just one example the so-called "Badass Teacher Association"—or the BATS, as they refer to themselves—a nationwide coalition composed primarily of leftist and radical leftist government-school teachers opposed to Common Core. Their logo: the infamous "socialist fist." With tens of thousands of members across America and various splinter groups, such as the Badass Parents Association, the group has already had an impact on the debate, especially in demolishing the essential Common Core claim that educators are largely unified in their support for the dubious standards.

"Never have I found myself finding so much common ground with people who call themselves conservative and libertarians—we all agreed public schools were going to be ruined by this," BATs cofounder Dr. Mark Naison, a professor at Fordham University with experience in public schools, told me (Alex). "This really represents the worst fantasies of both the right and left coming true: Big Government and Big Corporations imposing this terrible, untested, expensive plan using intimidation and bullying."[2]

Even Big Labor, generally strong allies of Obama on virtually everything, are calling for a moratorium on implementing some parts of the scheme—or even on Common Core altogether in some states. As this was being written, teachers' unions, faced with an uprising among their members, were beginning to jump off the Common Core bandwagon faster and faster despite major risks to funding from Bill Gates and other proponents of standards nationalization. The powerful Chicago Teachers Union officially announced its opposition in May 2014, slamming federal overreach, poor standards, damage to students, and more.[3]

It is also happening at the national level. In February 2014, for instance, National Education Association boss Dennis Van Roekel noted that, "in far too many states, implementation has been completely botched. Seven of ten teachers believe that implementation of the standards is going poorly in their schools." Members of the NEA, the nation's largest teachers' union, "have a right to feel frustrated, upset, and angry about the poor commitment to implementing the standards correctly," Van Roekel added.[4]

As usual, the criticism came along with demands for more taxpayer funds, which, as covered before, will do nothing to improve education but plenty to enrich the educational establishment. Still, it was an important development in the battle against Common Core. The NEA boss even suggested openness to having state governments modify the controversial standards, saying state policymakers should work with the NEA and "review the appropriateness of the standards and recommend any improvements that might be needed."[5]

About a year earlier, the American Federation of Teachers union, which received millions in funding from Bill Gates to push the scheme, was also forced to acknowledge that its membership was up in arms. "The Common Core is in trouble," admitted AFT boss Randi Weingarten. "There is a serious backlash in lots of different ways, on the right and on the left." According to Weingarten, the new standards are being poorly implemented, requiring a "mid-course correction" before the entire dream of supposed education reform crumbles.[6]

To get an idea of how badly it was going, consider that Weingarten argued that the implementation of the scheme has been "far worse" than the rollout of Obamacare. Among other concerns, the union boss said state governments were rushing out the Common Core–based tests without preparing teachers or designing new curricula to incorporate the national standards. In March 2014, the union finally stopped accepting Gates's money, citing outrage among its membership over Common Core.

AFT's affiliate, the New York State United Teachers (NYSUT), went much further than either of the two national unions. In late January, the union's board, which represents some six hundred thousand current and former educators in New York, voted *unanimously* to withdraw its support from Common Core. "We'll have to be the first to say it's failed," NYSUT boss Richard Iannuzzi told *Politico*, adding that union leaders in other states were considering doing the same. "We've been in conversations where we're all saying our members don't see this going down a path that improves teaching and learning." The board also adopted a motion of no confidence in the state education chief.[7]

In New York, which is further down the road toward full Common Core implementation than most other states, the dismal test scores apparently drove much of the unrest. Still, the outrage was so intense that even Gov. Andrew Cuomo, an ardent supporter of the standards, could no longer ignore the intensifying rebellion among parents, teachers, citizens, students and more. He created a "panel" to offer recommendations that would pretend to take the public into account while doing its best to shield Common Core from lawmakers facing a tsunami of complaints from constituents.

"The flawed implementation of the Common Core curriculum has resulted in frustration, anxiety, and confusion for children and parents," Cuomo said in a statement after his panel-released recommendations. "It is in everyone's best interest to have high, real world standards for learning and to support the Common Core curriculum, but we need to make sure that our students are not unfairly harmed by its implementation. The recommendations released by the Common Core Implementation Panel today seek to achieve this goal."[8]

Cuomo's deceitful retreat, designed to appease rebelling New Yorkers while preserving as much of the Common Core regime as possible, came after a special committee of legislators bypassed the governor and held a series of eleven public forums across the state. While a 2013 bill to stop Common Core went nowhere—that was before New Yorkers got a better handle on what was going on—lawmakers were working on new strategies by early 2014.[9]

Unsurprisingly, with the public increasingly disillusioned with Washington and the people's inability to control Leviathan, state capitols across America are where much of the action to stop Common Core has been taking place. As of spring of 2014, there was anti–Common Core legislation pending in more than half of all state legislatures. Many of the bills would kill the standards entirely in favor of new, better ones, while other bills would delay, defund, or review Common Core. Concerns over the massive costs of implementing Common Core—estimated at up to $16 billion or more—have also been coming into focus.

As this was being written, Indiana was in the process of supposedly killing the national standards. The legislature voted to scrap Common Core, and the governor, at least publicly, was fully onboard with the effort. However, criticism of the process was growing by leaps and bounds, too. Among other concerns, the new standards kept much from the national standards, simply piling more mandates on top of them. In some cases, as much as 90 percent of Common Core was in the supposedly "new" standards.

When Terrence Moore, a Hillsdale College professor and former public school leader, asked the state board in charge of the standards whether or not the phonics method would be used to teach children to read, they refused to offer a real answer.[10]

Separately, many states have also withdrawn from the two national testing consortia—the Smarter Balanced Assessment Consortium (SBAC) or the Partnership for Assessment of Readiness for College and Careers (PARCC). Because the Common Core–aligned tests are considered a crucial component of both the Common Core standards and the massive data-mining apparatus being erected across America, the significance of these developments could be major.

By late January of 2014, at least nine states had officially withdrawn from the federally funded ($360 million so far) assessment regimes under immense public pressure. Four had never joined in the first place, and many others were also considering backing out. As the tests go into effect across much of America in 2015, though, the uprising against Common Core will almost certainly accelerate.[11]

School districts, too, have been taking action to drop Common Core. Douglas County, Colorado, for instance, approved a resolution unanimously rejecting Common Core in favor of its own higher-quality standards. In Manchester, New Hampshire, the largest school district in the state, officials also voted in October 2013 to move beyond Common Core in favor of the "Manchester Academic Standards," becoming the second district in the state to do so. At least one school district in Wisconsin, a "local control" state, is also refusing to foist Common Core on its students despite the national testing regime.[12]

However, at the state and local levels, the battle against Common Core has also featured a huge amount of deception aimed at placating an outraged citizenry while keeping as much of the standards as possible. Many states, for example, were attempting to use what essentially amounts to public-relations gimmicks in an effort to soothe public fury. In both Oklahoma and Florida, among others, state officials simply renamed the Common Core standards while pretending to be concerned about federal intrusion. Oklahoma later repealed them in mid-2014.

The battle taking place outside of government schools has been intense as well. In recent years, the homeschooling community across America has been working hard to stop Common Core. Among other concerns, home education groups worry that the national standards will impact their freedom. With textbooks en masse and tests such as the ACT and SAT being aligned with Common Core, the national standards are already influencing home educators.

By the time this was being written, meanwhile, about half of America's Catholic dioceses had adopted Common Core—albeit with a supposed Christian spin—over massive parental objections, too. Still, a coalition of more than 130 of America's top Catholic educators have also rebelled against the standards, writing a stinging rebuke of the scheme in a letter to US bishops urging them to keep it out of Catholic schools.[13]

Among other concerns highlighted in the letter to church leaders, the Catholic educators warn that Common Core, which they said represents a "radical shift," is really a "step backwards" in terms of education. Beyond the particulars of the widely criticized standards, the powerful document points out that there are even greater fears about Common Core as it relates to the church and its institutions: the philosophy and aims of the reforms, and how they will "undermine" Catholic education while "dramatically" diminishing children's horizons. "In fact, we are convinced that Common Core is so deeply flawed that it should not be adopted by Catholic schools which have yet to approve it, and that those schools which have already endorsed it should seek an orderly withdrawal now," wrote the scholars, led by Notre Dame law professor Gerard Bradley and whose ranks include professors and leaders at many of America's most prestigious Catholic universities.

Most recently (as of this writing), a group of Senate Republicans had introduced a nonbinding "resolution" essentially complaining that the Obama administration was using bribes and coercion to push Common Core on states.

More serious efforts had started the year before. In the US Senate, Sen. Charles Grassley (R-IA) was among the leaders of the opposition to Common Core. In early 2013, Grassley began circulating a letter among his colleagues, calling for a prohibition on the Department of Education's bribes to state governments. The proposed measure would have also stopped federal funding of the nominally private entities working to develop the standards.[14]

The Grassley letter, dated April 26, was sent to the Senate Appropriations Committee's Education Subcommittee leadership. It was signed by eight other senators: Mike Lee (R-UT), Tom Coburn (R-OK), James Inhofe (R-OK), Deb Fischer (R-NE), Rand Paul (R-KY), Pat Roberts (R-KS), Jeff Sessions (R-AL), and Ted Cruz (R-TX). The coalition of senators sought an amendment to the appropriations bill funding the Department of Education that would restore state decision making.

"The decision about what students should be taught and when it should be taught has enormous consequences for our children," the senators wrote. "Therefore, parents ought to have a straight line of accountability to those who are making the decisions. State legislatures, which are directly accountable to the citizens of their states, are the appropriate place for those decisions to be made, free from any pressure from the U.S. Department of Education."[15]

Separately, a bill to stop Common Core was introduced in January 2014 in the Senate. Dubbed S. 1974, the "Learning Opportunities Created at Local Level Act" by Sen. Pat Roberts (R-KS) would prohibit federal involvement in state education through the use of various schemes—bribes, mandates, waivers, and more.[16] Of course, aside from being unconstitutional, federal involvement in state curricula is already unlawful, but laws seem to matter little to the Obama administration. Either way, the Senate bill never went anywhere.

In the House of Representatives, lawmakers were also working to stop Common Core. Led by Rep. Blaine Luetkemeyer (R-MO), a coalition including more than thirty members of Congress sent a letter to education secretary Arne Duncan outlining their concerns. The lawmakers also suggested that the Obama administration was moving forward with "education policy reform" without authorization or input from Congress.

"Such an action is, at best, in contravention with precedent," the representatives wrote, noting that the authority to move forward with some of the administration's schemes ended in 2008 without congressional reauthorization. "As representatives from states across the nation, we understand the diverse cultures and state-specific education needs that exist in America . . . Moreover, we believe that state-based education policies are vital to the successful education of a child. As with most one-size-fits-all policies, Common Core standards fail to address the specific needs of our states."[17]

The House of Representatives had also passed the Student Success Act on July 19, 2013, aimed at reducing the unconstitutional federal role in education while restraining the administration's abuse of "No Child Left Behind" waivers as a tool to coerce state governments. However, the legislation never went anywhere in the Democrat-controlled Senate, and even if it had, Obama had already threatened to veto the Student Success Act.

Efforts to simply defund the Department of Education and its Common Core bludgeons—perhaps the easiest and surest way to stop Obama's plot—have barely been mentioned in Congress, even with the House controlled by Republicans who claim to oppose it. In other words, Republicans at the federal level, despite outrage among their conservative base and the RNC's anti–Common Core platform, were not yet serious about slamming the brakes on the national standards.

As this was being written, though, the nationwide rebellion against Common Core was reaching unprecedented levels. In an effort to save Common Core from the public, Big Business announced that it was going all out, too. From chambers of commerce to the Business Roundtable, Big Business vowed to unleash a major advertising blitz in favor of the nationalization of education. Whether the business-led machinations will be effective—or will backfire, as some analysts suggested—was not yet clear by the time of this writing.[18]

Pro–Common Core propagandists and developers also have released a poll showing that even though most Americans were unfamiliar with the scheme, its popularity was down significantly over the previous round of surveys. The poll's analysis tried to spin the results, even pointing out that after a "factual" statement on Common Core was read to respondents, a majority favored the standards. However, the bogus statement was largely meaningless and deeply deceptive, relying on much of the same fraudulent marketing plan described in the previous chapter. As uninformed members of the public learn the truth, that shallow and largely bogus "support" tends to evaporate.[19]

At this point, it is safe to assume that the movement to stop Common Core will continue to grow, and the political class will have a tough time being able to resist public demands indefinitely.

If there is any bright side to the whole battle over Common Core, it is that parents are becoming increasingly suspicious of both the educational establishment and the politicians that fund it with ever-larger amounts of taxpayer money. The anger and suspicion are already translating into more scrutiny of government education more broadly—and that is, without doubt, a very positive development for anyone who truly values educational freedom and true academic achievement.

30

THE FUTURE OF EDUCATION: FREEDOM OR GLOBAL ENSLAVEMENT?

One of our immediate educational objectives must be the elimination of the competitive spirit, and the substitution of the cooperative consciousness.
—ALICE BAILEY, *EDUCATION IN THE NEW AGE*

Education—and the future of humanity, by extension—is at a crossroad today. On one side stand the United Nations, UNESCO, the Obama administration, Bill Gates, Common Core, Achieve, the Council on Foreign Relations, and the totalitarian-minded establishment. Their vision, as we shall show, involves centralizing education and all power over schooling for the purpose of creating what quite literally amounts to a global slave state. If that sounds like an exaggeration, continue reading and judge for yourself. The uneducated masses would be trained like Pavlov's dogs from a young age to fulfill their roles in what top establishment leaders regularly refer to as the "New World Order."

The other option is freedom. However, educational liberty, competition, proper instruction methods, and decentralization are the only way that freedom will survive into the future. Fortunately, there are encouraging signs that a global awakening is slowly and quietly taking place among parents and educators. The emergence of the worldwide homeschooling movement, for example—something that began its recent resurgence in the United States but is spreading across the globe like wildfire—is perhaps one of the brightest spots in an otherwise grim picture. We shall return to this in the next chapter.

First, let us begin by showing, using their own words and documents, what the would-be global education establishment is doing, and what it has in mind for the future. To do that, we can start by taking a look at UNESCO, the United Nations Educational, Scientific, and Cultural Organization. This, along with some other UN agencies, such as UNICEF, represents the nucleus of worldwide involvement in globalizing education.

From its earliest days, leaders of the self-styled global education agency have boldly proclaimed their intentions. Consider, as just one representative example among countless others that could be cited, the words of UNESCO's first boss, Sir Julian Huxley. (Not coincidentally, Julian's brother, Aldous Huxley, was the author of *Brave New World*.) The "task" before UNESCO, he explained in 1947, "is to help the emergence of a single world culture, with its own philosophy and background of ideas, and with its own broad purpose." He explained clearly that its outlook "must be" what he called "world humanism."[1] Huxley died in 1975.

Now, fast-forward ahead to today. The Obama administration, Bill Gates, and a broad coalition of establishment-minded forces have foisted Common Core on most of America. Despite growing resistance, the new national standards remain firmly in place across the vast majority of the nation. Critics have rightly condemned the machinations as a nationalization of US education. However, an even broader agenda—the globalization of schooling—has received far less attention.

Obviously, Common Core did not happen in a vacuum. In fact, the national standards represent merely the culmination of decades of quiet efforts by the globalist education establishment to foist its new values for its envisioned new society on the American people. In 1994, Democratic president Bill Clinton signed the "Goals 2000: Educate America Act" forcing an early version of "national standards" on schools across America. Then, Republican president George W. Bush signed the "No Child Left Behind Act" developing national "accountability" schemes to ensure that government schools were teaching what the federal government demanded.

Behind the scenes throughout all of it, though, were the UN, the Council on Foreign Relations, and the globalist forces working to centralize control over education—and every other facet of life. For decades now, the globalists at UNESCO and other UN outfits have been openly plotting to impose what they sometimes refer to as the "World Core Curriculum," or some variation of global education standards, on all of humanity.

In addition to gathering up unprecedented amounts of data on everyone, the global "education reform" movement is essentially seeking to instill radical new values in children—turning them into "global citizens" with views inherently at odds with biblical religion—to facilitate the total regimentation of human society. We shall return to the goals of that education in a moment. Countless UN programs and initiatives, such as "Education for All," though, are working hard toward making truly globalized education a reality.

In 1990, national governments and dictators from around the world came together at the World Conference on Education for All. At that summit, they agreed to the "World Declaration on Education for All: Meeting Basic Learning Needs" and to the "Framework for Action to Meet Basic Learning Needs" (the Jomtien Declaration). While obscure language is often used to conceal the agenda, it is not difficult to see through it.[2]

"Meeting basic learning needs constitutes a common and universal human responsibility," Article 10 of the declaration explains, suggesting that education is no longer the function of families or even local communities, but of the UN. "It requires international solidarity and equitable and fair economic relations in order to redress existing economic disparities." So what are "basic learning needs"? Article 1 says, "Basic learning needs . . . comprise both essential learning tools . . . and the basic learning content . . . required by human beings." In other words, if you skip through the propaganda, global institutions will decide what content and tools are "required" by your children and impose them upon them.

Even children who do not attend government schools must learn from the same standards, as the document makes clear. "Supplementary alternative programmes can help meet the basic learning needs of children with limited or no access to formal schooling, provided that they *share the same standards* of learning applied to schools," Article 5 explains (emphasis added).

A more recent UNESCO document adopted by governments in 2000, dubbed "The Dakar Framework for Action: Education for All: Meeting our Collective Commitments," follows up on the 1990 plan. While employing similarly opaque language, it also offers insight into the global plans. For instance, it demands that governments "implement integrated strategies for gender equality in education which recognize the need for changes in attitudes, values and practices." Later on, the same report explains that to achieve "gender equality" (read: radical feminist notions to support getting all women into the workforce and all children into "early childhood care"), "changes in attitudes, values and behaviour are required." "Required," of course, is the opposite of optional.[3]

In a section on "goals and strategies," the UN document explains that the plan is "designed to enable all individuals to realize their right to learn and to fulfill their responsibility to contribute to the development of their society. They are global in nature, drawn from the outcomes of the regional EFA conferences and the international development targets to which countries are already committed."[4]

"Governments and all other EFA partners," the agreement goes on, referring to international and regional governance mechanisms, national governments, and UN-approved "civil society" groups, "must work together to ensure basic education of quality for all." The quality, of course, will be established by those same partners, not local communities or parents. "Successful education" schemes, it continues, "require," among other elements, "a relevant curriculum that can be taught and learned in a local language," as well as "a clear definition and accurate assessment of learning outcomes, including knowledge, skills, attitudes and values."[5] Those definitions will not be set by your local school board, as we shall show shortly.

Despite the virtual media blackout, none of it is much of a secret—even in the United States. In fact, Obama's education secretary, Arne Duncan, even boasts openly that the US Department of Education he leads is "cooperating" with groups such as the United Nations, often dubbed a "dictators' club," to "improve" education in America. In a 2010 speech to UNESCO, Duncan even referred to the UN "education" agency as one of the administration's "global partners" in the effort to globalize schooling as part of the "cradle-to-career education agenda."[6]

"Today, education is a global public good unconstrained by national boundaries. . . . It is no surprise that economic interdependence brings new global challenges and educational demands," Duncan told the globalist UN bureaucrats, boasting of the billions of dollars US taxpayers were being forced to send foreign governments and institutions for "educational reform" abroad. "Our goal for the coming year will be to work closely with global partners, including UNESCO, to promote qualitative improvements and system-strengthening."[7]

More recently, a 2012 US Department of Education report made similar claims. "In today's globalized world, an effective domestic education agenda must address global needs and trends and aim to develop a globally competent citizenry," states the document, dubbed *Succeeding Globally through International Education and Engagement.*[8] In addition to boasting about globalizing US education and using Common Core to integrate American schools with the world, the document boasts of the education bureaucracy's collaboration with communist and socialist autocracies.

Unsurprisingly, billionaire UN devotee and population-control zealot Bill Gates—the primary financier of all things Common Core, other than US taxpayers via the federal government—is deeply intertwined with the planetary effort, too. According to the latest estimates, while his own children attend an elite, non–Common Core private school, the Microsoft founder has poured more than $2 billion into creating and promoting the dubious national standards for everyone else.[9]

In 2004, on behalf of Microsoft, Gates personally signed a "Cooperation Agreement" with UNESCO to accelerate the globalization of education through information technology and communication. "Together, UNESCO and Microsoft aspire for there to be a quantum leap in the quality of courses and in accelerating their uptake by educationalists . . . through the availability of standards, guidelines or benchmarks," the agreement explains, calling for the creation of a "master curriculum (Syllabus)." "UNESCO will explore how to facilitate content development," the document states.[10]

After signing the agreement, as reported by *Eagle Forum* chief Phyllis Schlafly in 2005, UNESCO director general Koichiro Matsuura gave a speech offering more insight into the plan. Among the goals of the partnership, the UN agency boss explained: "fostering web-based communities of practice including content development and worldwide curricula reflecting UNESCO values." As the document itself also explains, "Microsoft supports the objectives of UNESCO as stipulated in UNESCO's Constitution." Bill Gates is also a major financier of UNESCO, the UN Population Fund, UN ally and abortion giant Planned Parenthood, and more.[11]

More recently, in an official 2011 document about an advanced training program produced by UNESCO's International Institute for Educational Planning, the would-be global Department of Education even uses the term "Common Core." The course outline, which boasts that the UN institute had trained "more than 1,500 education planners and managers" from around the world, adds under the heading "Common Core": "Educational planners and managers need insight into the effects of demographic shifts, globalization, and social and political change on education."[12]

"The fourth part of the course presents the main development frameworks, including the 'new' international commitments as part of Education for All/ Fast Track Initiative, Poverty Reduction, Millennium Development Goals, and discusses their impact on the role and methods/instruments of educational planning," continues the document, which essentially outlines the training program being used to put legions of globalized education bureaucrats devoted to UNESCO's vision in key positions worldwide.[13]

UNESCO's vision for a truly global education regime under the "World Core Curriculum" or something similar goes back decades, too, as its officials openly admit. "In the middle of my life I discovered that the only true, objective education I had received was from the United Nations where the earth, humanity, our place in time and the worth of the human being were the overriding concerns," wrote the late Robert Muller, former UN assistant secretary-general and the architect of the "World Core Curriculum" plan. "So at the request of educators I wrote the World Core Curriculum, the product of the United Nations, the meta-organism of human and planetary evolution."[14]

Muller described his planetary Common Core–like scheme as "a curriculum of our universal knowledge which should be taught in all schools of Earth." One of his chief inspirations, he said, was former UN secretary-general U Thant, a Marxist radical, whom Muller quoted as saying: "The world will not change and find peace, if there is not a new education."[15] Another one of Muller's major inspirations was UN apparatchik and occultist Alice Bailey, who founded the Lucis Trust (formerly Lucifer Publishing Company) and claimed to channel spirits. If you really want to take a trip down the rabbit hole, spend some time researching Bailey and her books.

Bailey, a theosophist who played a key role in the emergence of the modern New Age movement, held deeply controversial views, to put it mildly. A brief examination of her work—she claimed it was provided to her by an ascended "Master of Wisdom" known as the "Tibetan," or Djwal Khul—offers a great deal of insight into the bizarre and potentially dangerous views of the increasingly influential global education establishment. Among other major motifs, Bailey devoted considerable effort to attacking the Judeo-Christian traditions of the West as the world moves toward her vision of a single global religion in preparation for the coming "Age of Aquarius." "There will not be any dissociation between the Universal Church, the Sacred Lodge of all true Masons and the inner circles of the esoteric societies," she wrote in *Externalisation of the Hierarchy*, perhaps her most important book. "In this way, the goals and work of the United Nations shall be solidified and a new Church of God, led by all the religions and by all of the spiritual groups, shall put an end to the great heresy of separateness."[16] For Christians and Jews, the implications should be obvious. In her book *Education in the New Age*, Bailey explains how attacking individualism is crucial on the road toward global government. "World Citizenship should be the goal of the enlightened, with a world federation and a world brain," she adds.[17] While the ideas may sound wild to Americans, Bailey's influence in the UN—and particularly in UNESCO and its education schemes—cannot be emphasized strongly enough.

UNESCO's use of the term "Common Core," too, goes back decades. In 1984, for example—the same year President Ronald Reagan withdrew US participation from the UN agency due to its anti-American, anti-freedom scheming—the outfit released a fifty-one-page document titled *A Methodological Guide to the Application of the Notion of Common Core in the Training of Various Categories of Educational Personnel*. That plot was aimed at training teachers worldwide using the same standards so that they, in turn, could fan out across the globe to "educate" students all over the world. President George W. Bush eventually rejoined UNESCO on behalf of the US government.

Even as far back as the late 1940s, UNESCO was actively promoting the use of globalized education as a means to achieve what its first secretary general, Huxley, described as "political unification in some sort of world government," which he claimed was "necessary."[18] In a widely quoted 1949 series on using the classroom to promote "world understanding," UNESCO said: "As long as the child breathes the poisoned air of nationalism, education in world-mindedness can only produce precarious results." So, to deal with that, schools should use various means to "combat family attitudes."[19] In other words, UNESCO wants to be the source of values for your child—and it wants to obliterate the values parents attempt to instill in their children. Countless other UNESCO officials and leaders have made that clear as well.

What are those UN values that should be instilled in your children? In essence, official UN documents and statements by top administration officials reveal a plan to transform American children, and students around the globe, into what globalists refer to as "global citizens" ready for the coming "green" and "sustainable" world order.[20]

In recent years especially, UN reports and top world leaders have been openly boasting of their globalist scheme to create a top-down, planned, and regimented society. By its nature, that vision is completely at odds with the US Constitution, national sovereignty, individual liberty, God-given rights, Judeo-Christian values, and Western traditions. It is also at odds with traditional notions of education, as we shall show.

A major component of the globalized education plan surrounds so-called sustainability and a radical UN program known as Agenda 21 encompassing virtually every facet of life. To prepare humanity for their vision, however, requires a new form of "education," the globalist education reformers admit. UNESCO calls the "new" system it seeks to foist on humanity "Education for Sustainable Development."[21]

On its website, the self-styled global education agency actually boasts of its plans. "The UN Decade of Education for Sustainable Development (2005–2014) seeks to mobilize the educational resources of the world to help create a more sustainable future," the UN outfit explains. "Many paths to sustainability . . . exist and are mentioned in the forty chapters of *Agenda 21*, the official document of the 1992 Earth Summit. Education is one of these paths. Education alone cannot achieve a more sustainable future; however, without education and learning for sustainable development, we will not be able to reach that goal."[22]

Digging into the actual text of the UN Agenda 21 agreement reveals even more. The UN plot was signed by Skull and Bonesman president George H. W. Bush. While never ratified by the Senate, it is nonetheless being implemented quietly at all levels of government across the United States. The scheme encompasses literally every aspect of human life, as the UN explains openly. Here, we shall concern ourselves only with the "education" component.

In chapter 25, which deals with children, the official UN Agenda 21 document states that governments must "ensure access for all youth to all types of education" and "ensure that education . . . incorporates the concepts of environmental awareness and sustainable development throughout the curricula."[23]

Chapter 36 is even more explicit, saying:

> Education is critical for promoting sustainable development and improving the capacity of the people to address environment and development issues. While basic education provides the underpinning for any environmental and development education, the latter needs to be incorporated as an essential part of learning. Both formal and non-formal education are indispensable to changing people's attitudes so that they have the capacity to assess and address their sustainable development concerns. It is also critical for achieving environmental and ethical awareness, values and attitudes, skills and behaviour consistent with sustainable development and for effective public participation in decision-making. To be effective, environment and development education should deal with the dynamics of both the physical/

biological and socio-economic environment and human (which may include spiritual) development, should be integrated in all disciplines, and should employ formal and non-formal methods and effective means of communication.[24]

Another key element will be ensuring that teachers worldwide are prepared to train students for the new sustainable order, as shown in the UNESCO "Guidelines and Recommendations for Reorienting Teacher Education to Address Sustainability."[25]

Before the term "sustainability" was in vogue, the late UN deputy secretary-general Muller of UNESCO's World Core Curriculum also offered some insight into the purpose of UN-led, globalized pseudoeducation. The goals, as he explained them: "Assisting the child in becoming an integrated individual who can deal with personal experience while seeing himself as a part of 'the greater whole.' In other words, promote growth of the group idea, so that group good, group understanding, group interrelations and group goodwill replace all limited, self-centered objectives, leading to group consciousness."[26] Put another way, the smashing of individualism and notions of individual rights, to be replaced with collectivism. Note the parallel with John Dewey's radical vision, sans occultism, described earlier in this book.

While the color red has fallen out of favor owing largely to its association with communist terror and mass murder, the same general goals now go under a new color: green. The self-styled "greens," however, are often referred to as "watermelons" for being green on the outside, and red on the inside. In 2014, UN climate change czar Christiana Figueres declared that Red China's political system was better suited than America's to fight "global warming."[27] Consider all of that as we use the reform architects' own words to describe the values at the heart of the globalized "green" education plan they are building at this very moment.

So what will children learn in the "green" world order? In a 2010 speech at a "Sustainability Summit," Obama Education Secretary

Duncan offered more than a few hints. He said the US Department of Education "is taking a leadership role in the work of educating the next generation of *green citizens* and *preparing them to contribute to the workforce through green jobs*" (emphasis added). Obama's former "Green Jobs" czar, Van Jones, of course, was eventually forced to resign after his own words exposed him as a "red" self-described "communist." As Duncan makes clear, central planners will determine what jobs citizens will have in the "green economy." And central planners will train them accordingly via their new "education" regime.[28]

The unconstitutional federal education bureaucracy is not alone in the plot to transform America's youth, Duncan continued, pointing to numerous other US agencies and departments that "have made important contributions linking education and sustainability." In the United States, he explained, like the imposition of Common Core on state governments, much of the federal effort to indoctrinate young Americans into the "sustainable development" agenda is being funded by the so-called stimulus plan (also known as the American Recovery and Reinvestment Act).[29]

At the global level, the World Bank, multiple UN agencies, Big Labor, Big Business, tax-funded so-called nongovernmental organizations, and more are all involved in harmonizing and globalizing education for "sustainability" as well.

"Historically, the Department of Education hasn't been doing enough in the sustainability movement," Duncan claimed in his speech, omitting the fact that the federal government has been lawlessly pushing similar schemes to transform and undermine values in US schools for decades now—under both Republican and Democratic presidential administrations. "Today, I promise you that we will be a committed partner in the national effort to build a more environmentally literate and responsible society."[30]

He added, "We must advance the sustainability movement through education," perhaps unaware that the vast majority of parents send their children to school to be educated, not to advance the sustainability movement. "We at the Education Department are energized about joining these leaders in their commitment to preparing today's students to participate in the green economy, and to be well-educated about the science of sustainability."[31]

The basic idea of the plotters is to restructure human civilization into a centrally planned global society under the control of international institutions such as the UN—all under the guise of "sustainable development." In fact, they say so themselves in countless reports and documents, even though, ironically enough, central planning has always and everywhere produced environmental devastation in addition to human misery, starvation, terror, death, and more.

Official UN documents show, for example, that under the "green economy" banner, literally everything about human existence must dramatically change: lifestyles, opinions, education, health, consumption, production, agriculture, diet, law, taxation, industry, governance, and much more. "Transitioning to a green economy requires a fundamental shift in the way we think and act," explains a 2012 UN report entitled *Working towards a Balanced and Inclusive Green Economy.*"[32] A more recent UN report, developed with help from Obama policy architect John Podesta, noted that the "worldview" and "behavior" of every person on earth must be "alter[ed] . . . dramatically."[33]

UN documents also make clear that national sovereignty, individual liberty, free markets, unalienable rights, traditional values, self-government, biblical religion, and more must all be pushed aside. Central planning will take its place. Even the UN's so-called Universal Declaration of Human Rights makes that explicit in Article 29, where it says: "These rights and freedoms may in no case be exercised contrary to the purposes and principles of the United Nations."[34]

Sex education, too, is a crucial component of the emerging new globalized education regime. The radical "National Sexuality Education Standards" being rolled out across America with Common Core, will ensure that American children get their dose of perversion and sexualization from kindergarten to high school.[35]

At the global level, UNESCO is working fiendishly to ensure that every child in the world receives his "fair share" as well—

much of it under the guise of supposedly preventing AIDS and other STDs. The contents would shock most parents. In the 2009 UNESCO report *International Guidelines for Sexuality Education*, one of many such documents, the UN outfit demands teaching children starting at age five that masturbation is "pleasurable." At age nine, they begin lessons on "aphrodisiacs," "homophobia," and "transphobia"—as well as the purported safety of legal abortion, and at age fifteen they learn how to "promote the right to and access to safe abortion."[36] Every type of perversion is included in the "guidelines" as well. So the kids will learn about sexualization *and* how to be good "green" and "global" citizens.

The 2012 US Department of Education document *Succeeding Globally through International Education and Engagement* states: "It is no longer enough to focus solely on ensuring that students have essential reading, writing, mathematics, and science skills." Now, in today's "globalized" world, "an effective domestic education agenda must address global needs and trends and aim to develop a globally competent citizenry."[37]

Traditional and classical notions of education have no place in the "sustainable" future being planned for humanity. In fact, a startling admission posted directly on UNESCO's website makes that about as explicit as can be.

"Generally, more highly educated people, who have higher incomes, consume more resources than poorly educated people, who tend to have lower incomes," the UN "toolkit" for global, "sustainable" education explains. "In this case, *more education increases the threat to sustainability*" (emphasis added).[38] In other words, more education leads to higher incomes, which leads to more consumption, and therefore, is not compatible with their vision of "sustainability."

As the UN makes clear in numerous documents, freedom, prosperity, and even the current population of about seven billion people are not compatible with "sustainability" either. In other words, poverty, illiteracy, and ignorance are good for sustainability.[39]

Open admissions about the purpose of the new, centralized vision of "education" being promoted and foisted on humanity—and on Americans—go back decades. The same ideas have been quietly burrowing their way into US schools for decades as well, even featuring largely the same cast of characters responsible for more modern manifestations of it all, such as Common Core.

Consider, for example, a 1989 speech given by Dr. Shirley McCune to a national education summit held in Kansas by the federally funded National Governors Association. She said, "What is happening in America today and what is happening to Kansas in the Great Plains is not simply a chance situation in the usual winds of change. What it amounts to is a *total transformation of our society.* So we have to anticipate what the future is and then move back and figure out what it is we need to do today. That's called anticipatory *socialization or the social change function of schools.*"[40]

Incredibly, the governors applauded upon being told that the purpose of education was now central planning and totally transforming society.

Dr. McCune, who has also worked with the National Education Association, the US Department of Education, and other top establishment entities behind the education regime, was not shy about sharing the long-term agenda with the nation's governors either. "You have to understand the breadth of the task that's before us," she continued. "You cannot think about restructuring of education without understanding that our total society is in a crisis of restructuring and you can't get away from it . . . what we are facing is a total restructuring of the society."

In 2004, meanwhile, the NGA, then chaired by Virginia governor Mark Warner, produced a report confirming yet again that the outfit's vision of government education was essentially to create a centrally planned society. Among the most astounding admissions highlighted by alarmed critics, the document celebrates:

- using schools to feed workers into selected corporations;

- identifying their state's key industries and needs for skilled workers in order to define a common agenda between their workforce and economic development programs;

- the integration of education, economic development, and workforce development policies;

- seamless connections between the components of the [education] system and with the skill demands of the workplace; and

- connecting workforce development to economic needs.[41]

If all of that sounds Maoist or Soviet-ish to you, good; it should. If it sounds suspiciously like the UN and UNESCO plots outlined previously, good; it should. How many parents, though, send their children to school so central planners can mold them into functionally illiterate cogs in a centrally planned machine, having just enough knowledge to do their preassigned tasks? How will such cogs be able to think critically, much less sustain liberty and the American experiment? The short answer is that they will not—and that is the point.

On the important subject of teaching reading, UNESCO has produced its own manual on the subject: *Guide to Teaching Reading at the Primary School Level* (2005) It advocates a "balanced approach" in which a whole-word method is mixed with phonetic information that adds up to the most confusing, irrational, and nonsensical reading program ever invented by so-called educators. In other words, high literacy is not the aim of the UNESCO program, which states:

The contemporary approach is a balanced one, which includes the strengths of previous methods. The method uses literature to teach skills and focuses on reading for meaning integrated with direct instruction in skill development for decoding and comprehension. Phonetics can be useful when incorporated into a balanced approach. However, *it should not share equal emphasis with reading comprehension.* The purpose of phonetics and other decoding strategies is to create additional means for improving reading comprehension and help learners understand the meaning of what they read. *Phonetics should not be viewed as skill pupils learn before using and interacting with authentic literature,* but rather is taught within the context of reading and writing (Irwin, 1967). Skill instruction should be mixed in reading and writing activities, and not presented as a separate activity. . . .

Children should be able to learn sight vocabulary in context rather than in isolation. Teachers could use word lists in order to compare and contrast, classify words or use tags and signs as a context for teaching sight vocabulary.[42]

Please note that according to the *New York Times* of June 22, 2014, Teachers College, Columbia, is offering the schools of New York City a new "balanced literacy" program similar to the one described by UNESCO.[43] It was at Teachers College that John Dewey and his colleagues launched their plan to dumb down America by changing the way children are taught to read. In other words, the conspiracy launched more than a hundred years ago is still being advanced by Dewey's present-day disciples.

At this point, we've established that the emerging global "education" paradigm intends to dumb down children and instill radical new values in all of humanity. Tyrants and would-be tyrants always understood that controlling education—and the minds of the young, by extension—was the key to maintaining power. From Marx and Stalin to Hitler, all of them knew that corrupting children was their path to total domination—that is why Marx included government schooling in his ten planks of the *Communist Manifesto.*

In his masterpiece *On Liberty* (1859), renowned British philosopher and parliamentarian John Stuart Mill succinctly explained the inherent problems with government schools even before those tyrants exploded on the scene with their murderous plans. He wrote:

"A general State education is a mere contrivance for moulding people to be exactly like one another; and as the mould in which it casts them is that which pleases the predominant power in the government . . . it establishes a despotism over the mind, leading by natural tendency to one over the body."

In sum, American progressives plan to hand over American children to a global education authority that will train them to become slaves in what globalists refer to as the "new world order." Children's attitudes and values will have been changed so that they will gladly give up the rights and protections of the US Constitution and comply with the dictates of global sustainability. This criminal plan to transform American children into slaves of world government must be exposed for what it is. The purpose of this book is to educate the American people, for as we are reminded by the prophet Hosea: "My people are destroyed for lack of knowledge" (Hosea 4:6).

31

THE FUTURE OF EDUCATION: HOPE REMAINS

Expect the rapidly expanding homeschooling movement to play a signifi-
cant role in the revolutionary reforms needed to build a free society with
Constitutional protections.
—REPRESENTATIVE RON PAUL IN HIS FAREWELL ADDRESS TO CONGRESS, 2012

Despite all of the utopian developments on the horizon, and
taking place at this very moment, there is one very bright
spot. That is the emergence of the fast-growing global homeschooling movement.

In the United States, official estimates suggest that there
are about two million children being homeschooled, with
those numbers climbing higher every year. According to a report
in *Education News*, the number of homeschooled US children grew
by 75 percent between 1999 and 2012, with about 4 percent of
students across America now educated at home.[1]

Even before Common Core, homeschooling numbers were growing about seven times faster than enrollment in government schools. According to expert Brian D. Ray, PhD, of the National Home Education Research Institute, homeschooling "appears to still be the fastest-growing form of education." It is great for taxpayers, too—with homeschoolers spending between $900 and $1,000 per year per student of their own money instead of more than $10,000 per year per student paid by taxpayers to produce illiterate "global" and "green" citizens.[2]

The horror stories surrounding Common Core are bound to convince many parents to consider homeschooling. Anecdotal evidence suggests that a significant move to homeschooling is already taking place. Many news reports in March 2014 reported the trend. The top three reasons cited by homeschooling families for educating at home are: "Can give child better education at home," "Religious reasons," and "Poor learning environment at school."[3]

Countless studies show that homeschoolers do very well academically. Indeed, in 2002, the College Board reported that homeschoolers scored an average of 71 points higher on the SAT than the national average—568 on the verbal section and 525 in math compared with the average of 506 and 514, respectively.[4] Data compiled by NHERI shows that homeschooled students typically score between 15 and 30 points higher than government-schooled kids on the government's own standardized tests.[5] They also scored better on the ACT, had higher GPAs in college, and graduated at a higher rate than others, according to a more recent study in 2010 published in the *Journal of College Admission*.[6] Homeschoolers tend to dominate academic competitions, such as the National Spelling Bee, too. Obviously, college recruiters have taken notice.

Around the world, the home-education movement is exploding as well. While international data about homeschooling is even more incomplete than data about the United States, what evidence does exist suggests the home-education phenomenon is spreading to every corner of the globe—and fast. The trend is especially well documented in English-speaking countries such as New Zealand, Ireland, Australia, the United Kingdom, Canada, South Africa, and more. Even in countries like Russia, home education is legal and growing at a tremendous pace.

In November 2012, I (Alex) had the opportunity to attend the first ever Global Home Education Conference in Berlin, Germany, as a media correspondent. The experience was encouraging, exciting, and depressing all at the same time. At the summit, some two hundred homeschooling leaders, attorneys, policymakers, human rights activists, parents, and experts from all over the globe united in support of one goal: the human right to educate one's own children. Even among many of those who came from nations where authorities restrict home education, the mood was generally optimistic.

"To experience that home educators from different faiths, motivations, methods and cultures have so much more in common than many may have believed was wonderful," said GHEC chairman Jonas Himmelstrand, also the president-in-exile of the Swedish Home Education Association. "Certainly the global home education movement has grown in conviction and strength through this conference."[7]

More than twenty-five countries from every continent except Antarctica were represented at this historic gathering. Among them: Brazil, Russia, Taiwan, South Africa, Canada, the Philippines, South Korea, Ireland, Australia, Switzerland, Luxembourg, Mexico, the United Kingdom, Morocco, France, Spain, Nepal, Bulgaria, Austria, Kenya, Finland, Sweden, the United States, Germany, Poland, and more.

The diversity—true diversity, not the type promoted by the educational criminals—among participants was a sight to behold, from conservative Christians to secular liberals and everything in between. While their views and beliefs varied as widely as their national origins, they all came together in support of the Berlin Declaration demanding that all governments around the world respect educational freedom and human rights.

The Berlin Declaration, the first of its kind endorsed by home-schooling leaders from every corner of the planet, argues that the right to home educate must be respected by every jurisdiction— after all, no government can legitimately violate the fundamental rights of citizens. Citing multiple human rights documents and a growing body of evidence showing the benefits of homeschooling, the document's signatories said the senseless persecution in certain rogue nations must come to an end. Even the controversial United Nations' so-called Universal Declaration of Human Rights, for example—while largely a list of government-issued privileges purportedly revocable on a whim—concedes that "parents have a prior right to choose the kind of education that shall be given to their children,"[8] as more than a few activists at the conference and the Berlin Declaration pointed out. Multiple European human rights treaties enshrine parental rights and home education as well.

Aside from the human rights angle, the Berlin Declaration also points to the well-documented success of homeschoolers academically and socially. "[We] further note that credible and scientific research indicate that home education is an effective means of educating children to become literate and productive citizens and members of civil society," it explains. "[We] commit to support freedom, diversity and pluralism in education through formal and informal coordination with the goal of making home education a legitimate educational option in every nation and the right of every family and child."[9]

Of course, the future of home education is still far from certain. In fact, despite its explosive growth in recent years, threats to homeschooling are growing in tandem—even in the United States, where certain members of the education establishment are becoming increasingly shrill about their desire to regulate or even quash home education. The reason: Consider the old story about the boy who pointed out that the emperor had no clothes. As an innocent, independent thinker, it was obvious to him, but once he pointed it out, suddenly everybody recognized what was going on. Thus, as long as even one child remains free from government indoctrination, there is always the risk that somebody might point out the absurdity of all the "sustainable development" hogwash being foisted on children worldwide.

In Germany, home education has been banned since the days of Adolf Hitler and his barbarian National Socialists, who were determined to ensure that every single child was properly indoctrinated into the Nazi/occultist pseudoreligion with its roots in theosophy and other anti-Christian dogmas. In response to those horrors, the UN adopted the section of its declaration enshrining the rights of parents to direct the upbringing of their children. Still, in Germany today, the persecution of home educators is ruthless, with authorities fining and jailing parents—and even kidnapping their children in some extreme instances.

When the Romeike family fled the German persecution to find educational freedom in America, a US judge initially granted them asylum, only to have the Obama administration fight it tooth and nail. It went all the way to the Supreme Court, which refused to hear the case. While the persecuted family was eventually granted indefinite "deferred action" on deportation, the case has troubling implications for the rights of US homeschoolers, too, and the administration has also made its attitudes on home education crystal clear.

Tragically, in 2010, the Swedish Parliament decided to follow German authorities down that dark road, passing a new education law essentially banning homeschooling and even religious instruction while foisting its bizarre curriculum on every child in the nation. Since then, home-educating Swedish families have either fled the nation or continue homeschooling in defiance of the ban. With the high-profile case of Domenic Johansson, who was abducted by authorities over home education, a cloud of fear always looms large. More recently, in early 2014, French politicians have also introduced similar legislation purporting to ban home education. So the threats are very real—and they are spreading almost as fast as home education.

Again Americans, and humanity at large, currently stand at

a turning point in human history, and education is at the center of it all. On the one side are Obama, Duncan, Common Core, UNESCO, the UN, the "progressive" Dewey legacy in the education establishment, tyrants, communists, Big Labor, Big Business, and other powerful interests determined to centralize and essentially destroy educational freedom. They have, as we hope this book has shown, created a gigantic criminal enterprise that will only get worse as it goes fully global.

On the other side of the battle is the growing global community of parents who seek educational freedom and real education. With liberty to educate, competition, and proper methods of instruction, this movement has the power to crush the criminal syndicate masquerading as the "education" establishment. Home education, private schools, and phonetic instruction methods (along with the high literacy they would produce) could be the key to reversing the trends.

The outcome of this battle between global education and home education has implications for all of humanity that are almost too monumental to contemplate—let alone fully comprehend. Now that you know, choose your side, and take action. There is still hope.

A TEACHER'S TESTIMONIAL ON THE TEACHING OF READING

by Paul Lukawski

have been a high school English teacher for years. I remember in college wanting to know how to teach children to read. I went to a teacher college established in 1910. The school had one of the oldest teacher colleges in the country. Its College of Education enjoyed an excellent reputation. I asked three different professors, "How do you teach reading?" I received three different vague responses. After I completed my second year of teaching, I realized that my students could not read. I taught grades nine through twelve. The second year, I had three classes of ninth graders. I assigned the novel *To Kill a Mockingbird* for them to read. I realized that most of my students could not read the novel's literate narrative.

It was during this time that I heard Samuel Blumenfeld interviewed on shortwave radio. At this time the Rodney King verdict had come in and there was rioting in the streets of L.A. He said that the reason the people were rioting was that they did not have jobs. They did not have jobs because they were illiterate. He said you could tell they were illiterate by listening to the lyrics of the songs they listened to and by the way they talked.

I was intrigued by what he said because it verified my experience as a high school teacher. He then said the schools were at fault because of the way they taught reading. I was again intrigued because of my experience in college trying to determine how to teach children to read. I was never taught it in college.

Mr. Blumenfeld had made two provocative statements on the radio, but I knew them to be true because of my personal experience. I then decided to buy a couple of his books, including *Alpha-Phonics*. My third year of teaching, I had a class of ninth graders that consisted of the worst performing students in the school. These students were in the dropout prevention program. They were waiting until they turned sixteen to drop out of school. I teach in our state's poorest county and our district at that time had a high drop out rate. Also in the class were several students from Mexico and one from Haiti. These students were speakers of other languages (ESOL). Their only problem was that they had a limited understanding of English. Every day in the class was a struggle with disruptive behavior; and if I could finish class without a student being sent to the office for discipline problems, I considered it a success.

The students had chronic discipline problems; they had trouble with the law, every problem you could imagine. After two months of getting absolutely nowhere with the students I decided that I would try an experiment. I was going to use *Alpha-Phonics* beginning with lesson one to teach those that wanted to learn how to read. I told the class that those that wanted to learn would sit on this side of the room, and those that did not were to sit on the opposite side of the room. The only rule was a student could not interfere with the *Alpha-Phonics* lesson.

Until this time, everyone sat scattered around the back of the room, as I did not have a seating chart. Any student, when given the option, will not sit in the front of the room with the teacher. The stage being set, I began the first day by reading the directions from the "Teachers Manual" to *Alpha-Phonics* and beginning with lesson one. I wondered what response I would get.

I was shocked by the response of the students. Nothing could have prepared me for what happened. If someone had told me what would happen I would not have believed them. With the exception of a few students who sat on the other side of the room because they did not want to participate, all of the students followed along as I wrote the lessons on the board. I would write the lesson on the board, read it out loud, and then have them read. The students leaned forward in their desks and followed along.

The next day the students all sat in the front of the room. Everyone would raise their hand and want to read. Indeed, after the first few days, the students would fuss among themselves to read aloud. They fought over who could write the lessons on the board. Everyone wanted to read aloud. Everyone sat in front of the room. There were no discipline problems. The entire class had been transformed. I had discovered a disturbing truth.

We worked through the book; and about halfway through the book, we began reading *Sounder* and *The Old Man and the Sea*. One youth in the class who could not read and who had been a behavior problem told me that every night he would sit with his dad as his dad read the sports section of the paper. He said he always wanted to read the paper with his dad, but he could not because he did not know how to read. A few weeks after starting *Alpha-Phonics,* he entered the class one day and told me that as he was driving down the road he began to sound out the words on the signs. He was excited because he was never able to do that before.

We had started *Alpha-Phonics* in October and the semester ended in December. I would not be seeing the students anymore. We had completed about three-fourths of the book and read the two novels. I would begin each class by doing about 15 minutes of *Alpha-Phonics* and then read from the novels. The students were eager and well behaved. The youth who began reading the signs told me that in the evening he could now sit with his dad and read the sports section along with him. They would talk about what they had read. Three Spanish-speaking students learned English this way.

The following year, I tried another experiment. I had one student who was identified as having ADD/ADHD. He was notorious. He was a ninth grader. This was his first year at our school. I had another student who was in trouble with the dean's office constantly. I gave both of them Sam's *Blumenfeld Oral Reading Test* (BORAT), and they scored between the first- and second-grade levels. I made an arrangement with other teachers to have both students come to my class for fifteen minutes while I did an *Alpha-Phonics* lesson with them.

Because I began in August, I was able to finish the whole book with them by Christmas. I gave both students the BORAT post-test. One boy had doubled his reading score and the other was close behind him. The boy with ADD/ADHD was never antsy or hyperactive when he was working on the lesson. He was a completely different child when he was with me. Indeed, his teacher would often allow him to stay the whole hour with me because he had many behavior problems in her class. He never had a behavior problem when working on *Alpha-Phonics*, neither [was] the other child who was constantly getting into fights and being suspended. When these two youngsters worked on *Alpha-Phonics* with me they were totally different children.

The following year, I worked with some other children. I had developed a system where I would set aside ten minutes each class period and do a few lessons while the rest of the class would work quietly on their own at their desks. I would use the BORAT to identify the illiterates in my class. I would then ask them if they had ever had an A in English. Invariably they would say, "No." I would ask them if they would want one. They would say, "Yes." I then would say that all they had to do was work with me for ten minutes a day on *Alpha-Phonics* until we were done with the book. When we were done with the book, I would choose several pages at random for them to read from. If they could read the pages to me, they would receive an A. I told them that that was all they had to worry about in the class. I was not interested in what they did regarding the usual coursework. That was the incentive I offered them. It was up to them.

One youth had failed the ninth grade and was taking his ninth-grade English class over again with me. He was also taking his tenth-grade English class. His tenth-grade class met next door to mine first period. He would then come to my class second period. His tenth-grade teacher was the same one he took the year before, the class which he had failed. He was working ten minutes a day on *Alpha-Phonics* for several weeks, when one day the door that communicated between my room and the neighboring room opened. It was his tenth-grade teacher. She called me over to her and asked what it was I was doing with him. I told her *Alpha-Phonics*. She said, "Look!" The whole class was watching Channel One and chatting. It was during homeroom. The whole class, except this youth, who was busy reading a book I had given him. The teacher was flabbergasted. She knew he was illiterate and could not believe that he was able to read.

One day I was working with this boy at my desk when we had a new student enter the class. He had just been released from juvenile detention. He knew the youth I was working with and sat by him as we worked together. He was curious about what we were doing, and I explained it to him. He said that he could not read either. He explained that he started having trouble reading in the third grade. He said that when the time came to read aloud he would intentionally get into trouble so he would be sent to the office so that he would not have to read. He could not take the embarrassment. He did not want anyone to know that he could not read. The boy I was working with chimed in and said that he was the same way. They both recounted events when they would get into trouble on purpose so they could avoid reading. They would even start fistfights. The boy who had been in juvenile detention was sent there because he had set fire to the junior high school.

The following year I had firmly established my regular ten-minute routine in my class, and every year after that I would have students who would participate. One year I was in a staffing meeting for a boy who was labeled as a special education student with learning disabilities. The special education staffer, whom I had never met before, asked me what I was doing with the boy. The reason she asked is that she was with the boy's science teacher when the science teacher had reported that the boy began volunteering to read aloud. The science teacher was astonished. We live in a small community and the teacher had known the boy ever since kindergarten and had known that he could not read, thus the placement in the special education program. Here he was volunteering to read aloud in her class. I told them what it was I was doing.

There is one case that haunts me. I had a big, strapping youth who was seventeen years old. He had failed ninth- and tenth-grade English because he could not read. He was in my ninth-grade English class. I had given him the BORAT test, and he was at about the first- or second-grade level: a typical case. We began working ten minutes a day. After a month I gave him the book *Sounder,* and he told me he was reading it at home. We were about halfway through the book when he no longer showed up in my class. I learned that he had moved away. I do not know if he ever completely learned how to read. He was a decent, well-mannered youth who would show up every day, was polite, and carried a big stack of books with him. He was waiting for someone to teach him to read.

My daughter was born in 1996. I remember seeing the little girl read in the *Hooked on Phonics* commercials and wished my daughter could read like her. When she was two, I began to teach her how to read during my summer vacation. She would take naps then, and I followed the advice in the teacher's manual. I set up a routine. Every day, before she took her nap, we would sit together. Following Sam's advice, I appealed to her intellect. I said, "It is time for our lessons." I began by following the alphabet prereading exercises in the back of the book. Again, following Mr. Blumenfeld's advice, I did not pressure her or scold her, regardless of her behavior. Some days, she would kick at the book and giggle. I would say, "You did a good job today!" And I put the book away. We would continue tomorrow. It went on like this for several months.

When school started again she would do the lessons with me before we went to bed. She enjoyed the routine and the lessons. One evening, while my wife was in the room, she took out the book on her own and began reading from lesson two: "Am, Sam, Hear the S sound," she said. Then, "Sam sat," etc. My wife could not believe it. "Did she memorize those words?" She asked. "No," I replied, and then explained the method.

When [our daughter] was three, we were driving down the road when she said, "Look, Momma," pointing to a sign, "*Marshall's*, there is your store!" My wife could not believe it. When she was three, there was one occasion when our daughter was at Sunday school. Her teachers were arguing over whether or not she was reading the colors on the crayons. "She's memorized them," said one. "No, she is reading them," said the other. The colors she was reading were purple, fuchsia and magenta. Magenta was her favorite.

The spring before my daughter began kindergarten she could read fluently any word in front of her. We were at a spring festival when my daughter and her friend bought soft drinks. My daughter read the inside of the cap, which told whether or not you had won a prize advertised on the side of the can. My daughter read the label effortlessly, which included the words *vacation* and *discovery*. "She is a genius!" exclaimed the [other girl's] father.

My daughter's friend asked her dad to read the soft drink label to her. I told the girl's father that his daughter could read as well if he used *Alpha-Phonics* with her. I said, "Follow the lesson manual and be patient, do not pressure your child, as Mr. Blumenfeld says, and in a year or so she will be like my daughter."

That fall I saw the girl's parents and asked how she was doing. He said his daughter had not really taken to the book yet. (His daughter had just started kindergarten, as mine had.) I said, "Be patient and keep going." Meanwhile, my daughter was reading at the second-grade level; and during kindergarten reading time, she would go to a second-grade class for reading instruction. The following year I saw the girl's dad again and asked him how she was doing in first grade. He said that his daughter was reading at a second-grade level and was being tested for gifted and talented.

Meanwhile my daughter entered the first grade and soon afterward was referred to the gifted and talented program. She won the spelling bee and Math bash just as she did in kindergarten. I used Samuel Blumenfeld's *How-to-Tutor* to instruct her in math. In second grade, she read at the seventh-grade level, won all of the reading, spelling, and math prizes, and was elected to the school's hall of fame. She has had straight As in every class. She learned to read with *Alpha-Phonics* and learned math with *How-to-Tutor*.

While my daughter was in first grade, I was asked to sit on a parent-teacher committee. While on the committee, the mayor of our town complained to the principal that he had been on the committee for three years and that the committee was always talking about doing something outside the box when it came to improving the school's reading scores. Regardless of what the committee did to improve reading scores, they were always the same. The principal said that he was open for suggestions outside the box.

No one had any suggestions, so I said that I was familiar with the method of reading instruction in the public schools and that was what was at fault. I said that I had a method that worked better. Indeed, I said that if I dropped my daughter off at school at 7:30, I could walk into any class, give a ten-minute lesson, and still arrive at the high school where I teach in time to sign in at 8:00 a.m. I said that, if anyone doubted me, I get a paycheck every two weeks with a comma in it; let's put it on the table and keep the tourists out. I wanted to let them know my intentions were serious.

They took me up on the offer, and a first-year teacher volunteered her class. I began the first Monday after spring break. I had only six weeks to work with the children. I made transparencies of the *Alpha-Phonics* lessons and followed the teacher's manual. I did only a ten-minute lesson. The first-year teacher combined her bottom-half students with the reading teacher's bottom-half students. After two weeks, the mother of one of the children approached me. She said, "I am glad you are working with my daughter. A while back the school called me up to their office and told me there was something wrong with my daughter. She had a learning disability. I cried for two days." I told her not to listen to anything the schools told her, to be patient and to watch what happens.

A week after school was over, I saw the mother again and I asked her how her daughter was doing. She said that the school had called her up again and told her that they had given her daughter an end-of-the-year reading test showing that she had a 40 percent improvement in her reading and they were going to put her into an advanced class.

The following year, I was asked to do the project again with a first-grade class. I worked ten minutes each morning. I was able to complete only three-fourths of the book. The school's diagnostic test revealed that, of the children who were able to complete the project successfully, not one had a reading disability. The makers of the diagnostic test said that you could expect 20 percent of the children to have reading disabilities.

I once was explaining to a student why children have reading problems. When I finished, a girl from the other side of the class, who I thought was not listening, said, "This is what happened to my brother. He is in the fourth grade, hates to read, and gets stomach-aches and headaches." I told her that his troubles were over and gave her a copy of *Alpha-Phonics*. Four months later, I asked how was her brother doing. She said he completed the book and reads just fine.

I had the same success with students in special education, who were labeled as learning disabled or educatably mentally retarded. I have 100 percent success with every student. The only variable is the speed at which students progress. You must follow Dr. Blumenfeld's advice and be patient. Do not pressure the child.

I have many other heartbreaking stories about children who have quit school because they did not know how to read, and no one will teach them. I have had children take a copy of *Alpha-Phonics* and keep it to teach their friends how to read. I encouraged everyone to try *Alpha-Phonics*. The results you see in the child are truly miraculous. It must be seen to be believed.

P.S. (August 17, 2013): I am currently tutoring several immigrant children from Bangladesh, including a kindergartener. I helped him complete *Alpha-Phonics* this summer. He can read all 124 lessons aloud with nary an error. I told the mother that this fall as he enters first grade the school will test him, and as a result of his reading ability he will be catapulted into the gifted program, as this happened to my daughter. She had completed *Alpha-Phonics* before kindergarten. Consequently, when her kindergarten class would spend their 30 minutes a day learning "reading," she was sent to a second-grade class to read. She is a senior in high school this year and scored a 31 on ACT, to the amazement of everyone. Yale is attempting to recruit her and she wants to be a cardiologist. *Alpha-Phonics* is first in line for any credit, as it maximized her nascent potential and linguistic development.

JOHN DEWEY'S PLAN TO DUMB DOWN AMERICA

THE PRIMARY EDUCATION FETICH
As It Appeared in the FORUM,
Vol. XXV, May 1898, Pages 315–328
(Reformatted by Bob Montgomery Thomas, April 30, 2013)

It is some years since the educational world was more or less agitated by an attack upon the place occupied by Greek in the educational scheme. If, however, Greek occupies the place of a fetich, its worshippers are comparatively few in number, and its influence is relatively slight. There is, however, a false educational god whose idolaters are legion, and whose cult influences the entire educational system. This is language-study—the study not of foreign language, but of English; not in higher, but in primary education. It is almost an unquestioned assumption, of educational theory and practice both, that the first three years of a child's school life shall be mainly taken up with learning to read and write his own language. If we add to this the learning or a certain amount of numerical combinations, we have the pivot about which primary education swings. Other subjects may be taught; but they are introduced in strict subordination.

The very fact that this procedure, as part of the natural and established course of education, is assumed as inevitable—opposition being regarded as captious and revolutionary—indicates that, historically, there are good reasons for the position assigned to these studies. It does not follow, however, that because this course was once wise it is so any longer. On the contrary, the fact, that this mode of education was adapted to past conditions, is in itself a reason why it should no longer hold supreme sway. The present has its claims. It is in education, if anywhere, that the claims of the present should be controlling. To educate on the basis of past surroundings is like adapting an organism to an environment, which no longer exists. The individual is stultified, if not disintegrated; and the course of progress is blocked. My proposition is, that conditions—social, industrial, and intellectual—have undergone such a radical change, that the time has come for a thoroughgoing examination of the emphasis put upon linguistic work in elementary instruction.

The existing status was developed in a period when ability to read was practically the sole avenue to knowledge, when it was the only tool which insured control over the accumulated spiritual resources of civilization. Scientific methods of observation, experimentation, and testing were either unknown or confined to a few specialists at the upper end of the educational ladder. Because these methods were not free, were not capable of anything like general use, it was not possible to permit the pupil to begin his school career in direct contact with the materials of nature and of life. The only guarantee, the only criterion of values, was found in the ways in which the great minds of the past had assimilated and interpreted such materials. To avoid intellectual chaos and confusion, it was necessary reverently to retrace the steps of the fathers. The régime of intellectual authority and tradition, in matters of politics, morals, and culture, was a necessity, where methods of scientific investigation and verification had not been developed, or were in the hands of the few. We often fail to see that the dominant position occupied by book-learning in school education is simply a corollary and relic of this epoch of intellectual development.

Ordinary social conditions were congruent with this intellectual status. While it cannot be said that, in the formative period of our educational system in America, authority and tradition were the ultimate sources of knowledge and belief, it must be remembered that the immediate surroundings of our ancestors were crude and undeveloped. Newspapers, magazines, libraries, art-galleries, and all the daily play of intellectual intercourse and reaction which is effective today were non-existent. If any escape existed from the poverty of the intellectual environment, or any road to richer and wider mental life, the exit was through the gateway of books. In presenting the attainments of the past, these maintained the bonds of spiritual continuity, and kept our forefathers from falling to the crude level of their material surroundings.

When ability to read and write marked the distinction between the educated and the uneducated man, not simply in the scholastic sense, but in the sense of one who is enslaved by his environment and one who is able to take advantage of and rise above it, corresponding importance attached to acquiring these capacities. Reading and writing were obviously what they are still so often called—the open doors to learning and to success in life. All the meaning that belongs to these ends naturally transferred itself to the means through which alone they could be realized. The intensity and ardor with which our forefathers set themselves to master reading and writing, the difficulties overcome, the interest attached in the ordinary routine of school-life to what now seems barren—the curriculum of the three Rs—all testify to the motive-power these studies possessed. To learn to read and write was an interesting, even exciting, thing: it made such a difference in life.

It is hardly necessary to say that the conditions, intellectual as well as social, have changed. There are undoubtedly rural regions where the old state of things still persists. With reference to these, what I am saying has no particular meaning. But, upon the whole, the advent of quick and cheap mails, of easy and continuous travel and transportation, of the telegraph and telephone, the establishment of libraries, art-galleries, literary clubs, the universal diffusion of cheap reading-matter, newspapers and magazines of all kinds and grades—all these have worked a tremendous change in the immediate intellectual environment. The values of life and of civilization, instead of being far away and correspondingly inaccessible, press upon the individual—at least in cities—with only too much urgency and stimulating force. We are more likely to be surfeited than starved: there is more congestion than lack of intellectual nutriment.

The capital handed down from past generations, and upon whose transmission the integrity of civilization depends, is no longer amassed in those banks termed books, but is in active and general circulation, at an extremely low rate of interest. It is futile to try to conceal from ourselves the fact that this great change in the intellectual atmosphere—this great change in the relation of the individual to accumulated knowledge—demands a corresponding educational readjustment. The significance attaching to reading and writing, as primary and fundamental instruments of culture, has shrunk proportionately as the immanent intellectual life of society has quickened and multiplied. The result is that these studies lose their motive and motor force. They have become mechanical and formal, and out of relation—when made dominant—to the rest of life.

They are regarded as more or less arbitrary tasks which must be submitted to because one is going to that mysterious thing called a school, or else are covered up and sugar-coated with all manner of pretty devices and tricks in order that the child may absorb them unawares. The complaint made by some, that the school curriculum of today does not have the disciplinary value of the old-fashioned three Rs, has a certain validity. But this is not because the old ideal has been abandoned. It is because it has been retained in spite of the change of conditions. Instead of frankly facing the situation, and asking ourselves what studies can be organized which shall do for to-day what language-study did for former generations, we have retained that as the centre and core of our course of study, and dressed it out with a variety of pretty pictures, objects, and games, and a smattering of science.

Along with this change in the relation of intellectual material and stimulus to the individual there has been an equally great change in the method and make-up of knowledge itself. Science and art have become free. The simplest processes and methods of knowing and doing have been worked out to such a point that they are no longer the monopolistic possessions of any class or guild. They are, in idea, and should be in deed, part of the social commonwealth. It is possible to initiate the child from the first in a direct, not abstract or symbolical, way, into the operations by which society maintains its existence, material and spiritual.

The processes of production, transportation, consumption, etc., by which society keeps up its material continuity, are conducted on such a large and public scale that they are obvious and objective. Their reproduction in embryonic form through a variety of modes of industrial training is entirely within the bounds of possibility. Moreover, methods of the discovery and communication of truth—upon which the spiritual unity of society depends—have become direct and independent, instead of remote and tied to the intervention of teacher or book. It is not simply that children can acquire a certain amount of scientific information about things organic and inorganic: if that were all, the plea for the study of the history and literature of the past, as more humanistic, would be unanswerable. No; the significant thing is that it is possible for the child at an early day to become acquainted with, and to use, in a personal and yet relatively controlled fashion, the methods by which truth is discovered and communicated, and to make his own speech a channel for the expression and communication of truth; thus putting the linguistic side where it belongs—subordinate to the appropriation and conveyance of what is genuinely and personally experienced.

A similar modification, almost revolution, has taken place in the relation which the intellectual activities bear to the ordinary practical occupations of life. While the child of bygone days was getting an intellectual discipline whose significance he appreciated in the school, in his home life he was securing acquaintance in a direct fashion with the chief lines of social and industrial activity. Life was in the main rural. The child came into contact with the scenes of nature, and was familiarized with the care of domestic animals, the cultivation of the soil, and the raising of crops. The factory system being undeveloped, the home was the centre of industry. Spinning, weaving, the making of clothes, etc., were all carried on there. As there was little accumulation of wealth, the child had to take part in these, as well as to participate in the usual rounds of household occupations. Only those who have passed through such training, and, later on, have seen children reared in city environments, can adequately realize the amount of training, mental and moral, involved in this extra-school life. That our successful men have come so largely from the country is an indication of the educational value bound up with such participation in this practical life. It was not only an adequate substitute for what we now term manual training, in the development of the hand and eye, in the acquisition skill and deftness; but it was initiation into self-reliance, independence of judgment and action, and was the best stimulus to habits of regular and continuous work.

In the urban and suburban life of a child to-day this is simply a memory. The invention of machinery; the institution of the factory system; the division of labor; have changed the home from a work-shop into a simple dwelling-place. The crowding into cities and the increase in servants have deprived the child of an opportunity to take part in those occupations which still remain. Just at the time when a child is subjected to a great increase in stimulus and pressure from his environment, he loses the practical and motor training neces-sary to balance his intellectual development. Facility in acquiring information is gained: the power of using it is lost. While need of the more formal intellectual training in the school has decreased, there arises an urgent demand for the introduction of methods of manual and industrial discipline which shall give the child what he formerly obtained in his home and social life.

Here we have at least a prima facie case for reconsideration of the whole question of the relative importance of learning to read and write in primary education. Hence the necessity of meeting the question at closer quarters. What can be said against giving up the greater portion of the first two years of school life to the mastery of linguistic form? In the first place, physiologists are coming to believe that the sense organs and connected nerve and motor apparatus of the child are not at this period best adapted to the confining and analytic work of learning to read and write. There is an order in which sensory and motor centres develop—an order expressed, in a general way, by saying that the line of progress is from the larger, coarser adjustments having to do with the bodily system as a whole (those nearest the trunk of the body) to the finer and accurate adjustments having to do with the periphery and extremities of the organism. The oculist tells us that the vision of the child is essentially that of the savage; being adapted to seeing large and somewhat remote objects in the mass—not near-by objects in detail. To violate this law means undue nervous strain: it means putting the greatest tension upon the centres least able to do the work. At the same time, the lines of activity which are hungering and thirsting for action are left, unused, to atrophy. The act of writing—especially in the barbarous fashion, long current in the school, of compelling the child to write on ruled lines in a small hand and with the utmost attainable degree of accuracy—involves a nicety and complexity of adjustments of muscular activity which can only be appreciated by the specialist. As the principal of a Chicago school has wittily remarked in this connection, "The pen is literally mightier than the sword." Forcing children at a premature age to devote their entire attention to these refined and cramped adjustments has left behind a sad record of injured nervous systems and of muscular disorders and distortions. While there are undoubted exceptions, present physiological knowledge points to the age of about eight years as early enough for anything more than an incidental attention to visual and written language-form.

We must not forget that these forms are symbols. I am far from depreciating the value of symbols in our intellectual life. It is hardly too much to say that all progress in civilization upon the intellectual side has depended upon increasing invention and control of symbols of one sort or another. Nor do I join in the undiscriminating cry of those who condemn the study of language as having to do with mere words, not with realities. Such a position is one-sided, and is as crude as the view against which it is a reaction. But there is an important question here: Is the child of six or seven years ready for symbols to such an extent that the stress of educational life can be thrown upon them? If we were to look at the question independently of the existing school system, in the light of the child's natural needs and interests at this period, I doubt if there could be found anyone who would say that the urgent call of the child of six and seven is for this sort of nutriment, instead of for more direct introduction into the wealth of natural and social forms that surrounds him. No doubt the skillful teacher often succeeds in awakening an interest in these matters; but the interest has to be excited in a more or less artificial way, and, when excited, is somewhat factitious, and independent of other-interests of child-life. At this point the wedge is introduced and driven in, which marks the growing divorce between school and outside interests and occupations.

We cannot recur too often in educational matters to the conception of John Fiske, that advance in civilization is an accompaniment of the prolongation of infancy. Anything which, at this period, develops to a high degree any set of organs and centres at the expense of others means premature specialization, and the arrest of an equable and all-around development. Many educators are already convinced that premature facility and glibness in the matter of numerical combinations tend toward an arrested development of certain higher spiritual capacities. The same thing is true in the matter of verbal symbols. Only the trained psychologist is aware of the amount of analysis and abstraction demanded by the visual recognition of a verbal form. Many suppose that abstraction is found only where more or less complex reasoning exists. But as a matter of fact the essence of abstraction is found in compelling attention to rest upon elements which are more or less cut off from direct channels of interest and action. To require a child to turn away from the rich material which is all about him, to which he spontaneously attends, and which is his natural, unconscious food, is to compel the premature use of analytic and abstract powers. It is willfully to deprive the child of that synthetic life, that unconscious union with his environment, which is his birth-right and privilege. There is every reason to suppose that a premature demand upon the abstract intellectual capacity stands in its own way. It cripples rather than furthers later intellectual development. We are not yet in a position to know how much of the inertia and seeming paralysis of mental powers in later periods is the direct outcome of excessive and too early to appeal to isolated intellectual capacity. We must trust to the development of physiology and psychology to make these matters so clear that school authorities and the public opinion that controls them shall have no option. Only then can we hope to escape that deadening of the childish activities, which led Jowett to call education "the grave of the mind."

Were the matter not so serious it would be ludicrous, when we reflect all this time and effort to reach the end to which they are specially consecrated. It is a common saying among intelligent educators that they can go into a schoolroom and select the children who picked up reading at home: they read so much more naturally and intelligently. The stilted, mechanical, droning, and sing-song ways of reading which prevail in many of our schools are simply the reflex of the lack of motive. Reading is made an isolated accomplish-ment. There are no aims in the child's mind which he feels he can serve by reading; there is no mental hunger to be satisfied; there are no conscious problems with reference to which he uses books. The book is a reading-lesson. He learns to read not for the sake of what he reads, but for the mere sake of reading. When the bare process of reading is thus made an end in itself, it is a psychological impossibility for reading to be other than lifeless.

It is quite true that all better teachers now claim that the formal act of reading should be made subordinate to the sense of what is read, that the child has first to grasp the idea, and then to express his mental realization. But, under present conditions, this profession cannot be carried out. The following paragraph from the report of the Committee of Fifteen on elementary education states clearly enough the reason why; though, as it seems to me, without any consciousness of the real inference which should be drawn from the facts set forth: "The first three years' work of the child is occupied mainly with the mastery of the printed and written forms of the words of his colloquial vocabulary,—words that he is already familiar enough with as sounds addressed to the ear. He has to become familiar with the new forms addressed to the eye; and it would be an unwise method to require him to learn many new words at the same time that he is learning to recognize his old words in their new shape. But as soon as he has acquired (before three years) some facility in reading what is printed in the colloquial style, he may go on to selections from standard authors."

The material of the reading-lesson is thus found wholly in the region of familiar words and ideas. It is out of the question for the child to find anything in the ideas themselves to arouse and hold attention. His mind is fixed upon the mere recognition and utterance of the forms. Thus begins that fatal divorce between the substance and the form of expression, which, fatal to reading as an art, reduces it to a mechanical action. The utter triviality of the contents of our school "Primers" and "First Readers," shows the inevitable outcome of forcing the mastery of external language-forms upon the child at a premature period. Take up the first half-dozen or dozen such books you meet with, and ask yourself how much there is in the ideas presented worthy of respect from any intelligent child of six years.

Methods for learning to read come and go across the educational arena, like the march of supernumeraries upon the stage. Each is heralded as the final solution of the problem of learning to read; but each in turn gives way to some later discovery. The simple fact is—that they all lack the essential of any well-grounded method, namely, relevancy to the child's mental needs. No scheme for learning to read can supply this want. Only a new motive—putting the child into a vital relation to the materials to be read—can be of service here. It is evident that this condition cannot be met, unless learning to read be postponed to a period when the child's intellectual appetite is more consciously active, and when he is mature enough to deal more rapidly and effectively with the formal and mechanical difficulties.

The endless drill, with its continual repetitions, is another instance of the same evil. Even when the attempt is made to select material with some literary or historic worth of its own, the practical outcome is much like making Paradise Lost the basis of parsing-lessons, or Caesar's Gallic Wars an introduction to Latin syntax. So much attention has to be given to the formal side that the spiritual value evanesces. No one can estimate the benumbing and hardening effect of this continued drill upon mere form. Another even more serious evil is the consequent emptiness of mind induced. The mental room is swept and garnished—and that is all. The moral result is even more deplorable than the intellectual. At this plastic period, when images which take hold of the mind exercise such suggestive motor force, nothing but husks are provided. Under the circumstances, our schools are doing great things for the moral education of children; but all efforts in this direction must necessarily be hampered and discounted until the school-teacher shall be perfectly free to find the bulk of the material of instruction for the early school-years in something which has intrinsic value—something whose introduction into consciousness is so vital as to be personal and reconstructive.

It should be obvious that what I have in mind is not a Philistine attack upon books and reading. The question is not how to get rid of them, but how to get their value—how to use them to their capacity as servants of the intellectual and moral life. The plea for the predominance of learning to read in early school-life because of the great importance attaching to literature seems to me a perversion. Just because literature is so important, it is desirable to postpone the child's introduction to printed speech until he is capable of appreciating and dealing with its genuine meaning. Now, the child learns to read as a mechanical tool, and gets very little conception of what is worth reading. The result is, that, after he has mastered the art and wishes to use it; he has no standard by which to direct it. He is about as likely to use it in one way as in another. It would be ungrateful not to recognize the faithfulness and relative success with which teachers, for the last ten or fifteen years, have devoted themselves to raising the general tone of reading with their pupils. But, after all, they are working against great odds. Our ideal should be that the child should have a personal interest in what is read, a personal hunger for it, and a personal power of satisfying this appetite. The adequate realization of this ideal is impossible until the child comes to the reading-material with a certain background of experience which makes him appreciate the difference between the trivial, the merely amusing and exciting, and that which has permanent and serious meaning. This is impossible so long as the child has not been trained in the habit of dealing with material outside of books, and has formed, through contact with the realities of experience, habits of recognizing and dealing with problems in the direct personal way. The isolation of material found in books from the material which the child experiences in life itself—the forcing of the former upon the child before he has well-organized powers of dealing with the latter—is an unnatural divorce which cannot have any other result than defective standards of appreciation, and a tendency to elevate the sensational and transiently interesting above the valuable and the permanent.

Two results of our wrong methods are so apparent in higher

education that they are worth special mention. They are exhibited in the paradox of the combination of slavish dependence upon books with real inability to use them effectively. The famous complaint of Agassiz—that students could not see for themselves—is still repeated by every teacher of science in our high schools and colleges. How many teachers of science will tell you, for example, that, when their students are instructed to find out something about an object, their first demand is for a book in which they can read about it; their first reaction, one of helplessness, when they are told that they must go to the object itself and let it tell its own story? It is not exaggerating to say that the book habit is so firmly fixed that very many pupils, otherwise intelligent, have a positive aversion to directing their attention to things themselves—it seems so much simpler to occupy the mind with what someone else has said about these things. While it is mere stupidity not to make judicious use of the discoveries and attainments of others, the substitution of the seeing of others for the use of one's own eyes is such a self-contradictory principle as to require criticism. We only need recognize the extent to which it actually obtains.

On the other hand, we have the relative incapacity of students to use easily and economically these very tools—books—to which most of their energies have been directed. It is a common experience with, I will not say only the teachers of undergraduate students, but of graduate students,—candidates for advanced degrees,—to find that in every special subject a large amount of time and energy has to be spent in learning how to use the books. To take a book and present an adequate condensed synopsis of its points of view and course of argument is an exercise, not merely in reading; but in thinking. To know how to turn quickly to a number of books bearing upon a given topic, to choose what is needed, and to find what is characteristic of the author and important in the subject, are matters which the majority of even graduate students have to learn over again for themselves. If such be the case—and yet attention to books has been the dominant note of all previous education—we are surely within bounds in asking if there is not something radically wrong in the way in which books have been used. It is a truism to say that the value of books consists in their relation to life, in the keenness and range that they impart to powers of penetration and interpretation. It is no truism to say that the premature and unrelated use of books stands in the way. Our means defeat the very end to which they are used.

Just a word about the corresponding evils: We have to take into account not simply the results produced by forcing language-work unduly, but also the defects in development due to the crowding out of other objects. Every respectable authority insists that the period of childhood, lying between the years of four and eight or nine, is the plastic period in sense and emotional life. What are we doing to shape these capacities? What are we doing to feed this hunger? If one compares the powers and needs of the child in these directions with what is actually supplied in the regimen of the three Rs, the contrast is pitiful, tragic. This epoch is also the budding-time for the formation of efficient and orderly habits on the motor side: it is preeminently the time when the child wishes to do things, and when his interest in doing can be turned to educative account. No one can clearly set before himself the vivacity and persistency of the child's motor instincts at this period, and then call to mind the continued grind of reading and writing, without feeling that the justification of our present curriculum is psychologically impossible. It is simply a superstition: it is a remnant of an outgrown period of history.

All this might be true, and yet there might be no subject-matter sufficiently organized for introduction into the school curriculum, since this demands, above all things, a certain definiteness of presentation and of development. But we are not in this unfortunate plight. There are subjects that are as well fitted to meet the child's dominant needs as they are to prepare him for the civilization in which he has to play his part. There is art in a variety of modes—music, drawing, painting, modeling, etc. These media not only afford a regulated outlet in which the child may project his inner impulses and feelings in outward form, and come to consciousness of himself, but are necessities in existing social life. The child must be protected against some of the hard and over-utilitarian aspect of modern civilization: positively, they are needed, because some degree of artistic and creative power is necessary to take the future worker out of the ranks of unskilled labor, and to feed his consciousness in his hours of contact with purely mechanical things.

Those modes of simple scientific observation and experiment which go under the name of "nature-study" are calculated to appeal to and keep active the keenness of the child's interest in the world about him, and to introduce him gradually to those methods of discovery and verification which are the essential characteristics of modern intellectual life. On the social side, they give the child an acquaintance with his environment—an acquaintance more and more necessary, under existing conditions, for the maintenance of personal and social health, for understanding and conducting business pursuits, and for the administration of civic affairs. What is crudely termed manual training—the variety of constructive activities, which, begun in the Kindergarten, ought never to be given up—is equally adapted to the characteristic needs of the child and to the present demands of associated life. These activities afford discipline in continuous and orderly application of powers, strengthen habits of attention and industry, and beget self-reliant and ingenious judgment. As preparation for future social life, they furnish insight into the mechanical and industrial occupations upon which our civilization depends, and keep alive that sense of the dignity of work essential to democracy. History and literature, once more, provide food for the eager imagination of the child. While giving it worthy material, they may check its morbid and chaotic exercise. They present to the child typical conditions of social life, they exhibit the struggles that have brought it into being, and picture the spiritual that it has culminated.

Due place cannot be given to literature and history until the teacher is free to select them for their intrinsic value, and not from the standpoint of the child's ability to recognize written and printed verbal symbols.

Here we have the controlling factors in the primary curriculum of the future—manual training, science nature-study, art, and history. These keep alive the child's positive and creative impulses, and direct them in such ways as to discipline them into the habits of thought and action required for effective participation in community life.

Were the attempt suddenly made to throw out, or reduce to a minimum, language-work in the early grades, the last state of our schools would undoubtedly be worse than the first. Not immediate substitution is what is required, but consideration of the whole situation, and organization of the materials and methods of science, history, and the arts to make them adequate educational agencies. Many of our present evils are due to compromise and inconsistency. We have neither one thing nor the other—neither the systematic, all-pervasive discipline of the three Rs, nor a coherent training in constructive work, history, and nature-study. We have a mixture of the two. The former is supposed to furnish the element of discipline and to constitute the standard of success; while the latter supplies the factor of interest. What is needed is a thoroughgoing reconciliation of the ideals of thoroughness, definiteness, and order, summed up in the notion of discipline, with those of appeal to individual capacities and demands, summed up in the word "interest." This is the Educational Problem, as it relates to the elementary school.

Change must come gradually. To force it unduly would compromise its final success by favoring a violent reaction. What is needed in the first place is that there should be a full and frank statement of conviction with regard to the matter from physiologists and psychologists and from those school administrators who are conscious of the evils of the present régime. Educators should also frankly face the fact that the New Education, as it exists to-day, is a compromise and a transition: it employs new methods; but its controlling ideals are virtually those of the Old Education. Wherever movements looking to a solution of the problem are intelligently undertaken, they should receive encouragement, moral and financial, from the intellectual leaders of the community. There are already in existence a considerable number of educational "experiment stations," which represent the outposts of educational progress. If these schools can be adequately supported for a number of years they will perform a great vicarious service. After such schools have worked out carefully and definitely the subject matter of a new curriculum—finding the right place for language-studies and placing them in their right perspective—the problem of the more general educational reform will be immensely simplified and facilitated. There will be clear standards, well-arranged material, and coherent methods upon which to proceed. To build up and equip such schools is, therefore, the wisest and most economic policy, in avoiding the friction and waste consequent upon casual and spasmodic attempts at educational reform.

All this amounts to saying that school reform is dependent upon a collateral wider change in the public opinion, which controls school board, superintendent, and teachers. There are certain minor changes; reforms in detail, which can be effected directly within the school system itself. But the school is not an isolated institution: it is one of an organism of social forces. To secure more scientific principles of work in the school, means, accordingly, clearer vision and wiser standards of thought and action in the community at large. The Educational Problem is ultimately, that society shall see clearly its own conditions and needs, and set resolutely about meeting them. If the recognition be once secured, we need have no doubts about the consequent action. Let the community once realize that it is educating upon the basis of a life which it has left behind, and it will turn, with adequate intellectual and material resources, to meet the needs of the present hour.

NOTES

INTRODUCTION

1. John Dewey, "The Primary-Education Fetich," *Forum* magazine, Vol. XXV, May 1898; *The Early Works of John Dewey*, vol. 5, *1882–1898* (Southern Illinois University Press, 2008), 254–69. You cannot really understand what has happened to American education unless you read John Dewey's seminal essay, which is reprinted in full in appendix B. It is Dewey's plan to change the character of Americans by turning individuals into collectivists, change our capitalist system into a socialist one, and dumb down Americans so that the plan could be implemented without opposition. In other words, what he planned was a criminal conspiracy to impose unconstitutional government on the American people.
2. "90 Million US Adults Called Barely Literate," *Boston Globe*, September 9, 1993: "Nearly half of all adult Americans read and write so poorly that it is difficult for them to hold a decent job, according to the most comprehensive literacy study done by the US government."
3. Dewey, "The Primary-Education Fetich," 268.
4. The National Commission on Excellence in Education, *A Nation at Risk: The Imperative for Educational Reform: A Report to the Nation and the Secretary of Education*, United States Department of Education (Washington, DC, April 1983), http://datacenter.spps.org/uploads/sotw_a_nation_at_risk_1983.pdf, 9. The publication of this report is considered a landmark event in modern American educational history. Among other things, the report contributed to the ever-growing assertion that American schools were failing, and it touched off a wave of local, state, and federal reform efforts, which led to no substantive improvement.

CHAPTER 1: TREASON: THE DELIBERATE DUMBING DOWN OF A NATION

1. The National Commission on Excellence in Education, *A Nation at Risk: The Imperative for Educational Reform: A Report to the Nation and the Secretary of Education*, United States Department of Education (Washington, DC, April 1983), http://datacenter.spps.org/uploads/sotw_a_nation_at_risk_1983.pdf, 9.
2. John Dewey, *Democracy and Education* (New York: Macmillan, 1916), 297.
3. John Dewey, *School and Society* (Chicago: University of Chicago Press, 1899), 14–15.
4. John Dewey, "The University School" *University Record* 1, no. 32 (University of Chicago Press) (November 6, 1896), 128.
5. John Dewey, "The Primary-Education Fetich," *Forum* magazine, May 1898.

6.   Andrew Lundeen, "Do the Rich Pay Their Fair Share?" *Tax Foundation* blog, April 17, 2014, http://taxfoundation.org/blog/do-rich-pay-their-fair-share.

7.   John Dewey, *Liberalism and Social Action* (New York: G. P. Putnam's Sons, 1935), 52, 54.

CHAPTER 2: HOW JOHN DEWEY CREATED A HOUSE OF LIES

1.   John Dewey, "The Primary-Education Fetich," *Forum* magazine, May 1898.

2.   Edmund Burke Huey, *The Psychology and Pedagogy of Reading*, special ed. (N.p.: International Reading Association, 2009), 200–1.

3.   Ibid., 202.

4.   Ibid., 223, 230.

5.   Ibid., 230–31.

6.   Carole Adelsky, Bess Altwerger, and Barbara Flores, *Whole Language: What's the Difference?* (Portsmouth, NH: Heinemann, 1991), 32.

7.   George Dykhuizen, *The Life and Mind of John Dewey* (Carbondale: Southern Illinois Univ. Press, 1973), 237–38.

8.   Ibid., 239.

9.   Jo Ann Boydston, ed., *The Later Works of John Dewey: 1925–1953,* vol. 9, *1933–34* (Carbondale: Southern Illinois Univ. Press, 1986), 102–6.

10. The National Commission on Excellence in Education, *A Nation at Risk: The Imperative for Educational Reform: A Report to the Nation and the Secretary of Education, United States Department of Education* (Washington, DC, April 1983), http://datacenter.spps.org/uploads/sotw_a_nation_at_risk_1983.pdf, 11.

11. Edward B. Fiske, "National Policy Urged to Combat Adult Illiteracy," *New York Times*, September 9, 1988, http://www.nytimes.com/1988/09/09/us/national-policy-urged-to-combat-adult-illiteracy.html.

12. "Nearly Half of U.S. Adults Lack Literacy," the *Washington Post*, September 9, 1993, as reported in the Miami *Sun-Sentinel*, http://articles.sun-sentinel.com/1993-09-09/news/9309090068_1_literacy-adults-americans.

13. National Center for Educational Statistics, "National Assessment of Adult Literacy (NAAL)," nces.ed.gov/naal/kf_demographics.asp#1; accessed August 20, 2014.

14. The National Endowment for the Arts, *Reading at Risk* (Washington, DC, 2007), http://arts.gov/publications/reading-risk-survey-literary-reading-america-0.

15. Michael Alison Chandler, "SAT reading scores drop to lowest point in decades," *Washington Post*, September 14, 2011, http://www.washingtonpost.com/local/education/sat-reading-scores-drop-to-lowest-point-in-decades/2011/09/14/gIQAdpoDTK_story.html.

16. This analysis of the SAT scores was first published in *The Blumenfeld Education Letter*, October 1994, 7, available online at http://www.howtotutor.com/bel/October_1994.pdf.

17. College Board, *2011 College-Bound Seniors Total Group Profile Report*, "Total Group Mean SAT Scores: College-Bound Seniors 1972–2011," http://media.collegeboard.com/digitalServices/pdf/research/cbs2011_total_group_report.pdf.

18. Ibid.

19. The College Board, *2013 SAT® Report on College & Career Readiness* (2013), https://www.collegeboard.org/sites/default/files/sat-report-college-career-readiness-2013_0.pdf.

20. James Vaznis, "Review finds Boston schools in disarray," *Boston Globe*, May 23, 2014, http://www.bostonglobe.com/metro/2014/05/22/report-slams-boston-schools-badly-fractured-distrustful-departments/osomKcf0MTHBYfJqKCyrnN/story.html.

21. Charlotte Iserbyt, "Charlotte Receives the "Pollyanna Medal,'" *ABCs of DumbDown* (official blog), May 19, 2014. Quoted with Charlotte Iserbyt's permission.

22. Orestes Brownson, *The Works of Orestes Brownson* (Detroit: Thorndike Nourse, 1884), 62, https://archive.org/stream/worksoforestesa05brow#page/48/mode/2up.

CHAPTER 3: PORTRAIT OF A FAILED SYSTEM

1.   Mary Sanchez, "Preschool Is an Investment in America," *Kansas City Star,* February 19, 2013.

2. David Silver, Marisa Saunders, and Estela Zarate. "What Factors Predict High School Graduation in the Los Angeles Unified School District ." Attendance Counts. Accessed February 26, 2014, http://www.attendancecounts.org/wordpress/wp-content/uploads/2010/04/LAUSD-Study-2008.pdf.

3. "Fast Facts: Education in the U.S. by the Numbers," Conservatives for Higher Standards, http://highercorestandards.org/fast-facts-education-in-us/.

4. Ibid.

5. "National Assessment of Adult Literacy," U.S. Department of Education Institute of Education Sciences National Center for Education Statistics, 2003, http://nces.ed.gov/naal/kf_demographics.asp.

6. National Center for Educational Statistics, "Reading 2009: National Assessment of Educational Progress at Grades 4 and 8," The Nation's Report Card, US Department of Education, http://nces.ed.gov/nationsreportcard/pdf/main2009/2010458.pdf.

7. "1992 National Adult Literacy Survey," May 5, 1999, http://nces.ed.gov/pubs2001/2001457_1.pdf.

8. "New ACT Study: Only 26 Percent of American High School Students Prepared for College," Foundation for Excellence in Education, August 22, 2013, http://excelined.org/news/press-release-new-act-study-only-26-percent-of-american-high-school-students-prepared-for-college/.

9. Programme for International Student Assessment (PISA) Results from PISA 2012, United States, Key Findings, http://www.oecd.org/unitedstates/PISA-2012-results-US.pdf.

10. "Fast Facts: Education in the U.S. by the Numbers," Conservatives for Higher Standards.

11. Ibid.

12. Ibid.

13. Ibid.

14. Ibid.

15. Ibid.

16. Javier C. Hernandez and Robert Gebeloff, "Test Scores Sink as State Adopts New Benchmarks in English and Math," *New York Times*, August 8, 2013.

17. "Mayor Bloomberg, Schools Chancellor Walcott Detail New York City Students' Results On New, More Rigorous State Tests Aligned To The Common Core Learning Standards," The New York City Department of Education, August 7, 2013, http://www.nytimes.com/2013/08/08/nyregion/under-new-standards-students-see-sharp-decline-in-test-scores.html?pagewanted=all&_r=0.

18. Michael Holzman, "SEGREGATION BY ANOTHER NAME: NYC EDITION," This is Dropout nation, March 14, 2014, http://dropoutnation.net/2014/03/14/segregation-by-another-name-nyc-edition/.

19. Jeb Bush, "Toward a Better Education System," *National Review Online*, August 19, 2013, http://www.nationalreview.com/article/356038/toward-better-education-system-jeb-bush.

20. John Taylor Gatto, *Dumbing Us Down: The Hidden Curriculum of Compulsory Schooling*, Collectors ed. (Gabriola Island, BC: New Society Publishers, 2005), xxxii.

21. Ibid., xxxiii.

22. Ibid., xxxiii–xxxiv.

23. Ibid., xxxiv.

24. Ibid., xxxv.

25. Ibid., 2.

26. Ibid., 4–5.

27. Eduardo Porter, "For Schools, Long Road to a Level Playing Field," *New York Times*, May 20, 2014, http://www.nytimes.com/2014/05/21/business/economy/for-schools-long-road-to-a-level-playing-field.html.

28. John Taylor Gatto, *Dumbing Us Down,* 5–6.

29. Ibid., 6–8.

30. Ibid., 9–10.

31. Ibid., 14, 16.

32. Barry Goldwater, *Conscience of a Conservative* (Sheperdsville, KY: Victor, 1960; Blacksburg, VA: Wilder, 2009), 45, 48–49. Citations refer to the Wilder edition.

CHAPTER 4: HOW DUMBED DOWN ARE WE?

1. E. D. Hirsch, Jr. *Cultural Literacy* (New York: Houghton Mifflin, 1987), 5.
2. Joel Cohen, David E. Bloom, and Martin B. Malin, eds., *Educating All Children: A Global Agenda*, American Academy of Arts and Sciences (Cambridge, MA: MIT Press, 2006).
3. Ibid., 3.
4. Hirsch, Cultural Literacy, 5.
5. Ibid., 6.
6. Jill Lepore. "The Commandments. The Constitution and its worshippers," *New Yorker*, January 17, 2011, 72, http://www.newyorker.com/magazine/2011/01/17/the-commandments.
7. Rick Shenkman, *Just How Stupid Are We?* (New York: Basic Books, 2008), 26–27.
8. Ibid., 117.
9. Lois Romano, "Literacy of College Graduates Is on Decline," *Washington Post*, December 25, 2005, http://www.washingtonpost.com/wp-dyn/content/article/2005/12/24/AR2005122400701.html.

CHAPTER 5: CHILD ABUSE: TURNING NORMAL CHILDREN INTO DYSLEXICS

1. Thomas H. Gallaudet, *The Mother's Primer* (Hartford: Daniel Burgess & Co., 1836). In my history of reading instruction, *The New Illiterates,* published in 1973, I was the first researcher to identify Gallaudet as the originator of the modern sight-reading method based on the needs of the deaf, which was later adopted by the progressives as the means of teaching children to read in the public schools.
2. Jules Abels, *The Rockefeller Millions* (London: Frederick Muller, 1967), 343.
3. David Rockefeller, *Memoirs* (New York: Random House, 2002), 27.
4. Ibid.
5. Nelson Rockefeller, *The Reading Teacher,* March 1972.
6. Samuel T. Orton, "The 'Sight Reading' Method of Teaching Reading as a Source of Reading Disability," *Journal of Educational Psychology*, February 1929.
7. "Dyslexia: Clinical gadgets amuse children while curing reading difficulties," *Life* magazine, April 10, 1944, 79.
8. Rudolf Flesch, *Why Johnny Can't Read* (New York: Harper & Brothers, 1955), 18.
9. Ibid., 9.
10. Anthony Oettinger, "Regulated Competition in the United States," *The Innisbrook Papers*, the edited proceedings of a Northern Telecom senior management conference on issues and perspectives for the 1980s, February 1982, 21.

CHAPTER 6: SIGHT VOCABULARY: THE POISON OF PRIMARY EDUCATION

1. Stanislas Dehaene, *Reading in the Brain: The New Science of How We Read* (New York: Penguin, 2010), 209.
2. Ibid.
3. Samuel Blumenfeld, *The New Illiterates and How You Can Keep Your Child from Becoming One* (New Rochelle, Arlington House, 1973), 201.
4. *Wikipedia*, s.v. "Dolch word list," http://en.wikipedia.org/wiki/Dolch_word_list; accessed August 21, 2014.
5. James McKeen Cattell, ed., Walter Dearborn, School and Society, Oct. 19, 1940, 368.

CHAPTER 7: HOW DO CHILDREN LEARN A SIGHT VOCABULARY? ANY WAY THEY CAN!

1. Walter Dearborn, "The Psychological Researches of James McKeen Cattell: A Review of Some of His Pupils," *Archives of Psychology* 30 (1914): 40–41.
2. Harold N. Levinson, *Smart but Feeling Dumb: New Research on Dyslexia—and How It May Help You*, rev. and upd. ed. (New York: Warner, 2003), xx.
3. Kenneth L. Goodman, "Reading: A Psycholinguistic Guessing, Game," http://readbysight.com/images/reading_a_psycholinguistic_guessing_game.pdf.

4. *Learning Disabilities: A Report to Congress. Interagency Committee on Learning Disabilities (U.S.)*, United States Department of Health and Human Services, 1987.
5. Don Potter, in an e-mail to the author.
6. "Reading Method Lets Pupils Guess; Whole-Language Approach Riles Advocates of Phonics," *Washington Post*, November 29, 1986.

CHAPTER 8: RIGHT BRAIN VS. LEFT BRAIN: HOW TO AVOID DYSLEXIA
1. Norman Doidge, *The Brain That Changes Itself: Stories of Personal Triumph from the Frontiers of Brain Science* (New York: Penguin, 2007), 70.
2. Ibid., 72.
3. Stanislas Dehaene, *Reading in the Brain* (New York: Viking Penguin Group, 2009), 327.
4. Doige, *The Brain That Changes Itself*, 41.
5. Dehaene, *Reading in the Brain*, 326.
6. Ibid., 3.
7. Ibid., 76–77.
8. Ibid., 197.
9. Ibid., 1–3, 4.
10. Ibid., 107.
11. Ibid., 244–46.
12. Ibid., 327.

CHAPTER 9: EDWARD MILLER PROVED THE SIGHT METHOD CAUSES DYSLEXIA
1. Samuel L. Blumenfeld, *New Illiterates and How You Can Keep Your Child from Becoming One* (New York: Arlington House, 1973), 315–51.
2. Mr. Miller was not an easy communicator, but I was able to work with him for over a decade, helping him develop his ideas for future publication. He spent much time and effort trying to convince the powers that be of the significance of his findings. However, the establishment proved immovable. He died in 2010, before the book could be completed. Miller also worked with Don Potter, who published his test. See http://www.donpotter.net/pdf/mwia.pdf.
3. Gretchen Davies, "Dr. Seuss: Celebrating His Birthday and True Literacy," *Examiner.com*, March 2, 2012, http://www.examiner.com/article/dr-seuss-celebrating-his-birthday-and-true-literacy.
4. Samuel L. Blumenfeld, "Can Dyslexia Be Artificially Induced in School? Yes, Says Researcher Edward Miller," *Blumenfeld Education Letter*, March 1992.
5. Ibid.
6. Ibid.
7. Ibid.
8. Ibid.
9. Betty Jean Foust, North Carolina consultant for reading communication skills, in a letter to Edward Miller, November 1989.
10. Blumenfeld, "Can Dyslexia Be Artificially Induced in School?"

CHAPTER 10: THE VICTIMS OF EDUCATIONAL MALPRACTICE
1. Lewis Schiff, *Business Brilliant: Surprising Lessons from the Greatest Self-Made Business Icons* (New York: HarperBusiness, 2013), 141–42.
2. Ibid., 143.
3. Ibid., 143–44.
4. Nancy Mather and Barbara J. Wendling, *Essentials of Dyslexia Assessment and Intervention* (Hoboken, NJ: John Wiley & Sons, 2011).

5.   Laura Kutney, "Mindfully Accepting My Learning Disability," January 1, 2014, *Elephant Journal*, http://www.elephantjournal.com/2014/01/mindfully-accepting-my-learning-disability/.
6.   "Henry Winkler on Dyslexia," *Instructor* magazine, February 2007.
7.   David Mamet, *The Secret Knowledge: On the Dismantling of American Culture*, (New York: Sentinel, 2012), 158.

CHAPTER 11: THE READING CONSPIRACY MARCHES ON

1.   Muriel Cohen, "Even best scores worse on SATs," *Ocala Star-Banner*, September 4, 1991, 3A.
2.   Martin G. Selbrede, "Education, Liberty, and the Bible," Chaldedon Foundation, https://sites.google.com/site/bibletruthsrestored/education-liberty-bible, accessed August 22, 2014.
3.   John B. Carroll and Jeanne S. Chall, *Toward a Literate Society. The Report of the Committee on Reading of the National Academy of Education* (New York: McGraw-Hill, 1975), 326.
4.   Ibid., 327.
5.   Rudolf Flesch, *Why Johnny* Still *Can't Read, A New Look at the Scandal of Our Schools* (New York: HarperCollins, 1981).
6.   National Commission on Excellence in Education, *A Nation at Risk: The Imperative for Educational Reform*, April 1983, 5.
7.   *National Commission on Teacher Education Act, Hearing Before the Subcommittee on Education, Arts and Humanities of the Committee on Labor and Human Resources, United States Senate, Ninety-Eighth Congress, Second Session on S.J. Res 138, Washington 1984*, p. 45, http://babel.hathitrust.org/cgi/pt?id=purl.32754076789308;view=1up;seq=1.
8.   Ibid.
9.   The National Endowment for the Arts, *Reading at Risk: A Survey of Literary Reading in America*, June 2004, http://arts.gov/publications/reading-risk-survey-literary-reading-america-0, vii.
10. Javier C. Hernández, "New York Schools Chief Advocates More 'Balanced Literacy.'" *New York Times*, June 26, 2014, http://www.nytimes.com/2014/06/27/nyregion/new-york-schools-chancellor-carmen-farina-advocates-more-balanced-literacy.html.
11. See "TC Reading and Writing Project's Albums," Vimeo, http://vimeo.com/tcrwp/albums; and in general, "Multimedia," Teachers College Reading and Writing Project, http://readingandwritingproject.com/resources/video-and-e-media.html.
12. "First Grade #3 – Shared Reading Experience," http://vimeo.com/85961675.
13. National Council of Teachers of English, "Remodeling Literacy Learning Together," National Center for Literacy Education, http://www.ncte.org/ncle.

CHAPTER 12: THE POLITICS OF THE WHOLE LANGUAGE METHOD

1.   Bess Altwerger, Carole Edelsky, and Barbara Flores: *Whole Language, What's the Difference?* (Portsmouth, NH: Heinemann, 1991), 32.
2.   Ibid., 19
3.   Ibid., 23
4.   James V. Wertsch, *Vygotsky and the Social Formation of Mind* (Cambridge, MA: Harvard Univ. Press, 1985), ix.
5.   A. R. Luria, *The Making of Mind: A Personal Account of Soviet Psychology*, eds. Michael Cole and Sheila Cole (Harvard University Press, 1979), chap. 3.
6.   Altwerger, Edelsky, and Flores, *Whole Language*, 67.
7.   Jane Baskwill and Paulette Whitman, *Evaluation: Whole Language, Whole Child* (New York: Scholastic, 1988), 19.
8.   Dianne Sirna Mancus and Curtis K. Carlson, "Politics and Reading Instruction Make a Dangerous Mix," *Education Week*, February 27, 1985, http://www.edweek.org/ew/articles/1985/02/27/05120016.h04.html?qs=language.
9.   Katherine Seligman, "3.1M in California 'functionally illiterate,'" *Patriot Ledger*, November 18, 1987, 35.

10. Frank Smith, "Overselling Literacy," *Phi Delta Kappan* 70, no. 5 (January 1989): 352–59, http://www.jstor.org/discover/10.2307/20403900?uid=3739968&uid=2&uid=4&uid=373 9256&sid=21104115803841.

11. Paulo Freire and Donaldo Macedo, *Literacy: Reading the Word and the World* (South Hadley, MA: Bergin & Garvey, 1987), vii.

12. Smith, "Overselling Literacy."

13. Kenneth Goodman, *What's Whole in Whole Language* (Portsmouth, NH: Heinemann, 1986), 37.

14. John Dewey, *Democracy and Education* (New York: Macmillan, 1916; Simon & Brown, 2012), 206. Citations are to the Simon & Brown ed.

15. Jan Allen, Patricia Freeman, and Sandy Osborne, "Children's Political Knowledge and Attitudes," *Young Children*, January 1989, 57.

16. William T. Fagan: "Empowered Students; Empowered Teachers," *Reading Teacher* 42, no. 8, (April 1989), 572–78.

17. Dewey, *Democracy and Education*, 315.

CHAPTER 13: CALIFORNIA'S LITERACY DISASTER: WHEN UTOPIANS RULE, THE CHILDREN SUFFER

1. Jill Stewart, "The Blackboard Bungle," *LA Weekly* 18, no. 14 (March 1, 1996).

2. Ibid.

3. Katherine Seligman, "3.1M in California 'functionally illiterate,'" *Patriot Ledger*, November 18, 1987, 35.

4. "Why the Latest Campaign Against Illiteracy Will Fail," *Blumenfeld Education Letter* 3, no. 9 (September 1988), www.howtotutor.com/bel/September_1988.pdf.

5. Stewart, "The Blackboard Bungle."

6. Ibid.

7. Ibid.

8. Ibid.

9. *Fresno Bee*, January 23, 1996.

10. Stewart, "The Blackboard Bungle."

11. Ibid.

12. Ibid.

13. Dan Walters, "California schools' test scores may drop again," *Sacramento Bee*, August 9, 2013.

14. Ibid.

15. Stewart, "The Blackboard Bungle."

16. Teresa Watanabe, "California sees a surprise drop in student test scores," *Los Angeles Times*, August 8, 2013, http://articles.latimes.com/2013/aug/08/local/la-me-test-scores-20130809.

CHAPTER 14: COOPERATIVE LEARNING: COMMUNIST IDEOLOGY IN THE CLASSROOM

1. Hughs Farmer of Henderson, Kentucky, has, over the years, sent me clippings from local newspapers on that state's ambitious education reform movement, which proved a failure.

2. Yael Sharan, "Cooperative Learning for Academic and Social Gains: valued pedagogy, problematic practice," *European Journal of Education* 45, no. 2 (2010): 300–313.

3. Eddie Price: Hancock teacher attacks Kentucky school reform, *The Hancock Clarion*, December 30, 1993, 1.

CHAPTER 15: THE GREAT AMERICAN MATH DISASTER

1. Pat Wingert, "A Dismal Report Card," *Newsweek*, June 17, 1991, http://www.newsweek.com/dismal-report-card-204422.

2. Amir D. Acze, *The Mystery of the Aleph: Mathematics, the Kabbalah, and the Search for Infinity* (New York: Washington Square Press, 2001).

3. Ian, Jill, and Dex, "What exactly was the 'new math'?" *Straight Dope* (blog), http://www.straightdope.com/columns/read/1529/what-exactly-was-the-new-math. Reprinted with permission.

4. See chapter 3; see also Michael Holtzman, "Segregation by Another Name: NYC Edition," Dropout Nation, March 14, 2014, http://dropoutnation.net/2014/03/14/segregation-by-another-name-nyc-edition/.

5. John Saxon, "Save our Mathematics!" *National Review* (August 8, 1983), 35.

CHAPTER 16: DRUG PUSHING: THE "CURE" FOR ADD AND ADHD

1. Peter Breggin, *Talking Back to Ritalin* (Monroe, ME: Common Courage Press, 1998), 3.

2. Pieter Cohen and Nicolas Rasmussen, "A Nation of Kids on Speed," *Wall Street Journal*, June 16, 2013, http://online.wsj.com/news/articles/SB10001424127887323728204578513662248894162.

3. Katherine Ellison, "We're not paying enough attention to ADHD," *Washington Post*, March 30, 2012, http://www.washingtonpost.com/opinions/were-not-paying-enough-attention-to-adhd/2012/03/30/gIQAh58qlS_story.html.

4. Claudia Wallis, "Life in Overdrive," *Time*, July 24, 1994, http://content.time.com/time/magazine/article/0,9171,164761,00.html.

5. Ibid.

6. Ellison, "We're not paying enough attention to ADHD."

7. Edward M. Hallowell and John J. Ratey, *Driven to Distraction* (New York: Pantheon, 1994), 269.

8. Ibid., 33

9. Ibid., 16

10. Edward M. Hallowell and John J. Ratey, *Driven to Distraction*, rev. and upd. ed (New York: Knopf Doubleday, 2011), 244.

11. Hallowell and Ratey, *Driven to Distraction* (1994), 237.

12. Dr. Peter Breggin, *Medication Madness* (New York: St. Martin's Press, 2008), 315, 20, 33, 34.

13. Breggin, *Talking Back to Ritalin*, 158.

CHAPTER 17: CONTRIBUTING TO THE DELINQUENCY OF MINORS

1. Akilah Johnson, "Teens ask for more sex ed, greater condom availability," *Boston Globe*, February 16, 2011, http://www.boston.com/news/local/massachusetts/articles/2011/02/16/teens_ask_for_more_sex_ed_greater_condom_availability/?page=1.

2. Ibid.

3. Ibid.

4. Ibid.

5. Ibid.

6. Sexuality Information and Education Council of the United States (SIECUS), "Questions and Answers: Adolescent Sexuality," accessed August 25, 2014, http://www.siecus.org/index.cfm?fuseaction=page.viewpage&pageid=627.

7. Neil Shah, "Birthrate for Girls 15 to 17 Fell to Record Low in 2013," *Wall Street Journal*, May 29, 2014, http://online.wsj.com/news/articles/SB20001424052702303633604579590470216215900.

8. "Sexual Risk Behavior: HIV, STD, & Teen Pregnancy Prevention," Centers for Disease Control Adolescent and School Health page, upd. June 12, 2014, http://www.cdc.gov/HealthyYouth/sexualbehaviors/.

9. Melissa Barnhart, "Chicago Public Schools Expand Sex Ed to Include Kindergarteners," *Christian Post*, March 12, 2013, http://www.christianpost.com/news/chicago-public-schools-expand-sex-ed-to-include-kindergarteners-91755/.

10. "Teen Drug and Alcohol Abuse Facts and Statistics," Teen Rehab website, accessed August 25, 2014, http://www.teendrugrehabs.com/facts-and-stats/.

11. Ibid.

12. National Institute on Alcohol Abuse and Alcoholism, "Underage Drinking," Alcohol Alert, January 2006, http://pubs.niaaa.nih.gov/publications/AA67/AA67.htm.

13. "Drug Alcohol Help and Information," http://www.addict-help.com/alcoholabusetreatment.asp, accessed August 25, 2014.

14. Michael S. Brunner, *Retarding America: The Imprisonment of Potential* (New York: Halcyon House: 1991), 29.
15. Joanne L. Rincker, Thomas F. Reilly and Sheldon Braaten, "Academic and Intellectual Characteristics of Adolescent Juvenile Offenders, *Journal of Correctional Education* 41, no. 3 (September 1990).
16. E. E. Gagne, *Journal of Special Education.*
17. A report to the Congress issued in 1977 by the Comptroller General.
18. Michael S. Brunner, Program of Research on the Causes and Correlates of Delinquency; Urban Delinquency and Substance Abuse, Washington, DC, US Dept. of Justice, 1991.

CHAPTER 18: DESTROYING A CHILD'S RELIGIOUS BELIEFS: A SPIRITUAL CRIME

1. Board of Educ. v. Mergens, 496 U.S. 226 (1990), https://supreme.justia.com/cases/federal/us/496/226/case.html.
2. Justin L. Barrett: *Born Believers: The Science of Children's Religious Belief* (New York: Free Press, 2012), 3, 9.
3. Dwight L. Evans, et al., *Treating and Preventing Adolescent Mental Health Disorders* (New York: Oxford Univ. Press, 2005), xxvii.
4. John Taylor Gatto, "Education and the Western Spiritual Tradition," in *The Underground History of American Education: An Intimate Investigation Into the Prison of Modern Schooling*, rev. ed. (New York: Oxford Village Press, 2003), 302.
5. Barrett, *Born Believers*, 199–201
6. Ibid., 225.
7. Ibid., 232.
8. Travis Loller, "Student's rights not violated in Tenn. Bible dispute," *Johnson City Press*, March 20, 2012, http://www.johnsoncitypress.com/article/99116.
9. Jack Hassard, "Creationism Creeps into Louisiana and Tennessee Science Classrooms," *Education Week*, April 24, 2012, available online on the Living in Dialogue blog, at http://blogs.edweek.org/teachers/living-in-dialogue/2012/04/jack_hassard_creationism_creep.html?cmp=soc-shr-tw.
10. Max Planck, *A Survey of Physical Theory* (New York: Dover, 2010), 62.
11. George Gilder: *Microcosm: The Quantum Revolution in Economics and Technology* (New York: Simon and Schuster, 1989), 17.
12. "Teen Depression Statistics," Teen Help website accessed August 17, 2014, http://www.teenhelp.com/teen-depression/depression-statistics.html.
13. http://www.addabilify.com/help-with-depression.aspx. Abilify (aripiprazole) is indicated for the treatment of schizophrenia in adults and adolescents thirteen to seventeen years of age.
14. Peter Finn, special to the *Inquirer*, Philly.com, September 23, 1990, http://articles.philly.com/1990-09-23/news/25875936_1_death-education-suicide-rate-public-schools.
15. Lisa Schencker, "Should students write obituaries for themselves?" *Bakersfield Californian*, October 26, 2006, http://www.bakersfieldcalifornian.com/local/x1393742538/Should-students-write-obituaries-for-themselves.
16. James Barron, "Suicide Rates of Teen-Agers: Are Their Lives Harder to Live?" *New York Times*, April 15, 1987, http://www.nytimes.com/1987/04/15/garden/suicide-rates-of-teen-agers-are-their-lives-harder-to-live.html.
17. American Academy of Child and Adolescent Psychiatry. "Teen Suicide," *Facts for Family*, no. 10, updated October 2013, http://www.aacap.org/AACAP/Families_and_Youth/Facts_for_Families/Facts_for_Families_Pages/Teen_Suicide_10.aspx.
18. Nina Rebak Rosenthal, "Death Education: Help or Hurt?" *Clearing House* 53, no. 5 (January 1980): 224–26.
19. Joanne M. Saldiveri, "Could 'Death Education' In Our Schools Also Be to Blame?" Western Journalism, January 12, 2013, http://www.westernjournalism.com/could-death-education-in-our-schools-also-be-to-blame/.
20. *Education Week*, December 14, 1988.
21. US Department of Education's Institute of Education Sciences and National Center for Education Statistics, "Fast Facts," 2014, http://nces.ed.gov/fastfacts/display.asp?id=372.

CHAPTER 19: THE UNSETTLING PHENOMENON OF TEEN SUICIDE

1. Justin Jouvenal and T. Rees Shapiro, "After Woodson High suicides, a search for solace and answers," *Washington Post*, April 11, 2014.

2. Ibid.

3. Benjamin Bloom, *Taxonomy of Educational Objectives: Cognitive and Affective Domains* (New York: David McKay, 1964).

4. Tom Rose, "Hidden Facets of the Littleton Tragedy," *Christian Statesman*, September–October 1999, cached on November 8, 2003, http://www.zoominfo.com/CachedPage/?archive_id=0&page_id=256227993&page_url=//www.www.natreformassn.org/statesman/99/facets.html&page_last_updated=2003-11-08T01:23:35&firstName=Tara&lastName=Becker.

5. Ibid.

6. Death education in the *NEA Journal*, March 1973.

7. Ibid.

8. Judith R. Hawkinson, Teaching About Death, *Today's Education*. Sept. - Oct. 1976, Vol. 65, No. 3, 41.

9. John M. McLure, "Death Education," *Phi Delta Kappan* 55, no. 7 (March 1974): 485.

10. Association of Death Education and Counseling (ADEC) Thanatology Association vision statement, http://www.adec.org/Vision_Statement.htm.

11. Association for Death Education and Counseling, "Riding the Dragon: End of Life and Grief as a Path to Resilience, Transformation and Compassion," 36th Annual Conference Final Program, 2014, http://www.adec.org/AM/Template.cfm?Section=Schedule_at_a_Glance&Template=/CM/ContentDisplay.cfm&ContentID=5291.

CHAPTER 20: THE MAKING OF THE BLACK UNDERCLASS

1. The U.S. Census statistics on illiteracy (1890–1930) were published in James McKeen Cattell's weekly publication, *School and Society* 35, no. 902 (April 9, 1932), in "Making the People Literate," by Dr. Robert T. Hill, 488–89.

2. Irwin S. Kirsch, *Adult Literacy in America*, 3rd ed. (National Center for Education Statistics, U.S. Department of Education, 2002). This report was front-page news at the *Boston Globe*, *Washington Post*, and *New York Times* on September 9, 1993. According to the authors of *Adult Literacy and Education in America: Four Studies Based on the National Adult Literacy Survey*, "Numerous reports published in the last decade—including *A Nation at Risk*, *The Bottom Line*, *The Subtle Danger*, *Literacy: Profiles of America's Young Adults*, *Jump Start: The Federal Role in Adult Education*, *Workforce 2000*, *America's Choice: High Skills or Low Wages*, and *Beyond the School Doors*—have provided evidence that a large portion of our population lacks adequate literacy skills and have intensified the debate over how this problem should be addressed." (Carl F. Kaestle et al. [National Assessment of Educational Progress, 2013]) http://nces.ed.gov/pubs2001/2001534.pdf, xix–xx.

3. The Nation's Report Card, Mathematics, *2013 Trial Urban District Snapshot Report*, http://nces.ed.gov/nationsreportcard/subject/publications/dst2013/pdf/2014468XN8.pdf.

4. *The Great Debaters* (2007), with Denzel Washington, a drama based on the true story of Melvin B. Tolson, a professor at Wiley College, Marshall, Texas. In 1935, he inspired students to form the school's first debate team, which went on to challenge Harvard in the national championship.

5. Professor G. Stanley Hall quoted in Mitford M. Mathews, *Teaching to Read Historically Considered* (Chicago: Univ. of Chicago Press, 1966), 136.

6. Anthony Oettinger, "Regulated Competition in the United States," *The Innisbrook Papers*, the edited proceedings of a Northern Telecom senior management conference on issues and perspectives for the 1980s, February 1982, 21.

7. Walter Williams: "Black Education," *FrontPage* magazine, December 31, 2009, http://www.frontpagemag.com/2009/walter-williams/black-education-by-walter-williams/.

8. Cindy Rodriguez, "Study shows US blacks trailing: Immigrants from Africa, Caribbean found to fare better," *Boston Globe*, February 17, 2003.

9. Walter Williams, "Black Education Disaster," December 22, 2010, http://econfaculty.gmu.edu/wew/articles/10/BlackEducationDisaster.
10. Williams: "Black Education."
11. *The Marva Collins Story,* Hallmark Hall of Fame Productions, 1981. The entire movie can be seen on YouTube: https://www.youtube.com/watch?v=uMjotCrGAOY.
12. Diane Rado and Alex Richards, "Illinois grade school test scores plunge—especially in poor communities," *Chicago Tribune,* October 21, 2013, http://articles.chicagotribune.com/2013-10-31/news/ct-met-school-report-card-scores-20131031_1_isats-test-scores-illinois-standard.
13. Charles Murray, *Coming Apart. The State of White America 1960–2010* (New York: Crown Forum, 2012), 181, 216, 285.
14. Ibid.
15. John Taylor Gatto, "Education and the Western Spiritual Tradition," in *The Underground History of American Education: An Intimate Investigation into the Prison of Modern Schooling,* rev. ed. (New York: Oxford Village Press, 2003), 300.
16. Theodore Dalrymple, *Life at the Bottom* (Chicago: Ivan R. Dee, 2001), viii.
17. Ibid., x–xi.
18. Ibid., xiv, 15.
19. Martin Newburn, in a Colin Flaherty article posted on the blog of *The Dave Levine Show,* December 7, 2013, http://thedavelevineshow.ning.com/profiles/blogs/lefty-librarian-beaten-to-a-pulp-in-knockout-assault-in-contra.

CHAPTER 21: EUGENICS AND THE CREATION OF THE BLACK UNDERCLASS

1. John Dewey, "My Pedagogic Creed," *School Journal* 54, no. 3 (January 16, 1897), 77–80.
2. R. Meade Bache, "Reaction Time with Reference to Race," *Psychological Review* 2 (1985), 481.
3. Henry Fairfield Osborn, Program of Second International Congress of Eugenics, 1921.
4. Edward L. Thorndike and Arthur I. Gates, *Elementary Principles of Education* (New York: Macmillan, 1929).
5. Edward L. Thorndike, speech on the theme of "Curriculum Research," October 19, 1928, during the third session of the sixty-fourth university convocation, recorded in the *University of the State of New York Bulletin,* no. 917 (February 1, 1929), 56, 64, in *Proceedings of the . . . Annual Convocation, Issues 56–64* (University of the State of New York).
6. Edward L. Thorndike, *Human Nature and the Social Order* (New York: Macmillan, 1940).
7. Lawrence A. Cremin, *A History of Teachers College* (New York: Columbia Univ. Press, 1954), 252.
8. Frank Smith: *Reading without Nonsense,* 4th ed. (New York: Teachers College Press, 2006), 23.
9. Jonathan Cott. *Dinner with Lenny* (New York: Oxford Univ. Press, 2013), 51.

CHAPTER 22: THE ROLE OF BEHAVIORAL PSYCHOLOGY IN THE DEWEY PLAN

1. John Dewey, "The Primary-Education Fetich," *Forum* magazine, May 1898; *The Early Works of John Dewey,* vol. 5, *1882–1898* (Southern Illinois University Press, 2008), 254–69.
2. Edward L. Thorndike, *Intellect (School and Society),* 28; (November 10, 1928), 575; *Animal Intelligence* (New York: Macmillan), 105.
3. John B. Watson, *Behaviorism,* rev. ed. (New York: W. W. Norton, 1970), ix.
4. John B. Watson, *Behaviorism,* 7th ed. (New Brunswick, NJ: Transaction), 11.
5. D. L. Schacter, D. T. Gilbert, and D. M. Wegner, *Psychology,* 2nd ed. (New York: Worth, 2011).
6. B. F. Skinner, *About Behaviorism* (New York: Alfred A. Knopf, 1974), 18–20.
7. B. F. Skinner, *Beyond Freedom and Dignity,* repr. ed. (Indianapolis: Hackett, 2002), 155.
8. A. R. Luria: *The Nature of Human Conflicts,* trans. and ed. W. Horsley Gantt (New York: Liveright, 1932), 206–7.
9. Alfred J. Marrow, *The Practical Theorist: The Life and Work of Kurt Lewin* (New York: Basic Books, 1969), 167.

10. Charlotte Thomson Iserbyt: *Back to Basics Reform, Or . . . Skinnerian International Curriculum?* p. 1. PDF available online on the Deliberate Dumbing Down website, at http://www.deliberatedumbingdown.com/MomsPDFs/Back%20to%20Basics%20Reform_Iserbyt_book.pdf.

11. Marrow, *Practical Theorist*, 122.

CHAPTER 23: WHY JOHNNY CAN'T TELL RIGHT FROM WRONG

1. Harriet Alexander et al., "Connecticut school shooting: troubled life of Adam Lanza, a fiercely intelligent killer," *Telegraph* (UK), December 15, 2012, http://www.telegraph.co.uk/news/worldnews/northamerica/usa/9747682/Connecticut-school-shooting-troubled-life-of-Adam-Lanza-a-fiercely-intelligent-killer.html.

2. Ibid.

3. Ibid.

4. Ibid.

5. "Timeline of Worldwide School and Mass Shootings: Gun-related tragedies in the U.S. and around the world," Infoplease.com, http://www.infoplease.com/ipa/A0777958.html; Mark Duell, Beth Stebner, and Meghan Keneally, "Dressed in a bulletproof vest: Ohio school 'outcast gunman' in first court appearance as THIRD classmate dies of wounds," *Mail Online* (UK), February 9, 2012, http://www.dailymail.co.uk/news/article-2107152/Chardon-High-School-shooting-THIRD-classmate-dies-TJ-Lanes-online-rantings-revealed.html; *Wikipedia*, s.v. "List of school shootings in the United States," accessed August 26, 2014, http://en.wikipedia.org/wiki/List_of_school_shootings_in_the_United_States; "Transcript: Chilling words from 'Elliot Rodger's Retribution,'" *Los Angeles Daily News*, May 25, 2014, http://www.dailynews.com/general-news/20140525/transcript-chilling-words-from-elliot-rodgers-retribution.

CHAPTER 24: BIG BROTHER'S DATA-COLLECTION SYSTEM AND THE ROAD TO TOTALITARIANISM

1. B. K. Eakman, *Educating for the New World Order* (Portland: Halcyon House, 1991).

2. Gerald Malitz, *Student Data Handbook for Early Childhood, Elementary and Secondary Education 1994* (Washington, DC: National Center for Education Statistics, July 1994).

3. Ibid.

4. CCSSO ARD Project and Beth Young, "Student Data Handbook for Elementary, Secondary, and Early Childhood Education: 2001 Update" (NCES 2000343REV), December 2001.

5. Samuel Blumenfeld, "Big Brother and Education Data Collection," *New American*, July 2012, http://www.thenewamerican.com/reviews/opinion/item/12092-big-brother-and-education-data-collection.

6. Nicole Shechtman et al., *Promoting Grit, Tenacity, and Perseverance: Critical Factors for Success in the 21st Century* (DRAFT) (US Department of Education, Office of Educational Technology), February 17, 2013.

7. Marie Bienkowski, Mingyu Feng, and Barbara Means, *Enhancing, Teaching and Learning through Educational Data Mining and Learning Analytics* (US Department of Education, Office of Educational Technology), October 2012.

8. Alex Newman, "Alongside Common Core, Feds Will Vacuum Up Data on Kids," *TSW* (*State Weekly* blog), October 28, 2013, http://thestateweekly.com/alongside-common-core-feds-will-vacuum-up-data-on-kids/.

9. National Education Goals Panel, *1995 National Education Goals Report*, US Department of Education, 119, http://govinfo.library.unt.edu/negp/reports/goalsv1.pdf.

10. National Education Association, *Reading At Risk: A Survey of Literary Reading in America: Research Division Report #46*, http://arts.gov/sites/default/files/ReadingAtRisk.pdf, xiii

CHAPTER 25: WHEN UTOPIANS ARE IN POWER, EXPECT TYRANNY

1. The Fabian Society Tract No. 1, quoted in A. M. McBriar, *Fabian Socialism and English Politics, 1884–1918* (Cambridge: Cambridge University Press, 1966), 9.

2. The Fabian Society credo, 1888. These original tracts have been digitized and are available on google: http://books.google.com/books?id=8EY5AQAAMAAJ&pg=RA1-PA58&lpg=RA1-PA58&dq=Fabian+society+tract+No.+1&source=bl&ots=XZEaRM4G79&sig=0NQg-Z0T.

CHAPTER 26: MULTICULTURALISM: HOW PUBLIC SCHOOLS ERADICATE AMERICANISM

1. Carolyn Brush and Julie Haynes, "Developing a Multicultural Curriculum," Everything ESL.net, http://www.everythingesl.net/inservices/multicultural_curr.php; accessed August 27, 2014.
2. David Gelernter, *Americanism: The Fourth Great Western Religion* (New York: Doubleday, 2007), 1.
3. Donna M. Gollnick, Multicultural Education in Teacher Education: The State of the Scene, American Association of Colleges for Teacher Education, Washington, DC, February 1978, http://files.eric.ed.gov/fulltext/ED206625.pdf, 16, 2–3.
4. NCATE, "Unit Standards in Effect 2008," http://www.ncate.org/Standards/UnitStandards/UnitStandardsineffect2008/tabid/476/Default.aspx.
5. Charles A. Tesconi, "Multiculturalism: A valued but problematic ideal," *Theory into Practice,* Vol. 23, no. 2 (Ohio State University, Spring 1984): 87–92; http://www.tandfonline.com/doi/abs/10.1080/00405848409543096?journalCode=htip20#.U6EUKZRdW-k.
6. Theresa E. McCormick, "Multiculuralism: Some principles and issues," *Theory into Practice* 23, no. 2 (Spring 1984): 92–97; http://www.tandfonline.com/doi/abs/10.1080/0040584840 9543097?journalCode=htip20#.U6EbU5RdW-k.
7. Sandra B. DeCosta, "Not all children are Anglo or Middle Class: A practical beginning for the elementary teacher," *Theory into Practice* 23, no. 2 (Spring 1984): 155–62, http://www.tand-fonline.com/doi/abs/10.1080/00405848409543107?journalCode=htip20#.U6EV05RdW-k.
8. Donna J. Cole, "Multicultural education and global education: A possible merger," *Theory into Practice* 23, no. 2 (Spring 1984): 151–54; http://www.tandfonline.com/action/doSearc h?quickLinkJournal=&journalText=&AllField=Donna+J.+Cole&publication=40000755.

CHAPTER 27: COMMON CORE: CONSUMER EXTORTION ON STEROIDS

1. Foundation for Excellence in Education, Newsroom, "Governor Jeb Bush Delivers Education Reform Address to the American Legislative Exchange Council," August 9, 2013, http://excelined.org/news/governor-jeb-bush-delivers-education-reform-address-to-the-american-legislative-exchange-council/.
2. Ibid.
3. Bill and Melinda Gates Foundation, http://www.gatesfoundation.org/How-We-Work/Quick-Links/Grants-Database#q/k=Common%20Core%20Standards%20grants.
4. Literacy Design Collaborative, http://ldc.org/.
5. National Governors Association, "Testimony—Economic and Employment Impact of the Arts and Music Industry," March 26, 2009, http://www.nga.org/cms/home/federal-relations/nga-testimony/edc-testimony-1/col2-content/main-content-list/march-26-2009-testimony--econom.html.
6. Paul Patton, "Reaching New Heights: Turning Around Low-Performing Schools," National Governors Association 2002–2003 Chairman's Initiative, http://www.nga.org/files/live/sites/NGA/files/pdf/INITIATIVEBROCHURE2002.pdf.
7. Common Core State Standards Initiative, "About the Standards," http://www.corestandards.org/about-the-standards/.
8. Bill and Melinda Gates Foundation, Common Core Grants, http://www.gatesfoundation.org/How-We-Work/Quick-Links/Grants-Database.
9. Common Core State Standards Initiative, "Developers & Publishers," http://www.corestandards.org/developers-and-publishers/.
10. Ibid.
11. Ibid.
12. National Governors Association, Richard Laine bio page, accessed August 27, 2014, http://www.nga.org/cms/home/about/contact-info/col2-content/nga-center-for-best-practices/education-division/richard-laine.html.

13. Editorial Board, "Starting Out Behind," *New York Times* Sunday Review, June 7, 2014, http://www.nytimes.com/2014/06/08/opinion/sunday/starting-out-behind.html.

14. Phyllis Schlafly, "Common Core Standards Aren't Cheap," *Education Reporter*, January 2012, http://www.eagleforum.org/educate/2012/jan12/common-core-standards.html.

15. Ibid.

16. Sam Blumenfeld, "The New Education Boondoggle: Common Core Standards," New American, February 13, 2012, http://www.thenewamerican.com/reviews/opinion/item/10923-the-new-education-boondoggle-common-core-standards.

17. Ibid.

18. Strauss, "Bill Gates."

19. Dana Goldstein, "The Schoolmaster," *Atlantic*, October 2012, http://www.theatlantic.com/magazine/archive/2012/10/the-schoolmaster/309091/.

CHAPTER 28: COMMON CORE STANDARDS: AN EDUCATIONAL FRAUD

1. Alex Newman, "Common Core: A Scheme to Re-write Education," *New American* magazine, August 2013, http://thenewamerican.com/culture/education/item/16192-common-core-a-scheme-to-rewrite-education.

2. Sandra Stotsky, Testimony to Texas Legislature for House Bill 2923, April 14, 2011, http://coehp.uark.edu/colleague/9863.php.

3. Ibid.

4. Ibid.

5. Sandra Stotsky, "Common Core Standards' Devastating Impact on Literary Study and Analytical Thinking," Heritage Foundation, December 11, 2012, http://www.heritage.org/research/reports/2012/12/questionable-quality-of-the-common-core-english-language-arts-standards.

6. Ibid.

7. Ibid.

8. Dr. James Milgram, a leading authority on math standards from Stanford University and member of the Common Core validation committee who refused to sign off on the math standards, testified in Eau Claire, WI, on October 23, 2013. See http://vimeo.com/78006951.

9. Newman, "Common Core."

10. R. James Milgram, "Review of Final Draft Core Standards," accessed August 19, 2014, ftp://math.stanford.edu/pub/papers/milgram/final-version-comments-final-draft-core-standards.

11. Ibid., 3.

12. Ibid., 4, 8, 10.

13. Ibid., 13.

14. Alice Whealey, "Joy Hakim Should Not Write about the History of Europe," *The Textbook Letter* 12, no. 1, http://www.textbookleague.org/121hakm.htm.

15. Joshua Rhett Miller, "New science standards have America's educational publishers turning the page," *Fox News*, April, 2013, http://www.foxnews.com/science/2013/04/12/new-science-standards-have-americas-educational-publishers-turning-page/.

16. David Whitehouse, "NASA and NOAA Confirm Global Temperature Standstill Continues," *Observatory*, January 21, 2014, http://www.thegwpf.org/nasa-noaa-confirm-global-temperature-standstill-continues/.

17. Frank Newport, "In U.S., 46% Hold Creationist View of Human Origins," Gallup Politics page, June 1, 2012, http://www.gallup.com/poll/155003/Hold-Creationist-View-Human-Origins.aspx.

18. Common Core State Standards for English Language Arts & Literacy in History/Social Studies, Science, and Technical Subjects, June 2, 2010, http://www.corestandards.org/assets/CCSSI_ELA%20Standards.pdf, 3.

19. Alex Newman, "New York Revolts Against Common Core," *New American*, February 7, 2014, http://www.thenewamerican.com/culture/education/item/17577-new-york-revolts-against-common-core.

20. Mercedes Schneider, "A Brief Audit of Bill Gates' Common Core Spending," Huffington Post The Blog, August 29, 2013, http://www.huffingtonpost.com/mercedes-schneider/a-brief-audit-of-bill-gat_b_3837421.html.

21. "Stunning revelation Bill Gates has spent $2.3 Billion on Common Core," *North Denver News*, March 17, 2014, http://northdenvernews.com/stunning-revelation-bill-gates-has-spent-2-3-billion-on-common-core/.

22. Bill Gates, speech before the National Conference of State Legislatures, July 21, 2009, http://www.gatesfoundation.org/media-center/speeches/2009/07/bill-gates-national-conference-of-state-legislatures-ncsl.

23. Bill Gates, "Bill Gates: Commend Common Core," *USA Today*, February 12, 2014, http://www.usatoday.com/story/opinion/2014/02/11/bill-melinda-gates-common-core-education-column/5404469/.

24. Louis V. Gerstner Jr., "Lessons From 40 Years of Education 'Reform,'" *Wall Street Journal*, December 1, 2008, http://online.wsj.com/news/articles/SB122809533452168067.

CHAPTER 29: REBELLION AGAINST "OBAMACORE" MAKES STRANGE BEDFELLOWS

1. Information and quotes in this chapter from this RNC resolution can be found at: Republican National Committee, "Resolution Concerning Common Core Education Standards," as adopted by the Republican National Committee on April 12, 2013, http://www.gop.com/wp-content/uploads/2013/04/2013_Spring-Meeting_Resolutions.pdf.

2. Alex Newman, "SPLC Launches Hysterical Attack on Common Core Critics," *New American*, May 8, 2014, http://www.thenewamerican.com/culture/education/item/18217-splc-launches-hysterical-attack-on-common-core-critics.

3. Stephanie Simon, "Nation's biggest teachers union slams 'botched' Common Core implementation," *Politico*, February 2014, http://www.politico.com/story/2014/02/national-education-association-common-core-103690.html.

4. Dennis Van Roekel, "NEA President: We Need a Course Correction on Common Core," NEAToday, February 2014, http://neatoday.org/2014/02/19/nea-president-we-need-a-course-correction-on-common-core.

5. Ibid.

6. Lyndsey Layton, "Turmoil swirling around Common Core education standards," *Washington Post*, April 29, 2013, http://www.washingtonpost.com/local/education/turmoil-swirling-around-common-core-education-standards/2013/04/29/7e2b0ec4-b0fd-11e2-bbf2-a6f9e9d79e19_story.html.

7. Simon, "Nation's biggest teachers union slams 'botched' Common Core implementation."

8. Alex Newman, "New York Revolts Against Common Core," *New American*, February 7, 2014, http://www.thenewamerican.com/culture/education/item/17577-new-york-revolts-against-common-core.

9. Ibid.

10. Joy Pullman, "Indiana's Attempt to Replace Common Core under Fire," *Human Events*, March 12, 2014, http://humanevents.com/2014/03/12/indianas-attempt-to-replace-common-core-under-fire/.

11. Shane Vander Hart, "What States Have Pulled Out of their Common Core Assessment Consortium?" Truth in American Education, January, 2014, http://truthinamericaneducation.com/common-core-assessments/what-states-have-pulled-out-of-their-common-core-assessment-consortium/.

12. Dr. Susan Berry, "School Districts Begin Exodus from Common Core," Breitbart.com, April 6, 2014, http://www.breitbart.com/Big-Government/2014/04/06/School-Districts-Begin-Exit-From-Common-Core.

13. Alex Newman, "Top Catholic Scholars Slam Common Core," *New American*, November 12, 2013, http://www.thenewamerican.com/culture/education/item/16927-top-catholic-scholars-slam-common-core.

14. Robby Soava, "Senate Republicans: No more Common Core 'coercion,'" *Daily Caller*, February 2014, http://dailycaller.com/2014/02/05/senate-republicans-no-more-common-core-coercion/.

15. Alex Newman, "Lawmakers and Activists Rally to Stop Obama-backed 'Common Core,'" *New American*, May 2, 2013, http://www.thenewamerican.com/culture/education/item/15277-lawmakers-and-activists-rally-to-stop-obama-backed-common-core.
16. See https://www.govtrack.us/congress/bills/113/s1974.
17. Newman, "Lawmakers and Activists Rally to Stop Obama-backed 'Common Core.'"
18. Stephanie Simon, "Big business takes on tea party on Common Core," *Politico*, March 14, 2014, http://www.politico.com/story/2014/03/big-business-takes-on-tea-party-over-common-core-104662.html.
19. "Voter Perceptions: Common Core State Standards & Tests, Achieve," March 2014. http://www.achieve.org/VoterPerceptionsCCSS.

CHAPTER 30: THE FUTURE OF EDUCATION: FREEDOM OR GLOBAL ENSLAVEMENT?

1. Julian Huxley, *UNESCO: Its Purpose and Philosophy*, 1947, http://unesdoc.unesco.org/images/0006/000681/068197eo.pdf, 61, 7.
2. *World Declaration on Education for All: Meeting Basic Learning Needs* and agreement on the *Framework for Action to Meet Basic Learning Needs* (the Jomtien Declaration), 1990, http://www.unesco.org/education/wef/en-conf/Jomtien%20Declaration%20eng.shtm.
3. *The Dakar Framework for Action: Education for All: Meeting Our Collective Commitments*, adopted by the World Education Forum Dakar, Senegal, April 26–28, 2000, http://unesdoc.unesco.org/images/0012/001211/121147e.pdf, 9, 16, 17.
4. Ibid., 15.
5. Ibid., 17.
6. Arne Duncan, "The Vision of Education Reform in the United States: Secretary Arne Duncan's Remarks to United Nations Educational, Scientific and Cultural Organization (UNESCO), Paris, France," November 4, 2010, http://www.ed.gov/news/speeches/vision-education-reform-united-states-secretary-arne-duncans-remarks-united-nations-ed.
7. Ibid.
8. U.S. Department of Education, "Succeeding Globally through International Education and Engagement: U.S. Department of Education International Strategy 2012–2016," November 2012, http://www2.ed.gov/about/inits/ed/internationaled/international-strategy-2012-16.pdf, 2.
9. Valerie Strauss, "Common Core backer: For public schools, it's great. For my private school, not so much." *The Answer Sheet blog, Washington Post*, March 30, 2014, http://www.washingtonpost.com/blogs/answer-sheet/wp/2014/03/30/common-core-backer-for-public-schools-great-for-private-school-not-so-much/.
10. Cooperation Agreement between the United Nations Educational, Scientific and Cultural Organization and Microsoft Corporation, November 17, 2004, http://www.unesco.org/new/fileadmin/MULTIMEDIA/HQ/CI/CI/pdf/strategy_microsoft_agreement.pdf.
11. Phyllis Schlafly, "Bill Gates Teams Up with UNESCO," Eagle Forum, November 30, 2005, http://www.eagleforum.org/column/2005/nov05/05-11-30.html.
12. UNESCO International Institute for Educational Planning, *Advanced Training Programme in educational planning and management: Diploma and Master at IIEP 2010/2011 Course Outline*, http://www.iiep.unesco.org/fileadmin/user_upload/Cap_Dev_Training/pdf/2010/Course_outline_2010.pdf, 3, 14.
13. Ibid., 17.
14. Robert Muller, "A Letter to All Educators in the World," July 2011, posted at Robert Muller's Schools International, http://www.unol.org/rms/rmltr.html.
15. Ibid.
16. Alice A. Bailey, *The Externalisation of the Hierarchy* (New York: Lucis, 2011).
17. Bailey, *Education in the New Age*.
18. Huxley, "UNESCO: Its Purpose and Philosophy," 17.
19. UNESCO, "In the Classroom with Children Under Thirteen Years of Age," Toward World Understanding, Vol. 5, 60, (Paris: United Nations Educational, Scientific and Cultural Organization, 1949) http://zannerman.files.wordpress.com/2008/12/unesco-toward-world-understanding.pdf.

20. See Allison Anderson, "Learning to Be Resilient Global Citizens for a Sustainable World," a "background paper prepared for the Education for All Global Monitoring Report 2013/4" (2013), http://unesdoc.unesco.org/images/0022/002259/225940e.pdf.

21. See UNESCO/Education/Education for Sustainable Development, About Us page, http://www.unesco.org/new/en/education/themes/leading-the-international-agenda/education-for-sustainable-development/about-us/; and the Education page at http://www.unesco.org/new/en/education/themes/leading-the-international-agenda/education-for-sustainable-development/.

22. "UNESCO Education About Us," http://www.unesco.org/new/en/education/themes/leading-the-international-agenda/education-for-sustainable-development/about-us/.

23. United Nations Sustainable Development: United Nations Conference on Environment & Development, Rio de Janeiro, Brazil, 3 to 4 June, 1992: Agenda 21, http://sustainabledevelopment.un.org/content/documents/Agenda21.pdf, 276.

24. Ibid., 320.

25. See http://unesdoc.unesco.org/images/0014/001433/143370e.pdf.

26. Henry Lamb, "U.N. Influence in U.S. Schools," UN Watch, January 26, 2004, http://www.unwatch.com/hl012604.shtml.

27. Michael Bastasch, "UN climate chief: Communism is best to fight global warming," *Daily Caller*, January 15, 2014, http://dailycaller.com/2014/01/15/un-climate-chief-communism-is-best-to-fight-global-warming/.

28. Arne Duncan, "The Greening of the Department of Education: Secretary Duncan's Remarks at the Sustainability Summit," September 21, 2010, http://www.ed.gov/news/speeches/greening-department-education-secretary-duncans-remarks-sustainability-summit.

29. Ibid.

30. Ibid.

31. Ibid.

32. *Working towards a Balanced and Inclusive Green Economy: A United Nations System-wide Perspective*, 2012, executive summary, 12, available for download http://www.unemg.org/index.php/working-towards-a-balanced-and-inclusive-green-economy-a-united-nations-system-wide-perspective.

33. *A New Global Partnership: Eradicate Poverty and Transform Economies through Sustainable Development: The Report of the High-Level Panel of Eminent Persons on the Post-2015 Development Agenda* (2013), 17, 10. Available for download from Fox News, at http://www.foxnews.com/politics/interactive/2014/02/12/report-high-level-panel-eminent-persons-on-post-2015-development-agenda/.

34. United Nations, The Universal Declaration of Human Rights, Article 29, http://www.un.org/en/documents/udhr/index.shtml#a29.

35. *National Sexuality Education Standards Core Content and Skills, K–12*, http://www.futureofsexed.org/documents/josh-fose-standards-web.pdf.

36. UNESCO, *International Guidelines on Sexuality Education*, 2009, http://www.foxnews.com/projects/pdf/082509_unesco.pdf, 43, 49, 32, 51, 42.

37. US Department of Education, Succeeding Globally through International Education and Engagement, 2.

38. UNESCO, *Education for Sustainable Development Toolkit*, 2006, http://unesdoc.unesco.org/images/0015/001524/152453eo.pdf, 12.

39. UNESCO, "Educating for a Sustainable Future: A Transdisciplinary Vision for Concerted Action," 1997, http://www.unesco.org/education/tlsf/mods/theme_a/popups/mod01t05s01.html.

40. Dr. Shirley McCune in a speech to the National Governor's Association, Kansas 1989; "Who Is Dr. Shirley McCune?" at http://www.learn-usa.com/relevant_to_et/ctd03.htm; emphasis added.

41. Schlafly, "Bill Gates Teams Up with UNESCO."

42. Kemba A. N'Namdi, *Guide to Teaching Reading at the Primary School Level* (Paris: United Nations Educational, Scientific and Cultural Organization, 2005, http://files.eric.ed.gov/fulltext/ED495644.pdf, 28; emphasis added.

43.   Javier C. Hernández, "New York Schools Chief Advocates More 'Balanced Literacy,'" *New York Times*, June 26, 2014, http://www.nytimes.com/2014/06/27/nyregion/new-york-schools-chancellor-carmen-farina-advocates-more-balanced-literacy.html.

CHAPTER 31: THE FUTURE OF EDUCATION: HOPE REMAINS

1.   Julia Lawrence, "Number of Homeschoolers Growing Nationwide," Education News, May 2012, http://www.educationnews.org/parenting/number-of-homeschoolers-growing-nationwide/

2.   Home School Legal Defense Association, "Homeschooling Research," http://www.hslda.org/research/faq.asp.

3.   Gallup, "Homeschooling: Expanding Its Ranks and Reputation," 2002, http://www.gallup.com/poll/5941/homeschooling-expanding-its-ranks-reputation.aspx.

4.   Ibid.

5.   Brian D. Ray, *Home Education Reason and Research: Common Questions and Research-Based Answers about Homeschooling* (Salem, OR: NHERI Publications, 2009), http://www.nheri.org/HERR.pdf, 2.

6.   Brian D. Ray, "Home-Educated Doing Well at College: Research by Michael Cogan," NHERI, August 7, 2010, http://www.nheri.org/research/nheri-news/home-educated-doing-well-at-college-research-by-michael-cogan.html.

7.   Alex Newman, "Parents shed tears over homeschool-crackdown horrors," WND, November 2012, www.wnd.com/2012/11/parents-shed-tears-over-homeschool-crackdown-horrors/.

8.   United Nations, The Universal Declaration of Human Rights, Article 26, http://www.un.org/en/documents/udhr/index.shtml#a26.

9.   The Berlin Declaration, November 3, 2012, http://www.theberlindeclaration.org/sites/default/files/Berlin%20Declaration%20--%20English.pdf, 2–3.

INDEX

A

Abels, Jules, 42
Abilify, 154, 330ch18n13
abortion, 136, 137, 165, 284
Achieve, Inc., 255, 257
ADD, xiv, 63, 64, 85, 197, 298
    intentional creation of, 127–34
    secondary symptoms asserted by educators,
       130
    two main classes of medications for, 132
Adderal, xiv, 135, 142
ADHD, xiv, 127–34, 197, 298
    diagnosing, 129
    intentional creation of, 127–34
    percentage of children with, 128
    symptoms of (according to *Time* magazine),
       128
"Adult Literacy in America," 18
African-American
    dropouts, 171
    population, illiteracy rates over time,
       169–70
    students who fail to graduate from high
       school in four years, 26
AIDS/HIV, 140, 189, 284
airport security, 227
alcohol use statistics for teens, 142–43
Agenda 21, 279, 280
Alinsky, Saul, 223
Alliance for Excellent Education, 27
Allport, Gordon, 119

alphabet, the key to the development of West-
    ern civilization, 189
Alpha-Phonics, 52, 67, 70, 89, 235, 296–99,
    301–4
"alternative" lifestyles, teaching, xiv
America
    dumbing down of. *See* dumbing down of
      America
    percentage of adult population who are
      functionally illiterate in, xii
American Academy of Arts and Sciences,
    35–36
American Academy of Child and Adolescent
    Psychiatry, 156–57
American consciousness, 230, 231
American history, the rewriting of, 232
Americanism, 226–27, 230–31
Americanism (Gelertner), 227
Americanization, 225, 229
American Principles Project, 261
Americans for Prosperity, 261
American Recovery and Reinvestment Act, 282
American Thinker, 262
Animal Intelligence (Thorndike), 182
arithmetic
    day-to-day uses of, 125
    key to its proficient use, 125
    versus math, 122–23
    why it is important to memorization the
      facts of, 125, 126
Arizona magazine, 76–77
Asian students, 28, 116, 117, 170, 172

Association for Death Education and Counseling, 166–67
atheism, xiv, 149–51, 156–57, 201, 230
    atheistic schools a danger to children's health, safety, and emotional lives, 160
Atlantic Monthly, 16, 163
attention deficit disorder. *See* ADD
attention deficit/hyperactivity disorder. *See* ADHD
Australia, 67, 291

B

Bache, R. Meade, 183
Back to Basics Reform (Iserbyt), 196–97
Badass Parents Association, 262
Badass Teacher Association (BATs), 262–63
Bailey, Alice, 271, 277–78
"balanced literacy," 98, 287
Bancroft, George, 147
Barrett, Justin L., 148, 149, 151–52
Beard, Charles, 16
Beck, Glenn, 261–62
Becker, Tara, 163–64
behavioral psychology: its role in the Dewey plan, 190–97
Behaviorism (Watson), 191–92, 193
Bell, Terrel H., 96
Bell Curve: Intelligence and Class Structure in American Life (Murray), 174
Bellamy, Edward, 2, 9, 16–17
Berlin Declaration, 291–92
Bernstein, Leonard, 189
Bible. *See chap. 18* (147–60)
    Americanism speaks on behalf of the, 227
    is the moral and spiritual foundation of the American system of government, 147–18
    not permitted in public schools but has been on the moon since 1971, 148
Bible clubs/studies, principals' refusal to allow, 147, 152–53
biblical morality, 177, 230
Big Brother (and data collection). *See chap. 24* (209–19)
Big Business, 269–70, 282, 294
Big Labor, 263, 282, 294
Bill and Melinda Gates Foundation, 234, 255.
    See also Gates, Bill
binocular imbalance, 46
births to high school girls, 139
Bishop, Amy, 205–6
"Blackboard Bungle." *See* Stewart, Jill
black underclass. *See also* African-American
    eugenics and the creation of the, 180–89
    the making of the, 168–79

Blaze, 262
Blue-Backed Speller (Webster), 40, 235
Bloom, Benjamin, 162–63
Bloomberg, Michael, 184
Blumenfeld Education Letter, 112
Blumenfeld Oral Reading Test (BORAT), 298, 300
Born Believers: The Science of Children's Religious Belief. See Barrett, Justin L.
Bolshevik Revolution, 9
"bootleg phonics," 64
Boston Globe, 21, 93, 172, 331ch20n1
brain
    importance of exercising the, 69
    plasticity, 67, 69
    right and left functions, 65
Bradley, Gerard, 267
Brain that Changes Itself, The (Doidge), 67
Brandon, Loyer D., 204
Branson, Richard (Virgin Airlines), 89
Brazill, Nathaniel, 203
Breggin, Peter, 128, 132–33
Brown, Todd, 205
Brownson, Orestes 23–24
Brunner, Michael S., 144, 145
Brush, Carolyn, 226–27
Burt, Jr., Donald R., 203
Buschbacher, Chris, 203
Bush, Elizabeth Catherine, 203
Bush, George H. W., 280
Bush, George W., 273, 278
Bush, Jeb, 26, 28, 233–34
Business Brilliant (Schiff), 88

C

Caldwell, Otis W., 42
California, literary disaster in, 110–17
Calkins, Lucy, 98
Canada, 67, 201, 291
Cantor, Georg, 123
capitalism, 9, 120, 221–22
Carnegie Foundation for the Advancement of Teaching, 158–59
Cassellius, Brenda, 250
Casserly, Michael, 171–72
Castro, Fidel, 2, 9
Cat in the Hat (Dr. Seuss), 76–77, 78
Cato Institute, 261
Cattell, James McKeen, 4, 40–42, 71,99, 181–82, 185, 188, 191, 331ch20n1
Centers for Disease Control and Prevention, 128
    troubling statistics from, 140
Chall, Jeanne, 113
Chanthabouly, Douglas, 204

charter schools, 33, 173, 188
Chen, Jack, 161–62
Cher, 89
Chicago Tribune, 175
Chicago Sun-Times, 174
child abuse (by deliberately harming children's brains), xiv, xv, 39–49, 129
childhood depression. *See* depression
chlamydia, 136–37
Cho Seung-Hui, 204
Christmas, school banning of the mention of, 156
class position, 31–32
Clinton, Bill, 214, 273
Coburn, Tom, 268
cocaine, xiv, 142
cognitive
    confusion / conflict, 51–52, 63, 130
    psychology refutes whole-language method, 71
Cognitive Neuro-Imaging Unit (France), 51
Colbert, Stephen, 249
Cole, Donna J., 231
Coleman, David, 236–37, 238, 240, 243–44
College Board, 18, 19, 20, 21, 93, 243, 290
Collins, Marva, 97, 173–75
Columbine High School killings, 133, 159, 163, 164, 199, 200, 201, 204
Coming Apart: The State of White America 1960–2010 (Murray), 175–76
Committee on Reading, 93
Common Core State Standards, xiv–xv, 28, 116–17, 212, 214, 215, 217, 233–71, 272–73, 276–77, 278, 282, 283, 285, 290, 294
    Catholic educators' concerns regarding, 267
    as consumer extortion, 233–44
    an educational fraud, 245–58
    estimated cost of implementing, 265
    on multiculturalism, 228–29
    problems with the history standards, 251–52
    problems with the math standards, 249–51
    problems with the science standards, 252
    rebellion against, 259–70
"Common Core State Standards Official Identifiers and XML Representation" (a report describing the complexity of trying to implement Common Core), 238–39
Common Core Validation Committee, , 247, 249
communism, 2, 9, 16, 17, 22, 120, 230
Communist Manifesto, 8, 287

communist ideology in the classroom. *See* chap. 14 (118–21)
competition, 120
Comte, Auguste, 181
conditioned reflex, 55, 194–95
condoms, 136, 137, 138, 159, 177
confusion (intentionally teaching out of context), 31
Congressional Budget Office, 240
Conscience of a Conservative (Goldwater), 34
congenital alexia, aphasia, word blindness, 46
contributing to the delinquency of a minor (teaching sex ed and alternative lifestyles), xiv, 136
Coon, Asa H., 204
cooperative learning, 109, 118–21
Cordova, Victor, Jr., 202
Core Knowledge Foundation (CKF), 235, 238
Cortez, Jesus, 113
Council of Chief State School Officers (CCSSO), 214–15, 236–37, 239, 255
Council on Foreign Relations, 48, 257, 271, 273
creationism, 153
credit card debt, 223
Cremin, Lawrence, 187
crimes being perpetrated against children, six, xiii–xv
Cruise, Tom, 89
Cruz, Ted, 268
Cuba, 9, 120, 221
Cultural Literacy (Hirsch), 35, 36–37
Cuomo, Andrew, 264–65
cutting, 143
Cylert, 132

D

Dade Christian School (Miami), 80–81
Daily Caller, 262
"Dakar Framework for Action: Education for All: Meeting our Collective Commitments," 274
Dalrymple, Theodore, 25, 176–77
Darwin, Charles, 180
Darwinism, 153
Das Kapital (Marx), 8, 16
data collection. *See* chap. 24 (209–19)
Davenport, Charles, 184
deaf-mute teaching method. *See* Gallaudet, Thomas H.
Dearborn, Walter, 55, 58
death education, 155–56, 157–58, 163–67, 200
    what it stirs up, 158
Death and Dying Education (Ulin), 165

debt pileup (under the Obama administration), 223
deception, xii–xiii, 26, 243, 246, 266
DeCosta, Sandra B., 230
Dehaene, Stanislas, 51, 67, 68, 69–72, 101, 104
Deliberate Dumbing Down of America: A Chronological Paper Trail (Iserbyt), 22, 118, 119
Deloitte study on life science and aerospace firms, 28
Democracy and Education (Dewey), 5–6, 108, 109
democracy as a euphemism for socialism, 105
Democratic Party, 30, 188
depression, xiv, 130, 149–50, 154–55, 156, 157, 158
    godless education leads to, xiv, 157, 162
"Developing a Multicultural Curriculum," 225–26
developmental alexia, 46
DeVivo, Olivia, 199
Dewey, John, xii, 1–9, 29, 34, 41, 42, 43, 76, 77, 96, 99, 105, 106, 108, 109, 120, 132, 135, 170, 175, 178, 181, 182, 187, 188, 219, 222, 223, 237, 281, 287, 294
    his plan to dumb down America ("Primary-Education Fetich"), 305–21, 322 pref. n. 1
    how he convinced educators to implement his plan, 11–24
    the role of psychology in his dumbing-down plan, 190–97
Dexedrine, 131
Diagnostic and Statistical Manual of Mental Disorders, IV, 133
Dick and Jane readers, 15, 40, 45, 50, 71, 90, 188
Dickson, Sue, 70
Discovery Institute, 153
discrimination, 166, 226, 229
disruptive behavior in the classroom, 158
Doidge, Norman, 67, 68, 69
Dolch, E. W., 54
Dolch list of basic sight words, 53
Driven to Distraction (Hallowell and Ratey), 129, 130, 132
Dr. Seuss, 71, 76–78, 84
drugs
    the crime of pushing powerful drugs on millions of schoolchildren. *See chap. 16* (127–34)
    education, 142
    impact on society of medicating millions of children with psychiatric, 132–33

drugs *(continued)*
    teen use statistics, 141–42
    two main classes for ADD, 132
dumbing down of America
    the deliberate, 1–10
    John Dewey's plan for the, 305–21, 322 pref. n. 1
    the role of psychology in Dewey's plan for the, 190–97
    when the plan was hatched for the, xii
Dumbing Us Down: The Hidden Curriculum of Compulsory Schooling, 29, 127, 135
Duncan, Arne, 217, 233, 259, 269, 275, 282, 294
Dykhuizen, George, 15–16
dyslexaphoria, 46
dyslexia, xiv, 39–51, 54, 60–62, 64–89, 114, 130, 133
    deliberate creation of. *See chap. 5* (39–49)
    how being forced to use the right brain to perform a left-brain function causes, 65–72
    proving that the sight method causes, 73–86
    symptoms of, 60–61
    what it does to the nonreader's brain, 51
    why it is seen among first graders, 84–85
Dyslexia Institute at Northwestern University, 46
dyslexics, some successful, 88–89

E

Eagle Forum, 163, 261, 276
Eakman, Beverly, 210
Earth Summit, 280
ecstasy, percentage of teens who know someone who has tried, 142
Educating All Children: A Global Agenda, 36
Educating for the New World Order (Eakman), 210
education
    the cost of public, 233–34
    fastest-growing form of, 290
    the future of
        (freedom or global enslavement?). *See chap. 30* (271–88)
        hope remains for. *See chap. 31* (289–94)
    most effective form in America today, 159
    purpose of (to our Founding Fathers), 49
    traditional philosophy, 162
Education Data System Implementation Project (EDSIP), 215
"educational dyslexia," 77, 78, 80, 81, 84
Education for All, 273, 277

educational malpractice, 44, 46, 87–91, 97, 128, 136, 144, 178, 188
Education in the New Age (Bailey), 271, 278
Education News, 289
Education Reporter, 241
Education for Sustainable Development, 279–80
Education Task Force of the American Legislative Exchange Council (ALEC), 242
Education Week, 104–5, 153
"Education and the Western Spiritual Tradition," 151, 175
Elementary Principles of Education, 185
Elementary and Secondary Education Act of 1965, xv, 92–93
Elementary and Secondary Integrated Data System, 210
Eliot, Charles W., 42, 184
emotional dependency, 32
"Empowered Students; Empowered Teachers" (Fagan), 109
England, 55, 67, 176, 184, 195, 200
Enhancing, Teaching and Learning through Educational Data Mining and Learning Analytics (DOE), 216
ethnocentrism, 226
eugenics and the creation of the black underclass, 180–89
Eugenics General Committee, 184
Evaluation: Whole Language, Whole Child, 104
evolution, 4, 24, 32, 152, 153, 162, 163, 180, 199, 252
ExPRESS (Exchange of Permanent Records Electronically for Students and Schools), 215
Externalisation of the Hierarchy (Bailey), 278
extortion (perpetrated by educators), xiv, 233–44 (Common Core), 245

F

Fabian Society, 222–23
facial expression camera, 216
Fagan, William T., 109
Farina, Carmen, 98
Farmer, Hughs, 328ch14n1
Fast ForWord (computer training program), 68
Fast Track Initiative, 277
Figueres, Christiana, 281
Finne, Liv, 242
Fischer, Deb, 268
Flesch, Rudolf, 16, 36, 39, 46–48, 72, 75, 78, 95, 96, 98, 113, 240
Flexner, Abraham, 42
"Framework for Action to Meet Basic Learning Needs" (the Jomtien Declaration), 273

Free Inquirer, 23
foreclosures, 223
Foundation for Excellence in Education, 26–28, 233
Foust, Betty Jean, 80
FreedomWorks, 261, 262
Freire, Paulo, 103, 106–7, 108
Fresno Bee, 114

G

Gagne, E. E., 144
Gallaudet, Thomas H., 39–40, 45, 66, 73, 325ch5n1
Galton, Francis, 180–81, 188
gangs, 145, 171
Gantt, W. Horsley, 195
gas prices, 223
Gates, Arthur I., 15, 185, 188
Gates, Bill, 233, 234–35, 237, 238, 239, 241, 243, 244, 249, 255–56, 257, 263, 264, 271, 272, 276
Gatto, John Taylor, 11, 29–33, 35, 151, 176
Gay, Lesbian, and Straight Education Network (GLSEN), 140
Gelernter, David, 226, 227
General Education Board, 42, 43
Gerstner, Louis, Jr., 257–58
Gilder, George, 154
Gioia, Dana, 19
Glazer, Nathan, 225
Global Home Education Conference, 291
global warming, 150, 153, 222, 252, 281
Goals 2000, 214, 218, 273
God
    Americanism speaks on behalf of, 227
    childhood depression a consequence of schools' rejection of, 149–50
    evolution teaches that there is no, 162
    people may be born believing in, 149
    primary purpose of language is to permit converation with, 7
    what happens in a school without, xiv, 158–59
Goldberg, Whoopi, 89
Goldman, Emma, 184
Goldwater, Barry, 34
Goodman, Kenneth L., 61, 107
Gore, Al, 222
Gorman, Michael, 38
goth subculture, 200
Graf, Al, 254
Grassley, Charles, 268
Gray, William Scott, 15, 188
"Great American Prophet" (Dewey), 16–17

Great Debate: Learning to Read, The (Chall), 113
Great Debaters, The (film), 170
green economy, 282, 283
Green Eggs and Ham (Dr. Seuss), 78
Groff, Pat, 57
Grubb, Mel, 111, 114
Grunow, Barry, 203
Guide to Teaching Reading at the Primary School Level (UNESCO), 50, 286–87

H

Hakim, Joy, 251–52
Hall, G. Stanley, 4, 12, 170, 181–83, 188, 191
Hallowell, Edward M., 129, 130, 132
hallucinogens, percentage of high school seniors who have used, 141
handwriting, 69
Harris, Eric, 133, 200
Hassard, Jack, 153, 256
Haynes, Judie, 225–26
Heartland Institute, 261
Heritage Foundation, 248, 251
heroin, 142
Hirsch, E. D., Jr. 35, 36–37, 235
Hirsch, John, 36–37
Hispanic students who fail to graduate high school in four years, 26
History of US, A (textbook series), 251–42
Hoffman, Emilio, 208
Hoffman, Jason, 203
Holmes, Dan, 201
Holmes, Oliver Wendell, 232
home foreclosures, 223
homeschooling, 121. *See chap. 31* (289–94)
    growth in enrollment compared to government school enrollment, 290
    home-school movement, 10, 121, 232, 242, 272, 289
    the most effective form of education today, 159
    top three reasons for, 290
    yearly cost to parents, 243, 267, 272
Home School Legal Defense Association, 261
homophobia, UN demand to teach children about, 284
Honig, Bill, 112–13, 115
Hooked on Phonics, 300
Hoover, Herbert, 184
House of Representatives, 219, 222, 268, 269
How to Tutor (Blumenfeld), 302
Huey, Edmund Burke, 12–14, 188, 191
Huffington Post, 255
Humanist Manifesto II, 192

Human Nature and the Social Order (Thorndike), 187
Huxley, Aldous, 272
Huxley, Julian, 272, 279

I

Iannuzzi, Richard, 264
Independence Institute, 261
indifference, 32, 130
individualism, whole language's purpose of getting rid of, 106
infants born out of wedlock to high school girls, 139
Infowars, 262
Ingram, Darrell, 202
Inhofe, James, 268
Institution for the Formation of Character (Scotland), 22
intellectual dependency, 32
intelligent design, 149, 153
Internal Revenue Service, 222
International Council for the Improvement of Reading Instruction, 46
International Guidelines for Sexuality Education (UNESCO), 284
International Institute for Educational Planning, 276
International Reading Association, 48
invented spelling, 31, 63, 83
Iserbyt, Charlotte, 21–22, 118, 119, 196–97
Islamists, 152
Izumi, Lance, 241

J

James, William, 42
Jenner, Bruce, 89
Jews, xi, 148, 149, 186, 231, 278
Jobs, Steve, 109
Johansson, Domenic, 293
Joint Committee on Taxation, 9
Jomtien Declaration, 273
Jones, Van, 282
Jordan, David Starr, 184
Jorgensen, Kari, 114
Joseph, Marion, 115
Journal of Educational Psychology, 44–45
Journal of College Admission, 290
Journal of Correctional Education, 144
Judd, Charles, 4, 15, 17, 188
Judeo-Christian tradition/values/worldview, 162, 229, 278, 279
Just How Stupid Are We? (Shenkman), 38

K

Kapital, Das (Marx), 8, 16
Kazmierczak, Stephen D., 205
Kentucky, 118–19, 121, 237, 328ch14n1
Keyes, Emily, 204
Khan, Sal, 32, 122
Kilby, Ivy, and son Cameron, 162
Kimble, Ramone, 202
King, Rodney, 145, 296
King James Version the greatest work of litera-
   ture of the Elizabethan era, 148
Kinsey, Alfred, 141
Kissinger, Henry, 43, 92
Klang, John, 204
Klebold, Dylan, 200
Kline, John, 217
"knockout game," 171, 178
Kok, Samnang, 204
Kromberg, Kyle, 199
K2, number of high school seniors who have
   used, 142

L

LA Times, 117
LA Weekly. See Stewart, Jill
Laboratory School (Univ. of Chicago), 4, 6, 41
Lane, T. J., 206
language, true purposes of, 5
Lanza, Adam, 199–201
Lanza, Marsha, 201
Lanza, Nancy, 200, 201
Lanza, Peter, 200
Lanza, Ryan, 200
LD(s). *See* learning disabled
learning disabled, 62, 64, 68, 71, 85, 133–34,
   177, 304
learning disorders, three main categories, 133
Lee, Mike, 268
Lenin, Vladimir, 2, 9, 22, 221, 253
Leno, Jay, 89
Levin, Elisheva H., 127
Levinson, Harold N., 60
Lewin, Kurt, 195, 196, 197
Liberalism and Social Action (Dewey), 9–10
Life at the Bottom (Dalrymple), 25, 176
Lincoln, Abraham, 3, 227
Lincoln School (Teachers College), 41–44
literacy
   in America, xii, 18–19, 331ch20n2
   learning, 98, 100
   why it was high in early America, 49
Literacy Design Collaborative, 234–35
Literacy: Reading the Word and the World, 106–7
Little, Rich, 89
Longfellow, Henry Wadsworth, 232

Looking Backward (Bellamy), 2, 8, 16
look-say, xii, 12, 14, 15, 40, 60, 69, 112, 178,
   188
Louis C. K., 249
Lowell, James Russell, 232
LSD, percentage of high school seniors who
   have used, 141
Luetkemeyer, Blaine, 268–69
Lukawski, Paul, 295
Luria, Alexander, 75, 103, 195, 196
Luther, Martin, 161

M

Macedo, Donaldo, 107
Macmillan Company, 188
Malkin, Michelle, 261–62
Mamet, David, 87, 90
Manual of Patriotism, 232
manufacturing jobs, number vacant for lack of
   qualified applicants, 27
Mao Tse-tung, 2, 9, 253
Marchese, Kimberly, 203
marijuana, percentage of eighth graders and
   high school seniors who have used, 141
Marrow, Alfred J., 196, 197
Marva Collins Story, The (Hallmark movie),
   173–74, 332n11
Marx, Karl, 8, 16, 22, 103, 287
masturbation, UN's demand to teach children
   about, 284
math. *See chap. 22, "The Great American Math
   Disaster"* (122–26)
   evolution of the teaching of math, 123–24
   "new math," 123
   versus arithmetic, 122–23
Mayo, Marion J., 185
MCAS, 21
McCormick, Theresa E., 230
McCune, Shirley, 285
McKinsey & Company, 27
McLaughlin, John Jason, 203
Mead, George Herbert, 119
Medical Dyslexic Treatment Center, 60
Medication Madness (Breggin), 132
Mein Kampf (Hitler), 253
Merzenich, Michael, 67–68
*Methodological Guide to the Application of the
   Notion of Common Core in the Training
   of Various Categories of Educational
   Personnel, A,* 278
Microsoft, 276
Milas, Gloria, 200
Milgram, James, 249, 250–51, 335ch28n8
Mill, John Stuart, 287–88
Millennium Development Goals, 277

Miller, Edward, 74–85, 326ch9n2
Miller Word Identification Assessment
    (MWIA), 78, 326ch9n2
military entrance exam, percentage of high
    school graduates who can't pass the
    US, 27
minimal brain damage, 46
Moore, Terrence, 266
moral absolutes, 230, 231
moral diversity, 229–30
Mother's Primer (Gallaudet), 40, 74
Muller, Robert, 277, 281
multicultural education, 226, 227–30, 231
"Multicultural Education and Global Educa-
    tion: A Possible Merger" (Cole), 231
multiculturalism. See chap. 26 (225–32)
Murray, Charles, 174, 175–76
My Pedogogic Creed (Dewey), 182

N

Naison, Mark, 263
National Academy of Education, 93
National Adult Literacy Survey, 26
National Assessment of Educational Progress
    (NAEP), 27, 28, 169–70
National Association for Remedial Teaching,
    46
National Center for Death Education, 166
National Center for Education Statistics
    (NCES), 18, 210, 211, 213, 214
National Commission on Excellence in Educa-
    tion, xiii , 96
National Commission on Teacher Education,
    97
National Council for Accreditation of Teacher
    Education (NCATE), 228–29
National Education Association (NEA), 10, 47,
    74, 45, 140, 164, 165, 185, 196, 218,
    231–32, 263, 285
National Endowment for the Arts, 19, 97, 218
National Governors Association (NGA), 236,
    239, 240, 255, 285
National Home Education Research Institute
    (NHERI), 290
Nationalist Clubs, 8–9
national pride, 232
National Sexuality Education Standards,
    139–40, 252–53, 283
National Socialism, 16, 186
National Society for the Study of Education, 3
National Spelling Bee, 290
National Training Laboratory, 165, 196
Nation at Risk, A, xiii, 5, 17–18, 96, 123, 218,
    322 pref. n4, 331ch2n2
Nature of Human Conflicts, The (Luria), 195

Nazism, 186
NEA. *See* National Education Association
NEA Journal, 164, 165
NEA: Trojan Horse in American Education
    (Blumenfeld), 10, 74
neuroplasticity, 67
New American, 262
Newburn, Martin, 177–78
New Education Data Improvement Project,
    215
New England Primer, 202
New Illiterates (Blumenfeld), 36, 50, 73, 113,
    240, 325ch5n1
"new math," 123, 124
New Republic, 15
New Right, 104–5
New World Order, 271, 288
New York City, 23, 29, 100, 149, 198, 210,
    226
    the "literacy learning"/"balanced literacy"
        approach to reading in, 98, 287
    percentage of black students who met pro-
        ficiency standards in math and English,
        28
    percentage of students who scored at
        Advanced levels in, 28, 169–70
New York Times, 18, 28, 98, 241, 287,
    331ch2n2
New Zealand, 67, 291
"Next Generation Science Standards," 252
nihilism, xiv, 176, 177, 200
Nixon administration, 94
No Child Left Behind, 218, 256, 259, 269,
    273

O

Obama, Barack, xv, 25–26, 28, 41, 120, 217,
    221, 222, 223, 249, 255, 256, 258,
    263, 268, 269, 271, 272, 275, 282,
    283, 293, 294
Obamacare, 213, 221, 224, 264
"Obamacore." *See* Common Core State Stan-
    dards
    rebellion against, 259–70
ocular blocks; ocular-manual laterality, 46
Oettinger, Anthony, 48–49, 171
Office of Educational Research and Improve-
    ment (OERI), 21
On Liberty (Mill), 287–88
Organization for Economic Cooperation &
    Development (OECD), 27
Orton, Samuel T., 44–45, 60, 72, 104
Osborn, Henry Fairfield, 180, 184
out-of-wedlock births by high school girls, 139
Owen, Robert, 22–23

Owen, Robert Dale, 23
Owens, Dedric, 202

P–Q

Padgett, Jared Michael, 207–8
Palmer, Julia, 63
parents, labeling of activist, 121
Parodi, Andrew, 135
Partnership for Assessment of Readiness for
    College and Careers (PARCC), 266
patriotism, 226, 227, 232
Patton, Paul, 236
Paul, Rand, 268
Paul, Ron, 289
Paulesu, Eraldo, 70
Pavlov, Ivan, 55, 75, 103, 191, 194, 195, 271
Pavlovian Society, 194
percent
    of alcohol consumed in the US by under-
        age drinkers, 143
    of American adults who are highly literate,
        18
    of American students now educated at
        home, 289
    of American students who are sexually ac-
        tive, 138
    of Americans who read at the lowest two
        literacy levels, 26
    of black and Latino students tested in NYC
        who scored at Advanced levels, 28
    of black students tested in NYC who are
        proficient in math and reading, 28
    of Boston's third- and fourth-graders profi-
        cient in reading on the MCAS, 21
    of Boston's high school students who have
        had sex, 136
    of children who will attend public elemen-
        tary and secondary schools, 159
    of college grads who can read a complex
        book and extrapolate from it, 38
    of eighteen-year-olds who are prepared for
        college coursework, 26
    of eighth graders who perform at grade
        level or above in math, 27
    of employers who felt their employees had
        been adequately trained by the educa-
        tional institutions, 27
    of growth in number of homeschooled
        children, 289
    of high school graduates who can't pass the
        US military entrance exam, 27
    of high school seniors who have abused
        alcohol, 143
    of high school seniors who have: abused a
        drug; used marijuana; used hallucino-
        gens; used LSD, 141

percent (continued)
    of high school students who have never had
        sex; who are sexually active, 138
    of decrease in test scores with Common
        Core testing, 116, 117
    of illiteracy among African-Americans in
        the 1800s and early 1900s, compared
        with today, 169
    of life science and aerospace firms reporting
        shortages of qualified workers, 28
    of minority youth who are functionally
        illiterate, 18
    of people polled who had never read the
        Constitution, 38
    or prisoners who read at the lowest two
        literacy levels, 26
    of public-school teachers who report
        disruptive behavior or student apathy
        in classrooms, 158
    of the reading under Common Core that
        will be "informational text," 246
    of recent college graduates who are jobless
        or underemployed, 244
    of SAT test takers who graduated prepared
        for college course work, 21
    of seventeen-year-olds who are functionally
        illiterate, 18
    of seventeen-year-olds who never read for
        pleasure, increase in, 19
    of sophomores who have abused alcohol,
        142
    of students who are prepared to succeed in
        America's high-tech economy, 27
    of students who fail to graduate from high
        school in four years, 26
    of students who have tried drinking alcohol
        by eighth grade, 142
    of students who report having been taught
        about HIV or AIDS in school, 139
    of teens who have used a family member's
        prescription painkillers, 142
    of teens who report keeping, selling, or
        using drugs at their school, 141
    of teens who use Adderall, 142
    of twelfth-graders who have used cocaine,
        crack, 142
    of US small-business owners who suffer
        from some form of dyslexia, 88
    of welfare recipients who read at the lowest
        two literacy levels, 26
    of young Americans who read a daily
        newspaper, 38
    of young college graduates working in jobs
        not requiring a college degree (2012),
        241

Perry, Rick, 260
Phi Delta Kappan, 106, 165–66
phonics, xii, 10, 44, 46, 48, 52–54, 58, 60, 62,
  64, 64, 67, 68, 70, 71, 72, 73, 77–81,
  84, 96, 98, 101, 104, 105, 107, 109,
  112–15, 134, 159, 169, 173, 174, 178,
  188, 198, 235, 266. *See also Alpha-
  Phonics*
Pinchot, Gifford, 184
Pioneer Institute, 261
Planck, Max, 154
Planned Parenthood, 140, 253, 255, 276
Podesta, John, 283
Pol Pot, 2
population control, 255, 276
positivism, 181
Potter, Donald, 62, 326ch9n2
poverty, xiv, 9, 120, 139, 168, 170, 221, 222,
  226, 284, 307
premarital sex, xiv
  alarming statistics on, 136, 138
  is a sin, 139
  public school's semipornographic sex
    education leads to, 135
  the single most pressing moral issue facing
    youth today, 136
"Primary-Education Fetich, The" (Dewey), xii,
  1, 8, 12, 175, 325 pref. n. 1
  full text of, 305–21
Principles of Learning Based upon Psychology
  (Thorndike), 191
private schools, number compared to number
    of public schools, 242
progressive bias in Common Core standards
    and curricula, 251, 252
"progressive education," xv, 1, 9, 34, 41, 43,
  96–97, 170, 186, 196
*Promoting Grit, Tenacity, and Perseverance:
  Critical Factors for Success in the 21st
  Century* (DOE), 215–16
provisional self-esteem, 33
Psychology and Pedagogy of Reading, The (Huey),
  12, 188, 191
public schools, four ways cripple youths brains
    and destroy their consciences, 135–36
Pyle, W. H., 185

R

Race to the Top, 237, 256, 259
Ratey, John J., 129, 130, 132
Ray, Brian D., 293
reading
  conspiracy, 92–100
  decline in SAT scores in, 19
  percent of third- and fourth-graders profi-
    cient in, 21
  United States place in world, 27

Reading in the Brain (Dehaene), 51, 67
"Reading Method Lets Pupils Guess: Whole-
    Language Approach Riles Advocates of
    Phonics," 63
Reading at Risk, 19, 97–99, 218–19
Reading Teacher, The, 44, 48, 105
Reagan, Ronald, 21, 96, 218, 278
reflexes, 54–55, 194–95
Regan, Dale, 206
reincarnation, 163–64
religious beliefs, destroy a child's, 147–60
Republican National Committee (RNC), 260,
  261
Research Center for Group Dynamics, 196
Right to Read program, 94
Riles, Wilson, 114
Riley, Richard W., 18
Ritalin, xiv, 85, 128, 132, 135–36, 142
Roberts, Carl Charles, 204
Roberts, Pat, 268
Rockefeller Mauzé, Abby (Babs), 43
Rockefeller, David, 43
Rockefeller, John D., Jr. 4, 42
Rockefeller, John D., III, 43
Rockefeller, Laurance, 42
Rockefeller, Nelson, 42, 43–44
Rockefeller Millions, The (Abels), 42
Rodger, Elliot, 207
Rolland, Kayla, 202
Romeike family, 293
Ronda-Clingman Elementary School (NC),
  79–80, 82, 84
Rosenthal, Nina Ribak, 157, 158
Rules for Radicals (Alinsky), 223
Rushdoony, R. J., 198, 208
Russia, 15–16, 120, 191, 195, 221, 291. *See
    also* Soviet Union
Russell, James E., 4, 42
Ryan, Nolan, 89

S

Saldiveri, Joanne, 157
Sanchez, Mary (*Kansas City Star*), 25
Sandy Hook massacre, 199, 201
San Francisco Examiner, 111
Sanger, Margaret, 184
satanism, xiv
SAT test, 243–44, 267
  scores, 18, 19 –21, 88, 93, 96, 172, 290,
    323n16
  verbal scores, 1941 and 2011 compared,
    20–21
Saxon, John, 125–26
Schiff, Lewis, 88
Schindler, Jayne, 163–64
Schlafly, Phyllis, 241, 276
school shootings, xiv, 152, 167, 198, 201–8

School and Society (Dewey), 6, 41
School and Society (weekly), 185, 331ch20n1
Schumerth, Shane, 206
Schwab, Charles R., 88–89
scientific creationism. *See* intelligent design
scientific racism, 183, 186
Scientific Learning, 68
Scott, David (Apollo 15 cmdr.), 148
secular humanism, xiv, 146
Segro, Eugene, 203
Senate Joint Resolution 138, 97
separation of church and state, 153
Sessions, Jeff, 268
sex. *See also* premarital sex
    among high school students, 136, 138
    education, xiv, 135, 136, 137, 138,
        139–41, 165, 167, 200, 251, 252–53,
        283
Sexuality Information and Education Council
    of the United States (SIECUS), 138,
    140
sexually transmitted diseases, 136–37, 140,
    141, 160, 284
Shaw, Clifford, 119
Sheets, James, 203
Shenkman, Rick, 38
Skinner, B. F., 22, 152, 176, 192–94, 197
Skinner, Charles R., 232
sight. *See also* whole-word
    method (reading instruction), xii, xiv,
        39–40, 44–45, 50, 55, 60–62, 67, 72,
        145, 181, 189, 325ch5n1
    how it was proven to cause dyslexia,
        73–86
    how it works, 58
    vocabulary, 50–56, 57–64, 66–67, 72,
        75–76, 84, 287
    words, 50, 53–54, 60, 62, 78–79, 82, 85
"'Sight Reading' Method of Teaching Reading
    as a Source of Reading Disability, The,"
    44
Sing, Spell, Read & Write program, 70
60 Minutes, 174
Smalls, Stacy, 202
Smart but Feeling Dumb (Levinson), 60
Smarter Balanced Assessment Consortium
    (SBAC), 266
Smith, Frank, 106–7, 189
Smith, Todd Cameron, 201
S. 1974 (the "Learning Opportunities Created
    at Local Level Act"), 268
socialism, 2, 5, 7–9, 11, 16, 23, 24, 109, 120,
    170, 222
    Dewey's euphemism for, 105
    objective of, 41
Solomon, Thomas, 202

Soviet Union, xi, 9, 15–16, 22, 103, 120, 194
Spielberg, Stephen, 89
Sprigg, Peter (Family Research Council), 141
S-R (stimulus-response) learning process, 42,
    188
Stalin, Joseph, 121, 221, 253, 287
STDs. *See* sexually transmitted diseases
Stein, Ben, 37
Stewart, Jill, 110–11, 112, 113–15, 116–17
stimulants, xiv, 132, 133, 135, 142
stimulus money, 261
stimulus bill/plan, 256, 282
stimulus-response (S-R), 42, 188
Stotsky, Sandra, 247–49, 251
Straight Dope (blog), 123–24
strephosymbolia, 46
Stuban, Steve, 162
Student Achievement Partners, 236–37
Student Data Handbook, 209, 210–12, 213
Student Success Act, 269
Succeeding Globally through International Edu-
    cation and Engagement, 275–76
suicide, xiv, 114, 133, 143, 150, 152, 155–57,
    159. *See esp.* chap. 19, "The Unset-
    tling Phenomenon of Teen Suicide"
    (161–67)
suicide bombers, 227, 228
Sulzberger, Arthur, 18
Summa, Cathy, 152–53
"sustainable development," 279–80, 282, 283,
    293
Sweden, 291, 293
synthetic marijuana (aka spice; K2), number of
    high school seniors who have used, 142

T

Talking Back to Ritalin (Breggin), 128, 133
Tax Foundation, 9
Taxonomy of Educational Objectives (Bloom),
    162–63
Teachers College, Columbia University, 3, 15,
    41, 42, 72, 98, 99, 182, 185, 187, 287
Teachers College Reading and Writing Project
    (TCRWP), 98–100
teacher's testimonial on the teaching of reading,
    295–304
teachers' unions, 132, 245, 263
Tea Party, 223, 261
teen depression. *See also* depression
    the most common disorder among teens,
    154
    symptoms of, 155
teen drug and alcohol use statistics, 141–43
Teen Help, 154–55
Teen Rehab, 141

teen suicide, xiv, 133, 143, 150, 152, 155–57, 159, 161–67, 204
Telegraph (UK), 199, 200
Tena, Araceli, 202
Ten Commandments, 146, 162, 230
Terman, Lewis, 183, 185
Tesconi, Charles A., 229
thanatology, 166, 167
Thant, U,
theft in schools, 158, 159
Theory into Practice (Tesconi), 229
Thiessens, Jay, 88
Thorndike, Edward L., 15, 41–42, 99, 182, 184–85, 187, 188, 191, 194
three Rs, 106, 108, 307, 308, 318, 320
thyroid treatments for dyslexia, 46
Time magazine, 128–29
To Kill a Mockingbird, 295
Tolson, Melvin B., 331ch20n4
Torlakson, Tom, 116
Toward a Literate Society, 93–94
Treadway, Jerry, 113–14, 116–17
treason (deliberate dumbing down of a nation), xiii, 1–10
Treating and Preventing Adolescent Mental Health Disorders, 150
Trickey, Seth, 202
tutoring programs, annual spending by parents in America, 27
20/20, 163

U

Ulin, Richard O., 165
underage drinking, annual youth deaths from, 143
UNESCO, 271, 272, 273, 274, 275, 276–77, 278–79, 281, 283–84, 286, 294
United Nations, 252, 255, 271, 275, 277, 278, 283, 292
United Nations Educational, Scientific, and Cultural Organization. *See* UNESCO
United States Constitution, xii, 34, 37–38, 105, 152, 184, 212, 213, 220, 257, 279, 288
United States Department of Education, 21, 22, 81, 119, 209, 210, 212, 213, 215–16, 217, 218, 237, 256, 268, 269, 275, 276, 282, 284, 285
Universal Declaration of Human Rights, 283, 292
University of Chicago, 4, 15, 17, 41, 58
UN Population Fund, 276
Urso, Catherine, 200
USA Today, 256
US Senate, 97, 267–68, 269, 280
utopianism, failure of, 221

V

values clarification, 136, 146, 163, 165, 182, 228
vandalism in schools, 158, 159
Van Roekel, Dennis, 263
venereal disease, xiv, 136. *See also* sexually transmitted diseases
Virginia Tech, 204, 206
voucher system for reading instruction, 94
Vygotsky, Lev, 103, 191

W–X

Waiting for Superman (film), 172–73
Wall Street Journal, 128, 257, 258
Walters, Dan (*Sacramento Bee*), 114–15
Warner, Mark, 285
Washington Post, 18, 19, 38, 63, 128, 129, 173, 331ch20n2
"watermelons," 281
Watson, John B., 119, 190, 191–92, 193
wealth, governments do not create, 221
Webster, Noah, 40, 235
Weeks, Edward, 16
Weingarten, Randi, 264
Weise, Jeffrey, 204
welfare recipients, percentage who read at the two lowest literacy levels, 26
Wertsch, James, 103
Western civilization, the key to the development of the, 189
Westside High School (Omaha, NE), 147
What's Whole in Whole Language (Goodman), 107
Whealey, Alice, 251–52
Whittier, John Greenleaf, 232
whole language, 14, 31, 62, 63
  political agenda of. *See chap. 12* (101–9)
  purpose behind, 106
  socialist purpose behind, 105–6
Whole Language: What's the Difference?, 14, 101–2
whole-word (reading), xii, xiv, 2, 12, 40, 45, 48, 54, 71, 72, 76, 90, 95, 108, 113, 114, 181, 286. *See also* sight
Why Johnny Can't Read (Flesch), 36, 46, 48, 75, 78, 113, 240
Why Johnny Still Can't Read (Flesch), 95
Wilhoit, Jim, 236–37
Williams, Charles Andrew, 203
Williams, Walter, 171–72, 173
Wingert, Pat, 123
Winkler, Henry, 89–90
WND, 262
word deafness, 46
Working towards a Balanced and Inclusive Green Economy (UN), 283

Workingmen's Party, 23
World Bank, 282
World Core Curriculum, 273, 277, 281
"World Declaration on Education for All: Meeting Basic Learning Needs," 273–74
Wright, Frances, 23
Wundt, Wilhelm, 4, 17, 40, 41, 71, 181, 182, 188, 191

Y

Ybarra, Aaron R., 207
Yerkes, Robert M., 184
Young, Loretta, 89

Z

Zawahri, John, 206–7
Zimba, Jason, 237
Zorinsky, Edward, 97
Zuckerberg, Mark, 109